Regulatory Impact Assessment

THE CRC SERIES ON COMPETITION, REGULATION AND DEVELOPMENT

Series Editors: Paul Cook, *Professor of Economics and Development Policy* and Martin Minogue, *Senior Research Fellow, Institute for Development Policy and Management, University of Manchester, UK*

Titles in the series include:

Leading Issues in Competition, Regulation and Development
Edited by Paul Cook, Colin Kirkpatrick, Martin Minogue and David Parker

The Politics of Regulation
Institutions and Regulatory Reforms for the Age of Governance
Edited by Jacint Jordana and David Levi-Faur

Regulating Development
Evidence from Africa and Latin America
Edited by Edmund Amann

Regulatory Governance in Developing Countries
Edited by Martin Minogue and Ledivina Cariño

Regulatory Economics and Quantitative Methods
Evidence from Latin America
Edited by Omar Osvaldo Chisari

Regulation, Markets and Poverty
Edited by Paul Cook and Sarah Mosedale

Competitive Advantage and Competition Policy in Developing Countries
Edited by Paul Cook, Raul Fabella and Cassey Lee

Regulatory Impact Assessment
Towards Better Regulation?
Edited by Colin Kirkpatrick and David Parker

Regulatory Impact Assessment

Towards Better Regulation?

Edited by

Colin Kirkpatrick

Hallsworth Professor of Development Economics, Institute for Development Policy and Management (IDPM) and Co-Director of the Regulation Research Programme, Centre on Regulation and Competition (CRC), University of Manchester, UK

David Parker

Research Professor in Privatisation and Regulation, Cranfield School of Management, Cranfield University and Co-Director of the Regulation Research Programme, Centre on Regulation and Competition (CRC), University of Manchester, UK

THE CRC SERIES ON COMPETITION, REGULATION AND DEVELOPMENT

Edward Elgar

Cheltenham, UK • Northampton, MA, USA

Published by
Edward Elgar Publishing Limited
Glensanda House
Montpellier Parade
Cheltenham
Glos GL50 1UA
UK

Edward Elgar Publishing, Inc.
William Pratt House
9 Dewey Court
Northampton
Massachusetts 01060
USA

A catalogue record for this book
is available from the British Library

Library of Congress Control Number: 2007921143

ISBN 978 1 84542 412 1 (cased)

Printed and bound in Great Britain by MPG Books Ltd, Bodmin, Cornwall

Contents

Contributors

Lorenzo Allio has previously worked as a Policy Analyst at the European Policy Centre (Brussels), where he was responsible for the EPC Better Regulation Programme from 2002 to 2006. Lorenzo Allio is also a PhD candidate at King's College London, where he writes on the emergence of Better Regulation in the European Union. He obtained his MA diploma in European Political and Administrative Studies at the College of Europe (Bruges), after graduating in Contemporary History and Economics at the University of Basel, Switzerland.

Cesar Cordova Novion is a Director of Jacobs and Associates, a consulting firm working on regulatory reform. He was Deputy Director of the OECD Programme on Regulatory Reform until 2003, where he directed the country review programme and carried out numerous reviews of RIA practices. Previously, he was Director of the Mexican Regulatory Reform Office.

Fabrizio De Francesco is an ESRC Research Fellow at the Centre for Regulatory Governance and doctoral candidate in the Department of Politics at the University of Exeter.

Rex Deighton-Smith is an independent public policy consultant, specializing in regulatory governance, regulatory impact assessment and competition policy. He formerly worked on the OECD's Programme on Regulatory Management and Reform and has also worked as the Director of the office of Regulation Reform in the Victorian State government, Australia.

Ed Humpherson heads the regulation practice at the National Audit Office, UK. He is responsible for leading the NAO's Better Regulation work, encompassing regulatory impact assessment and the costs of regulation. He also leads the NAO's assessments of independent regulators such as Ofcom, Ofgem and the Financial Services Authority.

Colin Jacobs has worked in the public sector for over 20 years and has a doctorate in public administration. Dr Jacobs heads the international team at the UK Evaluation Society and is a Chartered Fellow at the Chartered Institute of Personnel and Development (CIPD). He worked from 2004 to 2005 at the

Regulatory Impact Assessment (RIA) Unit at the UK's Cabinet Office, to review monitoring and evaluation (M&E) systems and strengthen evidence-based impact assessments. Dr Jacobs is an Associate at the Institute of Development Policy and Management, University of Manchester, UK.

Scott H. Jacobs is a leading international expert on regulatory reform. He directed the Programme on Regulatory Reform at the OECD from 1995 to 2001. From 2001, he has been Managing Director of Jacobs and Associates, a consulting firm working on regulatory reform in over 70 countries.

Colin Kirkpatrick is Hallsworth Professor of Development Economics and Director of the Impact Assessment Research Centre at the Institute for Development Policy and Management, School of Environment and Development, University of Manchester, UK. He is also Co-director of the Regulation Research Programme at the Centre on Regulation and Competition, University of Manchester.

Malathy Knight-John is a Research Fellow and Head of Industry, Public Enterprise Reform and Regulatory Policy Research at the Institute of Policy Studies, Colombo, Sri Lanka. She is currently reading for a PhD in Development Policy and Management at the University of Manchester, UK.

Peter Ladegaard is a Senior Investment Policy Officer at the Investment Climate Department of the World Bank Group. Before joining the World Bank Group in April 2005, Peter Ladegaard worked for the OECD's Regulatory Reform Programme. Peter Ladegaard specializes in policy advice and technical assistance on regulatory management and reform.

David Parker is Research Professor in Privatisation and Regulation and Director of the Centre for Competition and Regulation Research at the Cranfield School of Management, Cranfield University, UK. He is also Co-director of Regulation Research at the Centre on Regulation and Competition at the University of Manchester and a member of the UK Competition Commission.

Claudio M. Radaelli is Professor of Political Science and Jean Monnet Chair at the University of Exeter, UK, and Director of the Centre for Regulatory Governance.

Margo Thomas is FIAS/World Bank Group Regional Program Coordinator and Business Enabling Environment Manager for South East Europe, responsible for providing advice and technical assistance on business environment policy and regulatory reform. In 2004–5 Margo Thomas was a visiting researcher at the University of Manchester's Centre on Regulation and Competition.

Darren Welch is Deputy Director at DAI Europe Ltd, responsible for work on policy and regulatory reform. He has advised on these issues in Africa, Asia and Europe. Darren Welch is a former member of the Cabinet Office of the UK where he was Head of the Better Regulation Unit's EU and International Branch.

Preface

Issues of regulation and competition have long been matters of both public policy debate and academic research in developed economies, but until recently were relatively unexamined in relation to developing economies. The Centre on Regulation and Competition (CRC) of the University of Manchester, UK, has been conducting research into regulatory development and competition issues since 2001, with a primary focus on changes and reforms in developing countries, working together with partners both in the UK and overseas in China, Ghana, India, Malaysia, the Philippines, South Africa and Sri Lanka. This work has been funded primarily by the UK's Department for International Development, with support from the UK Foreign and Commonwealth Office's Global Opportunities Fund, and from the British Council. Other collaborating agencies include the Foreign Investment Advisory Service of the World Bank and the Competition Division of the United Nations Committee on Trade and Development (UNCTAD).

This book series is one of the many ways in which the work of the CRC and its partners is disseminated, complementing conferences, workshops, journal publication and policy briefs. This edition brings together the research of CRC on regulatory impact assessment (RIA). Introduced in the 1990s in a number of OECD countries, the purpose of RIA is to create a culture within government conducive to weighing up both the costs and benefits of a new regulation before it is introduced. Also, RIA can be used to assess the continuing need for existing regulation.

While there is growing interest in the principles and practice of RIA there is very little accessible literature on the subject. This book provides an analysis, supported by case studies, of the principles of better regulation. A key feature of the book is its focus on the problems of applicability and adaptation of RIA practice in developed, developing and transitional economies.

Paul Cook and Martin Minogue
CRC, University of Manchester, UK

Acknowledgements

We are grateful for the financial support provided by the UK Department for International Development (DFID) to the CRC. This has enabled the CRC to fund research and host conferences from which the contributions for this book have been drawn. We would also like to express our thanks to Pam Johnson who has provided support in the preparation of this book.

1. Regulatory impact assessment: an overview

Colin Kirkpatrick and David Parker

INTRODUCTION

The potentially damaging effects on economic growth resulting from excessive government regulation have attracted increasing attention from policy-makers in recent years. Starting with the Reagan administration in the USA and followed by the Thatcher government in the UK, a rapidly growing number of governments around the world have adopted measures to improve the quality of both existing regulations and proposals for new regulations. A core component of these programmes for regulatory reform is regulatory impact assessment (RIA). RIA is a method of policy analysis, which is intended to assist policy-makers in the design, implementation and monitoring of improvements to regulatory systems, by providing a methodology for assessing the likely consequences of proposed regulation and the actual consequences of existing regulations.

RIA was originally conceived as an instrument for identifying the costs of regulation on the business sector, which would be followed by a process of deregulation aimed at reducing the regulatory 'burden' on the private sector and thereby improving competitiveness. Over time, however, the definition and purpose of RIA have been refined and widened. First, the focus has shifted from the costs of regulation alone, to a consideration of both benefits and costs. This reflects a recognition that regulation is not bad per se; rather, each regulation needs to be assessed on a case by case basis in terms of how it contributes to the objectives of public policy. Second, the public objectives to which regulation can contribute have been widened beyond the single objective of private sector competitiveness. Typically, RIA will now consider the potential or actual impacts (positive and negative) of a regulatory measure in terms of the three pillars of sustainable development, namely, economic, social and environmental. This broadening of the definition and coverage of RIA has been mirrored at the level of regulatory reform by the shift in focus from 'less regulation' to 'better regulation'.

The rapid spread of RIA has been an important part of the more general process of public sector management reform and better governance. By requiring a systemic examination of the consequences of regulatory choices, RIA is seen as a tool for strengthening evidence-based policy-making. It also contributes to the core principles of good governance, by increasing the transparency and accountability of political decisions on the choice of regulatory measures and policies.

The aim of this volume is to provide a comprehensive account of the principles and practice of RIA. The standard characteristics of the RIA approach to regulatory decision-making are explained, together with a discussion of the principles relating to quality evaluation of RIA processes. There is a strong comparative dimension to the analysis, detailed case studies draw from developed, transitional and developing countries. Besides describing the system of RIA in a range of different economic and political environments and contexts, the case studies also provide an analysis of the factors that have influenced the adoption of RIA and an evaluation of the results of the particular RIA system in practice. The remaining sections of this introductory chapter provide a background overview of the principles and practice of RIA, which are then developed in more detail in the other chapters of the book written by international experts in RIA.

THE REGULATORY IMPACT ASSESSMENT (RIA) APPROACH TO POLICY-MAKING

'Good' regulation will be both *effective* and *efficient*. Effective in the sense of achieving its planned goals and objectives, and efficient in terms of achieving these goals at least cost, in terms of government administrative costs and the costs imposed on the economy in terms of complying with regulations. There is, therefore, a compelling case for the systematic appraisal of the positive and negative impacts of any proposed or actual regulatory change. Regulatory impact assessment (alternatively referred to as *regulatory impact analysis* or *impact assessment*) provides a methodological framework for undertaking this systematic assessment of benefits and costs of regulation, and for informing decision-makers of the consequences of a regulatory measure.

There is no single or generally agreed definition of regulatory impact assessment or of the 'regulations' that are covered by RIA. The UK defines RIA as 'a tool which informs policy decisions. It is an assessment of the impact of policy options in terms of the costs, benefits and risks of a proposal' (Cabinet Office, 2003, p. 5). The OECD, which has been active in developing 'best practice' guidance on RIA as part of its programme on regulatory reform practice, defines regulation broadly in the following terms: 'regulation refers to the diverse set of instruments by which governments set requirements on enterprises and citizens' (OECD, 1997). Regulation therefore, extends beyond sector-specific regulation to include any government measure that affects individual or group behaviour. With this broader definition of 'regulation', RIA is perhaps better understood as a tool of public policy analysis, which contributes to better policy selection.

RIA can contribute to both the *outcome* and the *process* dimensions of policy. By providing a methodological framework of rational policy selection, RIA allows for the outcomes (ex ante or ex post) to be assessed against the goals that are set for regulatory systems. The process contribution of RIA can be assessed in terms of the principles of 'good governance'. There is a broad consensus that these principles encompass proportionality (the regulation should be appropriate to the size of the problem it is intended to address); targeting (the regulation focuses on the problem and does not cause unintended consequences in other areas of the economy or society); consistency in decision-making (to avoid uncertainty); accountability for regulatory actions and outcomes; and transparency in decision-making (Parker, 2002).

The purpose of an RIA is:

> to explain the objectives of the [regulatory] proposal, the risks to be addressed and the options for delivering the objectives. In doing so it should make transparent the expected costs and benefits of the options for the different bodies involved, such as other parts of Government and small businesses, and how compliance with regulatory options would be secured and enforced. (NAO, 2002, p. 51)

A properly conducted RIA, therefore, systematically examines the impact arising or likely to arise from government regulation and communicates this information to decision-makers. It also involves public consultation to identify and measure benefits and costs and thereby has the potential to improve the transparency of governmental decision-making. It can promote government accountability by reporting on the information used in decision-making and by demonstrating how the regulation will impact on society. The result should be an improved and more consistent regulatory environment for both producers and consumers. It is important to recognize, however, that RIA, even when operated well, is not a tool that substitutes for decision-making. Rather, it should be seen as an integral part of the policy-making, which aims to raise the quality of debate and therefore the quality of the decision-making process (Kirkpatrick and Parker, 2004). As S. Jacobs (2004, p. 287) points out, 'the most important contributor to the quality of government decisions is not the precision of calculations, but the action of asking the right questions, understanding real-world impacts, and exploring assumptions'.

Typically, RIA will involve a number of tasks to be carried out at each stage of the process:

- a description of the problem and the objective of the proposal;
- a description of the options (regulatory and non-regulatory) for achieving the objective;
- an assessment of the significant positive and negative impacts, including an assessment of the incidence of the benefits and costs on consumers, business and other interests groups;
- a consultation process with stakeholders and other interested parties;
- a recommended option, with explanation of why it has been selected.

This framework, which is common to most RIA procedures, should not be interpreted as advocating a 'one-size-fits-all' best practice approach to regulatory assessment. Rather, it should be viewed as a guide to developing an RIA system that meets the particular needs and resource constraints of an individual country. The process of adapting the general framework to meet country-specific requirements can be informed by a number of practical lessons drawn from the experience of countries that have implemented some form of RIA.

First, RIA needs the development of RIA skills within the government machinery, including skills in enumeration and valuation of costs and benefits. Generally, qualitative effects will involve more judgmental or subjective evaluation and physical units introduce serious problems of aggregation. There may be a temptation, therefore, to diminish the RIA to include only an evaluation of measurable financial costs and benefits. Or, the assessment may be reduced to looking solely at the cheapest way of achieving the regulatory outcome (in effect providing a cost-effectiveness study only) in which the benefits are taken as given. This lesser form of RIA risks ignoring important differential benefits from different forms of regulation.

Second, RIA requires the extension of consultation procedures to ensure that appropriate information is collected and analysed in reaching a view on the regulatory impact. There may be little tradition of consulting widely before undertaking regulation, or those chosen for consultation in the past may have been selected on political grounds. The need to consult and evaluate can be time-consuming and resource-heavy within hard-stretched governments. RIAs may involve multiple stages with each new regulation facing an initial RIA, another RIA after consultation and redrafting and a final RIA on the legislation as passed by the legislature. A sensible approach to minimize these costs is to prioritize where detailed RIA should be undertaken, by using a screening procedure to identify when a regulation is likely to have major effects on the economy, society or the environment. It is important, however, that the decision on when to use an RIA is not made simply on political grounds.

Third, RIA needs to be championed across government if it is to be used consistently and become a normal feature of regulatory policy-making. It therefore needs clear and powerful political support within government if it is to overcome bureaucratic and political inertia. More generally, to achieve these improvements in regulatory governance may require a cultural change within government, involving more open policy-making as part of a broader process of governance reform.

Finally, RIA must also confront the possibility of 'regulatory capture'. In practice, the nature and content of regulation may be 'captured' by special interest groups, who have the time, resources and incentives to invest in influencing the regulatory process. In market economies, resources flow to where the perceived returns are highest and this is no less true in the shaping of regulation policy. There will be constant pressure from external groups and their spokespersons within the legislature and government to advance regulations that promote their members' economic rents. For this reason, regulatory policy-making may not be the objective and rational process that RIA presumes, with its emphasis on fact-finding and disinterested decision-making. At the same time, however, RIA can help to control rent-seeking activity within government by promoting wider consultation and by requiring the explicit identification and evaluation of costs and benefits. RIA, by making the regulatory process more transparent and accountable, provides a means of weakening regulatory capture.

EVALUATING THE QUALITY OF RIA

The growth in RIA practice has been accompanied by increasing recognition of the importance of establishing procedures for monitoring and ex post evaluation. Ex post evaluation can support better regulation policy if the results and lessons for improvement are used to inform the design and implementation of future regulatory proposals. Also, if the evaluation results are accessible by external stakeholders, the policy-makers can become more accountable for their regulatory decisions. The OECD defines regulatory quality as follows:

> *Regulatory quality* refers to the extent to which a regulatory system pursues its underlying objectives. These objectives involve the specific policy objectives which the regulatory tool is being employed to pursue and the efficiency with

which these objectives are achieved, as well as governance based objectives including transparency and accountability. (OECD, 2004, p. 8)

The purpose of the evaluation of RIA, therefore, is to improve the effectiveness and efficiency of the RIA system, in terms of the policy objectives that are set for it. These objectives can be defined at several levels. In a restricted sense, the objectives can be expressed in terms of contributing to 'better' regulation and regulatory governance. In a broader sense, the evaluation can be in terms of the societal goals of economic growth, environmental sustainability and/or social justice to which RIA and regulatory reform can contribute.

Evaluation can be conducted, therefore, at several different levels, each with its own set of indicators of performance:

- *Content evaluation* is input-based, and checks the content of the RIA report for compliance with the RIA procedures and process.
- *Output evaluation* goes beyond the question of formal compliance with procedural requirements, and measures the quality of the analysis undertaken.
- *Outcome evaluation* assesses the actual effect of RIA in terms of the quality of the regulatory outcomes.
- *Impact evaluation* assesses the impact of the change in regulation quality on the broader economic, social and environmental goals.

In practice, the problems of obtaining quantifiable performance indicators and of attributing causal links between each stage of the evaluation become increasingly difficult as one moves from content evaluation through output and outcome evaluation to impact evaluation. Consequently, most evaluation studies of RIA have concentrated on the content and output stages of evaluation.

Content evaluation typically involves a 'scorecard' assessment against published guidelines for RIA good practice, such as the OECD checklist for regulatory decision-making shown in Box 1.1 (OECD, 1995).

In the UK, the National Audit Office (NAO) has prepared a number of reports on RIAs produced by UK government departments and agencies, by applying a series of content questions, as shown in Box 1.2 (NAO, 2004, 2006).

Perhaps not surprisingly, the NAO studies have identified the use of a number of practices and approaches across UK government departments, evidence of good practice and areas in need of improvement. There were a number of main findings (Humpherson, 2004). First, RIA was well embedded within government as part of the policy-making process and all new

BOX 1.1 OECD RIA CHECKLIST

1. Is the problem correctly defined?
2. Is government action justified?
3. Is regulation the best form of government action?
4. Is there a legal basis for regulation?
5. What is the appropriate level (or levels) of government for this action?
6. Do the benefits of regulation justify the costs?
7. Is the distribution of effects across society transparent?
8. Is the regulation clear, consistent, comprehensible and accessible to users?
9. Have all interested parties had the opportunity to present their views?
10. How will compliance be achieved?

regulations are subject to RIAs. Second, within the sample of RIAs the NAO studied, there was an insufficient degree of attention paid to the generation of alternative options, including 'do nothing' (don't regulate), and to the analysis of options. Third, there had been improvement in the form, content and timing of consultations, although there was scope for improvement in the integration of consultations into the final RIA report. Fourth, quantifying costs and benefits was weak. Quantification of risks and hazards that the regulation was intended to reduce was attempted in some cases, but benefits were rarely quantified. Data uncertainties were often ignored and excessive accuracy was attached to the quoted figures rather than providing a range of possible values. Finally, there was insufficient consideration given to the enforcement, sanctions and evaluation of the RIAs.

Similarly, Lee and Kirkpatrick (2006) carried out a performance evaluation of a sample of 'extended impact assessments' undertaken by the European Commission. The reports were evaluated in five main areas, each of which was disaggregated into more detailed subcategories. The study identified a number of areas of weakness, including poor identification of the problem, unbalanced coverage of different types of impacts and lack of clarity in the explanation of the analysis, and weaknesses in the presentation of the RIA findings.

Output evaluations attempt to demonstrate the difference that the RIA has made to the quality of the regulatory system. The most frequently used method of evaluating RIA outcomes is to assemble data on the frequency with which regulatory proposals are revised or abandoned as a result of an RIA. This type of evaluation faces the standard methodological difficulty of determining whether the observed change is the direct result of the RIA, or

BOX 1.2 NATIONAL AUDIT OFFICE, UK: FRAMEWORK OF QUESTIONS

1. Was the RIA process started early enough?

Did the department have clear objectives for the regulation?
Did the department allow a realistic timetable for the RIA process?
Did the department consider the risks?
Did the RIA consider a range of options?
Were alternatives to regulation considered?
Were alternative regulatory tools considered?

2. Was consultation effective?

Was effective consultation started early in the process?
Did the department use appropriate consultation techniques?
Did the department explain clearly the impact of the regulation?
Did the department consult all interested groups of stakeholders?
Did the department consider the impact on small businesses?
Were the results of the consultation used well in formulating the regulation?

3. Did the RIA assess the costs thoroughly?

Were the implementation and policy costs on all affected taken into account?
Did the department identify all parties on whom costs would fall?
Did the department consider the costs to small businesses?
Did the department identify all likely costs?
Did the department assess the costs of all options?

4. Did the RIA assess benefits realistically?

Did the department identify all parties who would benefit?
Were the benefits realistic and relevant to the regulation?
Was the methodology for quantifying/scoring the benefits robust?

5. Did the RIA realistically assess compliance?

Was possible non-compliance factored into the analysis?
Did the department assess the existing level of compliance?
Were ways of increasing compliance considered?

6. Will the regulation be effectively monitored and evaluated?

Did the RIA contain procedures for monitoring and evaluating the extent to which the regulation meets its objectives?

Source: Humpherson (2004).

whether other factors have influenced the output. Also, a part of the impact will be unobservable, if regulatory proposals are withdrawn in anticipation of an unfavourable RIA. Ambler, Chittenden and Shamutkova (2003) examined a sample of 200 RIAs conducted by UK government departments between the mid-1998 and mid-2002. They found little evidence that RIAs had caused legislation to be aborted, with only 11 cases of final RIAs being identified where this was a possibility. However, this may understate the impact of the RIA process, since the authors were unable to track initial and partial RIAs that were subsequently withdrawn. Vibert (2004) evaluated the first year of extended impact assessments undertaken by the European Commission, and found that 'there is not a single case where EU action has been assessed to have negative net benefits or where the inability to quantify the net benefits has led to the conclusion that the measure should be withdrawn or that no policy would be the best policy' (p. 9).

A second method of evaluating outputs is to conduct an audit trail in relation to the RIA process and focus on how suggested changes to the initial regulatory proposal have been dealt with. This approach has the advantage of reviewing the process of managing the consultation suggestions and the internal decision-making involved in the preparation of the RIA. It is likely, however, to be relatively resource-intensive (Yarrow, 2004). It also requires access to the key actors within government, which external evaluators may have difficulty in obtaining, since it increases the pressure on the regulators to be transparent and to justify their decisions.

By extending the audit trail method, it may be possible to test the effect of the RIA on the organizational and regulatory culture; that is, 'how and whether RIAs are instrumental in instilling a greater appreciation and understanding of the benefits of the RIA process, and thereby encouraging a proactive rather than reactive use of the RIA as a policy development tool' (OECD, 2004, p. 38). This type of evaluation is largely qualitative in nature, which can pose problems in the interpretation of the results. It does have the merit, however, of providing a more direct measure of the extent to which the overriding goal of RIA, to change the assessment of regulatory initiatives, has been achieved. Interestingly, the National Audit Office, which has legal authority to investigate internal procedures within UK government, found that its RIA evaluations had a significant impact on accountability – 'in essence, therefore, the fact of the NAO evaluation can help concentrate the minds of departments: a point borne out by the feedback discussions held with departments whose RIAs were in the pilot sample, following the completion of the first year's work by the NAO' (Humpherson, 2004, p. 281).

Evaluation at the outcome level involves assessing the impact of RIA on the regulatory environment and on the benefits that this provides, in terms of the goals of the regulatory reform process. This approach to evaluation is considerably more complex and methodologically challenging than the content and output approaches that have been discussed above. The methodological problems of establishing a counterfactual baseline from which to assess changes, and the difficulties of attributing changes to the initial RIA process, have limited the application of this evaluation approach to RIA.

The challenge of attribution becomes even more evident if the evaluation is extended from outcomes to impacts in terms of the broad goal of sustainable development.

The OECD country reviews of regulatory reform have provided empirical evidence of a relationship between regulatory reform and better economic performance. Gains in terms of higher productivity and economic growth are found in countries such as Canada, the USA and the UK, which have had a lengthy period of RIA. The general conclusion is that 'countries with explicit regulatory policies consistently make more rapid and sustained progress than countries without clear policies. The more complex the principles, and the more concrete and accountable the action program, the wider and more effective was reform' (OECD, 2002, p. 40). Evidence of the relationship between regulatory reform, particularly as it affects the business sector, and economic performance in a large number of developing and transitional countries, has been assembled by the World Bank (2004). However, the supporting data are largely associative in nature, and provide little convincing evidence of causality.

To conclude this section, a common limitation of most RIA systems is the limited attention given to the monitoring and evaluation of results. This is a significant weakness, given that the systematic and transparent evaluation of ex post impacts can contribute to a better understanding of successes and failures, and thereby to improved performance of RIA and regulatory systems. However, establishing the links between RIA and improvements in the quality of the overall regulatory environment, and between the regulatory environment and society's economic, social and environmental goals for national development, is a highly challenging exercise.

THE INTERNATIONALIZATION OF RIA

The use of RIA as a tool of public sector management and decision-making is widespread, and the majority of OECD countries have adopted formalized RIA arrangements. In March 1995, the Council of the OECD adopted a *Recommendation on Improving the Quality of Government Regulation*, which made reference to the use of RIA (OECD, 1995). In 1997 ministers of the Member countries endorsed the OECD *Report on*

BOX 1.3 COMMON CHARACTERISTICS OF RIA

1. *Statement of problem*. Is government intervention both necessary and desirable?
2. *Definition of alternative remedies*. These include different approaches, such as the use of economic incentives or voluntary approaches.
3. *Determination of physical effects of each alternative, including potential unintended consequences*. The net should be cast wide. Generally speaking, regulations or investments in many areas of public policy can have environmental implications that must be kept in mind.
4. *Estimation of benefits and costs of each alternative*. Benefits should be quantified and where possible monetized. Costs should be true opportunity costs. Not simply expenditures.
5. *Assessment of other economic impacts*. Including effects on competition, effects on small firms, international trade implications.
6. *Identification of winners and losers*. Those in the community who stand to gain and lose from each alternative and if possible, the extent of their gains and losses.
7. *Communication with the interested public*. Including the following activities: notification of intent to regulate; request for compliance costs and other data; public disclosure of regulatory proposals and supporting analysis; and consideration of and response to public comments.
8. *A clear choice of the preferred alternative*. Plus a statement defending that choice.
9. *Provision of a plan for ex post analysis of regulatory outcomes*. It is important, for example, to establish current conditions to have a benchmark to measure performance against. Planning is needed to ensure that procedures are in place for the collection of data to permit such benchmarking.

Source: OECD (2004, p. 27).

Regulatory Reform, which recommended that governments 'integrate regulatory impact assessment into the development, review, and reform of regulations' (OECD, 1997). S. Jacobs (2002) reports that 20 out of the then 28 OECD countries were using RIA in some form by 2001, although Radaelli (2002) found that national guidelines for undertaking RIAs existed in only nine of these countries. While the detail of the way in which RIA is being applied varies between countries, there is a degree of commonality in terms of the main characteristics of the procedures that have been adopted, as summarized in Box 1.3.

The origins of RIA can be traced to the USA. There the formal adoption of RIA in the 1970s was in response to a perceived increase in the regulatory burden associated with a surge in regulatory activity since the mid-1960s, together with concerns that this might be adding to inflationary pressures in the US economy (Anderson, 1998). Since 1995 the Office of Management and Budget (OMB) has been required to report on the costs and benefits of government regulations and in 2000 the OMB published guidance on how to conduct RIAs. This widened the scope of RIA to include non-quantifiable costs and benefits and put more emphasis on risk assessment and the quality of information collection (OMB, 2001).

In the UK the systematic assessment of the impact of regulation by government began in the 1980s as part of the Conservative government's Deregulation Initiative. The Better Regulation Task Force (BRTF) was established as an independent advisory body in 1997 to advise government on regulatory issues, supported by a Regulatory Impact Unit (RIU) located in the Cabinet Office. In 1998, the Prime Minister announced that no proposal for regulation should be considered by Ministers without a regulatory impact assessment being carried out. Guidelines for carrying out RIAs were published, and encompassed risks, and costs and benefits not only to business but more widely. The RIA reports are published for public scrutiny.

In January 2006 the UK government established the Better Regulation Commission (BRC), which has taken over from the BRTF to provide independent advice to government about new regulatory proposals, and to review the government's overall regulatory performance (Parker, 2006). Alongside the BRC operates the Better Regulation Executive (BRE) within the Cabinet Office, which was established in May 2005. This is tasked with promoting the Government's better regulation agenda. The BRE also takes forward the work previously carried out by the RIU.

In the European Union, regulatory impact assessment is an important part of the 'better governance' agenda, which aims to improve the quality of legislation and make governance more transparent, responsive and accountable (Radaelli, 2003). The Goteborg European Council meeting in June 2001 agreed that 'sustainable development should become the central objective of all sectors and policies . . . careful assessment of the full effects of a policy proposal must include estimates of its economic, environmental and social impacts inside and outside the EU' (EC, 2001), and established procedures to ensure that each major legislative proposal is informed by an assessment of the potential impacts of the measure, both inside and outside the Union. The 2002 Communication of the European Commission on impact assessment commits the Commission to undertake an impact assessment of all major policy proposals in order 'to improve the quality and coherence of the policy development process' and to 'contribute to an effective and efficient regulatory environment and further, to a more coherent implementation of the European strategy for Sustainable Development' (EC, 2002). In June 2005, the Commission issued new impact assessment guidelines, which began to be implemented in August 2005 (EC, 2005). The new guidelines are to be applied to all items on the Commission's Work Programme, covering regulatory proposals, White Papers, expenditure programmes and the negotiating of international agreements. In addition, the Commission may decide, on a case by case basis, to carry out an impact assessment of a proposal that does not appear on the Work Programme.

Although the transitional economies of Central and Eastern Europe share a common history of Soviet or communist rule, there are considerable variances in the use of RIA, which suggests that history alone is not a sufficient explanation of the way reforms develop within government. Issues of administrative capacity, institutional infrastructure and incentives to carry out an RIA, all affect the reform process in transitional economies (Jacobs, C., 2005). The adoption of RIA is also seen as advantageous in terms of promoting the democratic principles of 'good government'. RIAs support legal government, which observes the rule of law with proportionate and equitable law. An accountable government is promoted through assessing direct costs and benefits that citizens will incur and selecting policies on the basis of best value for money, taking into account redistribution effects – that is, who gains and who loses. Consultation with consumers, business and civil society also helps build legitimacy and promotes issues of equity and fairness among citizens. This is particularly important in transition economies where NGOs and voluntary non-state institutions have been sluggish to develop and the role of civil society in shaping government is incipient and weak (Jacobs, S., 2004).

In developing countries there is a growing recognition among policy-makers that RIA can be used in the design and implementation of regulatory reform programmes to bring about improvements in the quality of regulatory governance and policy-making (World Bank, 2004, pp. 73–4). However, evidence on the use of RIA in developing countries is limited (Kirkpatrick, Parker and Zhang, 2004). Where evidence is available, it suggests that the coverage of RIA, both in terms of types of regulation and number of regulation proposals appears, however, to vary widely between countries, and few countries appear to be applying RIA consistently to regulatory proposals affecting economic, social and environmental policies. While there is a general recognition of the desirability of including benefits as well as costs in an RIA, methods of quantification are generally under-developed.

CONCLUSIONS

Globally, the past decade has seen a major shift in the role that the state plays in the process of economic growth and development. This has led to interest in new approaches to policy-making with the aims of improving the quality of legislation and making governance more transparent and accountable. Regulation impact assessment has been at the centre of this move towards 'better' policy and governance. RIA provides an analytical framework for assessing the effects that the introduction of a new regulation is likely to have, and also for assessing the actual impact of existing regulatory measures. By providing decision-makers with evidence on the effects of their regulatory choices, RIA can contribute to more informed policy choices, thereby improving the efficiency and effectiveness of regulation policy.

RIA was initially adopted in the OECD countries but is now being used in a growing number of transitional and developing economies. The way in which RIA has been implemented has varied between countries, reflecting differences in the objectives selected, institutional capacity and resource constraints. For many of these countries, RIA has been adopted within government only recently, and there is limited evidence available so far on the impact that it has had in terms of improving the quality of regulation decision-making. But for those countries where there is sufficient experience on which to make an evaluation of RIA performance, the results suggest that the impact has been positive in terms of more efficient regulation and also in the contribution to the broader goal of better governance.

This book is intended to increase our knowledge and understanding of this international trend towards the use of RIA as a tool for regulatory reform and better policy-making. Many of the issues that have been introduced in this chapter are discussed in detail in the remaining chapters of the volume. Together, the chapters provide a wealth of detailed information on the international experience with RIA, derived from country case studies and cross-country comparative analyses for developed, developing and transitional economies.

RIA is a relatively new concept and experience, and in most countries it is characterized by an ongoing process of adaptation, learning and improvement. At the same time, the evidence provided in the chapters of this volume confirms a common purpose to integrate RIA into the policy-making process with the aim of raising the quality of the regulatory environment and in this way contributing to society's goal of economic, social and environmental advancement.

REFERENCES

Ambler, T., Chittenden, F. and Shamutkova, M. (2003), *Do Regulators Play by the Rules? An Audit of Regulatory Impact Assessments*, London: British Chambers of Commerce.

Anderson, J.E. (1998), 'The Struggle to Reform Regulatory Procedures, 1978–1998', *Political Studies Journal*, **26** (3), 482–98.

Cabinet Office (2003), *Better Policy Making: A Guide to Regulatory Impact Assessment*, London: Regulatory Impact Unit.

EC (European Commission) (2001), *Communication: A Sustainable Europe for a Better World: A European Union Strategy for Sustainable Development*, COM(2001)264 Final, Brussels.

EC (2002), *Communication from the Commission on Impact Assessment*, Brussels, 5 June, 2002.

EC (2005), *Impact Assessment Guidelines*, SEC (2005) 791, Brussels: EC.

Humpherson, E. (2004), 'The National Audit Office's Evaluation of RIAs: Reflections on the Pilot Year', *Public Money & Management*, **24** (5), 277–82.

Jacobs, C. (2005), 'Improving the Quality of RIA in the UK', Draft paper for Centre for Regulation and Competition, Manchester University, January 2005.

Jacobs, S. (2002), 'Convergence in Impact Analysis: Toward an Integrated Framework for RIA and SIA in European Institutions', Paper presented at the *Sustainability Impact Appraisal Seminar*, British Embassy, Brussels, April 2002.

Jacobs, S. (2004), 'Regulatory Impact Assessment and the Economic Transition to Markets', *Public Money & Management*, **24** (5), 283–90.

Kirkpatrick, C. and Parker, D. (2004), 'Regulatory Impact Assessment and Regulatory Governance in Developing Countries', *Public Administration and Development*, **24**, 333–44.

Kirkpatrick, C., Parker, D. and Zhang, Y.F. (2004), 'Regulatory Impact Assessment in Developing and Transitional Economies: A Survey of Current Practice', *Public Money and Management*, **24** (5), 291–6.

Lee, N. and Kirkpatrick, C. (2006), 'A Pilot Study of the Quality of European Commission Extended Impact Assessments', *Impact Assessment and Project Appraisal*, **24** (1).

NAO (National Audit Office) (2002), *Better Regulation: Making Good Use of Regulatory Impact Assessments*, London: Report by the Comptroller and Auditor General HC 329 Session 2001–2002, November.

NAO (2004), *Evaluation of Regulatory Impact Assessments Compendium Report 2003–04: Report by the Comptroller and Auditor General*, HC 358 Session 2003–2004, 4 March, 2004.

NAO (2006), *Evaluation of Regulatory Impacts Assessments 2005–06*, London: Report by the Comptroller and Auditor General, HC Session 2005–06, 28 June, 2006.

OECD (1995), *Recommendation on Improving the Quality of Government Regulation*, Paris: OECD, 9 March.

OECD (1997), *The OECD Report on Regulatory Reform: Synthesis*, Paris: OECD.

OECD (2002), *Regulatory Policies in the OECD Countries: From Intervention to Regulatory Governance*, Paris: OECD.

OECD (2004), 'Regulatory Performance: Ex Post Evaluation of Regulatory Tools and Institutions', *Working Party on Regulatory Management and Reform*, Draft Report by the Secretariat, Paris: OECD.

OMB (Office of Management and Budget) (2001), *Making Sense of Regulation: 2001 Report to Congress on the Costs and Benefits of Regulations and Unfunded Mandates on State, Local and Tribe Entities*, Washington, DC: Office of Information and Regulatory Affairs, OMB.

Parker, D. (2002), 'Economic Regulation: A Review of Issues', *Annals of Public and Cooperative Economics*, **73** (4), 493–519.

Parker, D. (2006), 'Regulatory Impact Assessment – A False Dawn?', *Occasional Lecture 15*, Centre for the study of Regulated Industries, University of Bath School of Management.

Radaelli, C. (2002), 'The Politics of Regulatory Impact Analysis in the OECD Countries', Mimeo, University of Bradford.

Radaelli, C. (2003), 'Impact Assessment in the European Union: Innovations, Quality and Good Regulatory Governance', Paper prepared for DG Enterprise, Brussels: European Commission.

Vibert, F. (2004), *The EU's New System of Regulatory Impact Assessment – A Scorecard*, London: European Policy Forum.

Yarrow, G. (2004), 'Evaluation of Regulatory Communication and Consultation Mechanisms: Approaches, Methodologies and some Guiding Principles', Paper prepared for the OECD Project on Ex Post Evaluation of Regulatory Tools and Institutions, Paris: OECD.

World Bank (2004), *World Development Report 2005*, Washington, DC: World Bank and Oxford University Press.

2. Current trends in the process and methods of regulatory impact assessment: mainstreaming RIA into policy processes

Scott H. Jacobs

INTRODUCTION

Regulation is the defining characteristic of modern governance. Most of the important public policy concerns facing governments – environment quality, consumer rights, definition of property rights, control of new technologies, integration into global markets – are regulatory issues. The success of modern governance depends essentially on the performance of regulation. This is certainly true in the industrialized countries: in the United States, despite its unwarranted reputation for deregulation, around 115 000 new regulations have been adopted at federal level since President Reagan was elected in 1981, and in the European Union over 130 000 pages of regulation now comprise the European Single Market,

The dominance of the regulatory state is also true in developing countries where regulation of private behaviour is one of the most consuming of government activities. Businesses usually face not dozens, but hundreds or even thousands of regulatory obligations from all levels of government, and more are added daily.

Tackling the regulatory reform agenda is among the most difficult challenges facing governments since regulatory systems, while large, tend to be highly decentralized among numerous institutions, non-transparent, easily captured and based in enduring habits of public sector behaviour. The clearest lesson of the last 20 years is that modernizing the regulatory role of the state requires a sophisticated 'good governance' agenda, not a narrow 'deregulation' agenda. Successful regulatory reform has become a multi-faceted strategy that includes better regulation, deregulation, re-regulation, simplification and institution building (including public sector reforms that realign incentives). In the modern practice, regulatory reform is not about limiting the role of the state but about redefining the capacities and the role of the state to meet evolving needs.

This kind of agenda requires substantial learning on the part of the public sector and key stakeholders who interact in a new dynamic of public–private problem-solving and accountability. To be successful in managing limited resources, governments must learn better and faster about how to solve problems. For example, governments must learn when and how to regulate well in a market economy and not to abandon their legitimate roles in the face of evolving market forces.

RIA has become one of the methods through which societies speed up learning. Because it is an open and consultative technique, RIA stimulates social learning, in which various stakeholders involved in the issue gain a clearer sense of the options, and trade-offs, and the consequences of solutions, than in the past. Because it increases opportunities for debate, RIA contributes to the development of a degree of social consensus that allows difficult public policy decisions be made. Because it is an evidence-based approach, RIA fosters the development of new and open channels of information-gathering and data-sharing across interests.

The usefulness of RIA in speeding up critical learning is one reason why it has spread so quickly across developed countries and increasingly in developing countries. One result of this imperative of learning is that in many countries, RIA is now being mainstreamed into policy processes. That is, RIA is becoming routinized into the machinery of policy development. Mainstreaming of RIA is a positive development because good RIA is an effective tool for improving the quality of public policy. But mainstreaming raises new methods and tensions as RIA becomes more responsive to political concerns such as highly visible paperwork burdens and as wider circles of civil servants are required to deal with analytical techniques for which they have not been adequately prepared.

In this kind of system of results-oriented policy-making based on learning, the nature of RIA is also changing. In most countries RIA has evolved from narrow technical methods aimed at cutting costs toward more flexible and sophisticated techniques of problem-solving aimed at fostering a richer and more informed public debate about important public policy issues. The 'smart regulation' movement is aimed at improving the performance of the 'regulatory state' that is everywhere under pressure to produce more results at lower cost.

The wider role of RIA means that the value of RIA is increasingly due to process rather then method. Functionally RIA is now seen less as an analytical method of arriving at precise answers to quantitative questions and more as a three-stage learning process: asking the right questions in a structured format to support a wider and more transparent policy debate;

systematically and consistently examining selected potential impacts arising from government action or non-action; and communicating the information to decision-makers and stakeholders.[1]

The essential question facing governments in their use of RIA is: how can RIA be used most effectively to speed up learning about problem-solving? The answer to that question lies in the processes of RIA and the techniques of RIA, which are discussed in the rest of this chapter.

PROCESSES FOR RIA

To answer this question this chapter reviews international trends in four elements of the RIA process:

- targeting and scope;
- public consultation processes;
- quality control of RIA;
- data collection methods and data quality standards.

These four elements are increasingly seen as the key design elements of an effective RIA programme. For RIA to succeed in improving public policy, these four elements must work together within a systemic process.[2]

Targeting and Scope of RIA

RIA has become more widespread at the same time as it has become more targeted. That is, basic RIA is being applied to more regulations while a higher standard of quantitative analysis is being applied to fewer regulations. This is accomplished through application of principles of 'proportionality' and 'significance'.

It is generally accepted that all regulations with more than trivial impacts should undergo sufficient analysis to allow for informed debate and decision-making. In most countries some form of RIA has been generally applicable to most regulations for years. For example, in the United Kingdom, RIAs must be completed for all policy changes whether European or domestic, that could affect the public or private sectors, charities, the voluntary sector or small businesses. In the European Commission however, RIA became a general requirement only in 2005. Its 2005 policy greatly expanded the scope of RIA to all policies included in the Commission's annual work programme.

At the same time, standards of RIA quality and the depth of external scrutiny have recently increased significantly for the most important regulations. This selective targeting has shifted RIA resources to where they can do the most good. Australia, the United Kingdom, the European Commission, Ireland, New Zealand and the United States are all using stricter and clearer targeting strategies combined with higher analytical standards for important regulations. Most are using a monetary trigger to establish an objective threshold in combination with subjective thresholds using words like 'major' and 'significant' applied to various kinds of impacts. In federal Australia for example, RIA resources are more targeted toward 'significant' changes and proportional analysis and more effort is being given to improving analysis of the most 'significant' regulations.[3] In the European Commission, since 2005, a 'roadmap', or partial RIA is required for all proposals to better inform other services and the public of the issue at hand, policy options, likely impacts, assessments and consultations to be undertaken, and their timing. This is followed by a fuller 'impact assessment' in which the depth of analysis depends on the importance of the proposal.

Public Consultation Processes

Public consultation is the means by which RIA fosters public debate. Public consultation linked to RIA has become simultaneously more multilayered, which allows it to become more open and more targeted.

It has become more open in the sense that RIA is pushing consultation to occur sooner, more systematically and more transparently. In the United States, the United Kingdom and the European Commission, draft RIAs are published on Internet sites for maximum public access. The record however, is far from perfect: in Sweden, only 48 per cent of RIAs in 2005 reported on how consultation had occurred, up from 35 per cent in 2004. In New Zealand only final RIAs must be published on the Internet (since 2001).

Consultation has become more targeted in the sense that some forms of consultation are structured to link information needs with particular stakeholders who hold information. These structured approaches include test panels in Denmark, the United Kingdom, Germany and the Netherlands, and focus groups (Sweden, Victoria State in Australia).

These newer multilayered consultation strategies – based on minimum and consistent standards of openness but allowing more flexible adaptation to target key groups – seem to be more effective and accessible than earlier consultation strategies based on standardized consultation methods. The minimum standards for publication of RIA open up access by preparing the public to participate more effectively while the more structured and tailored forms permit more intensive dialogue and better information collection.

Quality Control of RIA

Quality control is necessary if RIA is to be carried out at a reliable level of consistency and quality. However, incentives to conduct good RIA are weak and often perverse in traditional civil services, and many RIA failures have been traced to the lack of an effective quality control and incentives system in the civil service.

RIA-related reforms in recent years have focused on increasing oversight and quality control of RIA through several methods, described below.

Strengthening the challenge function from a central RIA watchdog

It is accepted now that the RIA oversight body is most effective when placed at the centre of government where authorities for inter-ministerial oversight are already well established. But even these central bodies have struggled to maintain RIA quality and as a result, several countries have strengthened central oversight mechanisms.

In the United States, the Office of Information and Regulatory Affairs (OIRA) has done this largely through the mechanism of the 'return letter', in which OIRA publicly details its concerns and criticism about the regulation in the RIA. While OIRA does not have formal approval authority over regulations, its central role in the process of regulatory development and its proximity to the White House makes it difficult for a regulator to ignore its public advice. Furthermore, OIRA has moved to increase scrutiny of regulatory quality by setting a higher level of data quality standards and it has multiplied the challenge function through scientific peer review.

The UK government now has no fewer than three challenge units at the centre and a series of challenge functions built into the policy-making process. First in 2005, the Better Regulation Executive (BRE) in the Cabinet Office replaced the Regulatory Impact Unit (RIU). The BRE is intended to provide stronger central coordination of delivery and implementation of regulatory reforms, challenge departments on their progress with regulatory reform and work with departments to change regulatory culture and processes. The incentives of the Cabinet Office to monitor RIA are strengthened by a Public Service Agreement target (performance measure) for the Cabinet Office to achieve 100 per cent compliance with the RIA requirements. Second, a Small Business Service reviews proposals that affect small firms. Third, all regulatory proposals likely to impose a major new burden on business require clearance from the Panel for Regulatory Accountability, chaired by the Prime Minister. The Panel will monitor the new requirement for 'compensatory simplification' – the 'one in, one out' approach to new regulations – for every new proposal. At the level of the government departments (ministries), 'better regulation' ministers and units are accountable for delivering reductions in administrative burdens and achieving regulatory simplification. Finally, the Better Regulation Task Force (BRTF) became permanent in January 2006 as the new Better Regulation Commission, with additional responsibilities to challenge departments and regulators on their performance against the better regulation targets.

Strengthening the challenge function in the European Commission has been difficult due to complex governing relations, the relatively decentralized structure of the Commission and the weakness of horizontal management functions. An 'inter-institutional agreement (IIA) on better regulation', agreed in December 2003 by the three EU institutions (European Parliament, Council and Commission), established a global strategy for better law-making throughout the entire EU legislative process. But there was no creation in the IIA of a central RIA oversight body in the Commission or anywhere else. As an alternative, the Commission has stated that 'it is important to reinforce the quality control by Commission departments of impact assessments before releasing these for interdepartmental scrutiny' (CEC, 2005a).[4]

Involvement in RIA quality control and monitoring by other institutions

Other than a central reform body, institutions with quality control functions can be divided into four categories. First, political-level and policy-level bodies that provide oversight of the regulatory reform programme as a whole and of the work of the central unit. These include committees of the Cabinet (such as the Special Committee of Council in Canada), high-level commissions (such as the Competitiveness Council in the European Commission), high-level inter-ministerial bodies (such as the Implementation Group of Secretaries General in Ireland), and activist committees and bodies of the parliament (such as the General Accounting Office in the United States; the Standing Joint Committee of the Senate and the House of Commons for the Scrutiny of Regulations in Canada; and Committees of the European Parliament).

Second, ad hoc inter-ministerial working groups that are put together to coordinate and advise on major regulatory initiatives. Examples include the cross-departmental steering groups in Ireland and ad hoc inter-service coordination groups in the European Commission.

Third, ministerial- or departmental-level regulatory reform units, which are responsible for carrying out the regulatory policy and RIA quality oversight at the level of the ministry or regulator.

Finally, private sector groups, advisory bodies, think tanks, or other research bodies who support the regulatory reform agenda can be helpful in identifying priorities and proposing reforms. The OECD highlighted the UK's Better Regulation Task Force (BRTF) as an example of an oversight body that has played a 'large role' in advocacy of regulatory reform, that is: 'the promotion of long term regulatory policy considerations, including policy change, development of new and improved tools and institutional change' (OECD, 2002a). The BRTF and its successor, the Better Regulation Commission, are independent advisory bodies established to advise the government on actions to improve the effectiveness and credibility of regulation. Its advocacy and monitoring functions have been highly effective in the United Kingdom in maintaining attention on RIA quality. The general trend in recent years seems to be for bodies in these four categories to be more proactive at higher levels (in the sense of more intense monitoring and higher expectations) but without a parallel activism at lower levels (in the sense of more effective decentralized departmental quality efforts and regulatory RIA bodies).

Early planning and preparation of RIA

Some of the problems with RIA stem from poor timing of the RIA process, in particular the failure to start RIA early enough to integrate its results into policy decisions. Such failure seems to be less of a problem in countries with annual regulatory planning activities. A regulatory planning process provides early notification to the public about regulatory initiatives at a time when it is still possible to revise fundamentally the regulatory decision. In the governments reviewed for this chapter, only three have such plans:

- In Canada, each department and agency must prepare a one-year Report on Plans and Priorities (RPP) to be tabled in parliament. The RPP offers an opportunity to advise parliamentarians and interested groups and individuals, of upcoming regulatory initiatives. The RPP is supplemented by the more detailed Departmental Regulatory Plan, which is placed on a website.
- The United States has had since 1984 a regulatory planning process in which very early RIA summaries are published twice a year in the Unified Agenda of Federal Regulations (also known as the Semiannual Regulatory Agenda). The Unified Agenda summarizes the rules that each federal agency expects to issue during the next six months. The agenda is also placed on a central website.
- The European Commission in 2005 put considerable effort into earlier preparation and planning for RIA. Major impact assessments are integrated into the Commission's annual Strategic Planning and Programming (SPP).

There is a clear trend toward earlier planning and launching of RIA, particularly the preparation of early 'light' RIAs, called 'initial RIAs' in the United Kingdom, 'screening RIAs' in Ireland, 'roadmaps' in the European Commission and 'consultation RIAs' in Australia. Early screening RIAs support a policy of proportional analysis and open the way for earlier and more meaningful public consultation on alternatives and regulatory design.

Monitoring compliance followed by public reporting of performance

Closely related to the challenge function is the RIA monitoring function. There is a close relationship between the central RIA units who are more proactive in challenging low-quality RIAs and the units who actively monitor compliance and report on performance. In the most advanced RIA systems, regulators with poor RIA performance are identified publicly and regularly and follow-up action is planned. The most public regulatory review on a case by case basis is that carried out by OIRA in the United States. OIRA's 'return letters' containing the results of its reviews, including blunt criticism of the quality of the analysis, are publicly available on its website.

A more common and perhaps more effective approach is to issue performance evaluations based on the quality of RIAs. The US OIRA, the European Commission and Australia's Office of Regulation Review (ORR) issue annual reports on RIA quality and compliance status. Probably the most advanced institution in the world in monitoring and reporting is Mexico's Federal Commission of Better Regulation (COFEMER), which has implemented a simple internal RIA scoring system and sends fortnightly reports on RIA compliance to the Comptroller General.

A country not included in this list is the United Kingdom. The United Kingdom's Better Regulation Executive says that it 'carries out regular exercises to establish the level of compliance' with RIA processes and publishes the results. Compliance ranges from 92 per cent in 2002 to 100 per cent in 2004 and 2005. This monitoring is not however, nearly as detailed as that carried out in Australia or the United States and the score of 100 per cent for two years raises doubts as to its rigour. Similarly, neither Canada nor New Zealand have any equivalent for these reports. Monitoring of RIA quality and compliance is still considered to be an internal matter rather than a public responsibility of importance to effective governance and hence a matter to be tracked publicly.

Better use of scientific input through peer review

Regulatory matters have become increasingly technical and science-based over the past decade. This trend has placed increasing strains on regulators who often do not have the skills needed to access, interpret and apply the science underlying a regulatory decision. Increasing access to scientific expertise in regulatory decision-making has become, in a few countries, an important quality strategy. One technique for this is peer review. A peer review group that builds up expertise in a particular area such as risk assessment or data quality can be expected to produce better review results at lower cost than a series of ad hoc peer review groups scattered through the public administration.

The US government has issued government-wide guidance aimed at enhancing the practice of peer review of government science documents to improve the quality of published information (OMB, 2003). The guidance requires that important scientific information shall be peer reviewed by qualified specialists before it is disseminated by the federal government, recognizing that different types of peer review are appropriate for different types of information.

The European Commission announced in 2005 its intent to use scientific peer review, not of data quality, but of the RIA methodology designed for specific major regulations. It announced that it would 'improve the intrinsic quality of the impact assessment of EU legislation by ensuring on a case by case basis the ex ante validation by external scientific experts of the methodology used for certain impact assessments' (EC, 2005a). This peer review process has not yet been launched.

RIA training and guidance

Quality of RIA is dependent on the skills of the regulators. Building the skills needed for good RIA takes time and investment, which most governments have failed to provide. Following years of neglect of RIA training there is a small but growing emphasis on better RIA training. For example, the Australia ORR provides training and guidance to regulatory officials and 'plans to enhance its ongoing RIS [regulatory impact statement] training for departments and agencies' (2005). Training is at a robust level: in 2004–05, the ORR provided formal training on RIA and regulatory best practice to 415 officials, a slight reduction from previous years. However, this may be insufficient, since businesses still complain that 'greater education, skill development, resources and priority within agencies is needed' to address problems of 'poor RIS compliance and policy design'. The European Commission is investing a small but growing amount in RIA training. Most of this training is decentralized to the various Directorate Generals and hence there are no consolidated figures on the number of officials trained. In the United Kingdom, the RIU (Regulatory Impact Unit) runs seminars, formal training sessions and workshops on RIA. The RIU is also involved in training officials through the Civil Service College's training courses on policy-making.

Following a period of relative quiet in the early 2000s, there has been in the past two years considerable investment in producing new and better guidance on RIA. There appear to be three major trends in the content of the new RIA guides. First, compared with earlier guides, there is much more attention to the process of RIA. More guidance is given about when to start RIA (early), the consultation process and the review process. This illustrates the point that the process of RIA has become just as important to the process of government learning as the quantitative content of RIA. Second, there is more detail and assistance in quantifying impacts. All of the evaluations of RIA have shown that lack of quantification continues to be weak. These guides provide more examples of how to quantify and more precise instructions on how to present qualitative impacts. Third, there is more attention to assessing alternatives, although this aspect continues to be the weakest part of every RIA guide.

Data Collection Methods and Data Quality Standards

The most expensive and time-consuming component of the entire RIA process is the collection of relevant and reliable data. Collecting data is something that all regulators must do in the course of their day to day activities. Therefore, they most develop the skills and the contacts to identify data needs, identify data sources and present the inevitable uncertainties associated with data. The choice of which data to collect and the data collection method are not isolated decisions in the regulatory process because they influence the whole process.

Most RIAs will require a mix of already available information and very specific information that is tailored to the micro-impacts of the proposal in terms of benefits, costs or risks. This means that some original data collection is usually needed, either by formal means, such as statistical methods, or by informal means such as by public consultation. Usually a mix of formal and informal means will be needed. Yet regulators are often poorly prepared to collect high-quality data. Criticism of RIA in specific proceedings often appears as concerns about low data quality.

Defining standards of data acceptability in advance, as well as the quality control process for data use, are critical to boosting RIA credibility and reliability. The most common data quality standard is 'transparency'. Several countries require that underlying data and assumptions be made explicit in the analysis so that readers can easily understand how conclusions were reached.

The United States government has adopted general information quality standards based on 'objectivity, utility and integrity'. Under these guidelines, 'information quality' means 'utility' (usefulness to its intended users), 'integrity' (security), and 'objectivity'. 'Objectivity' focuses on whether the disseminated information is accurate, reliable and unbiased as a matter of presentation and substance. OMB's government-wide guidelines cover the quality of information disseminated by federal agencies. More critical 'influential' information is subject to higher quality standards.

Both the United States and the European Commission require that 'best available data' be used. Other data quality standards used include: reproducibility, acceptance by independent experts, collected according to good statistical practices such as random sampling and presentation of best estimates reflecting expected values (as distinct from 'worst case' or conservative estimates), along with plausible ranges. A general rule is that survey data should not be used for RIAs unless the sampling method, the instrument itself and the raw data are available to the regulator for quality checking.

Data needs and quality should be included in the design of the RIA system. The means by which data are collected and the standards of quality that define acceptable data should not be ad hoc decisions decided for every RIA but a matter of RIA policy that aims to produce the best-quality data at the lowest cost possible.[5]

TECHNIQUES OF RIA

The main analytical methods used in RIA programmes are:

- forms of benefit–cost analysis, integrated impact analysis (IIA) and sustainability impact analysis (SIA) to integrate issues into broad analytical frameworks that can demonstrate links and trade-offs among multiple policy objectives;
- forms of cost-effectiveness analysis based on comparison of alternatives to find lowest-cost solutions to produce specific outcomes;
- a range of partial analyses such as SME tests, administrative burden estimates, business impact tests and other analyses of effects on specified groups and stemming from certain kinds of regulatory costs;
- risk assessment and uncertainty analysis. Risk assessment is aimed at characterizing the probability of outcomes as a result of specified inputs. On the other hand, various forms of sensitivity or uncertainty are used to project the likelihood of a range of possible outcomes due to estimation errors. Uncertainty analysis is used to provide policy-makers with a more accurate understanding of the likelihood of impacts.

Benefit–Cost Analysis

The economics thrust of RIA has always favored benefit–cost analysis (BCA) as the most inclusive and socially responsible method of public decision-making. BCA is the method long used by governments in assessing investment projects such as roads and dams, and was adapted to regulatory policy issues in the 1970s.

While there are continual concerns about over-monetization of impacts that can be legitimately presented in other metrics, this is a concern that is easily met. Mainstream benefit–cost analysis as used in RIA today is a soft form of BCA, in which quantitative and qualitative metrics are combined and presented systematically. There is no country in which modern BCA insists on the monetization of all benefits and costs. That is why the author calls this method soft benefit–cost analysis.

Soft BCA is the method best adapted to protecting a broad range of interests. One of the key advantages of benefit–cost frameworks is that they encompass the broadest range of impacts across the socioeconomic environmental spectrum, hence they are in line with nearly universal political demands that RIA methods address a wider range of public interests. BCA also offers the important advantage of comparing costs and benefits occurring at different points in time.

The BCA framework is the most inclusive and integrated form of RIA and provides the best information on which to make sound policy decisions. The fact that countries with strong environmental protection standards and records are pushing toward more integrated RIA frameworks based on soft BCA and stronger emphasis on quantitative measures of impacts suggests that such a framework is fully consistent with high values of social and environmental protection.

But the general move toward more integrated forms of RIA through soft BCA is only one strand in current trends in RIA methods. RIA trends today show a diversification, sometimes even a fragmentation, among the several analytical methods listed above. The main reason for the divergence of methods is that RIA is entering the mainstream of policy, and is coming under pressure from the many groups who now understand that they have a direct stake in RIA. That is, RIA is being democratized from its origins as a rather technocratic tool into a political and policy tool. Table 2.1 below shows how the different sources of interest in RIA lead to different goals and kinds of analysis.

Diversification of methods is not a bad trend as long as the other RIA methods act as inputs into a broader benefit–cost framework. There are sound reasons for some aspects of analytical diversification such as concerns about how regulations will affect larger social goals and concerns

Table 2.1 Pressures on RIA methods

Pressures on RIA		Goals		Analytical Method
Neoclassical economics	=	Maximization of social welfare among multiple goods and bads (Pareto optimum)	=	Benefit–cost analysis, integrated impact assessment including multiple policy objectives
New public management	=	Cost and performance disciplines	=	Cost-effectiveness analysis on various options
Competitiveness, microeconomic policies	=	Minimizing business costs	=	Business impact, SME tests, administrative burden tests
Social consensus, interest group pressures	=	High valuation of impacts on selected groups	=	Distributional analysis, partial analyses

Source: Jacobs (2006).

about the disproportionate effects of fixed regulatory costs on small businesses. In some cases a focus on specific kinds of impacts is merited because regulators have neglected those impacts in the past. In such cases, partial analysis can be seen as an attempt to rebalance the inputs into good regulatory decisions.

However, in some countries, diversification is driven in part by competitiveness issues and in part by political intent to serve vocal constituencies. This has resulted in fragmentation of methods into competing policy agendas. In such cases RIA is weakened by over-reliance on partial, uncertain and inappropriate analytical methods that are not based on a coherent view of the use of RIA in public policy. Reliance on such methods creates risks of systematic errors in policy decisions. Such errors reduce the benefits of government action and increase the likelihood of policy failure.

The conclusion here is that governments should develop what the European Commission calls integrated impact analysis (IIA), in which economic, social and environmental impacts are assessed together within a transparent benefit–cost framework. In this approach the RIA becomes the framework through which trade-offs are identified and benefits are maximized across a range of policy objectives.

Another important issue is analytical quality within the method chosen. In the countries with the most investment in RIA, there are continual efforts to increase the quality of RIA through more quantification, more precise requirements and higher-quality data. In Australia for example, since the mid-1990s the ORR has progressively raised the minimum information requirements of RISs, with the objective of improving the quality of RISs and their usefulness to decision-makers. For example, for regulatory proposals that generate additional compliance costs on business, since 1 July 2004, the ORR has advised regulators that quantitative data about such costs must be included in RISs (or, alternatively, a clear statement be made that the regulator is unable to estimate such costs).

Similarly the United States' OMB's guidelines for RIA increased emphasis on cost-effectiveness analysis as well as benefit–cost analysis. Specifically the new guidelines emphasize monetization and 'net benefits' criteria while clarifying the presentation of non-quantifiable factors. Cost-effectiveness analysis was mandated for all major health and safety standards to provide a clearer comparison of the cost for risk reduction. This step was intended to increase incentives for regulators to set priorities addressing more important risks or risks that could be mitigated at lower cost, and reducing incentives to address high-profile but less important risks with higher costs.

Cost-effectiveness Analysis and Comparing Policy Options

Cost-effectiveness analysis (CEA) is a technique that is used to compare the costs of different options with the same or similar outputs or benefits. It is a useful but limited method because it does not determine if the action is worth taking (that benefits justify costs) and does not resolve the choice of the optimal level of benefits. But it can reduce the costs of problem solutions to the lowest level. That is, whereas BCA helps governments decide what to do, CEA helps governments decide how to do it. One of the primary functions of CEA is to compare systematically and transparently many options. Comparing options is among the most difficult tasks of RIA. The most rigorous and data-intensive approach is taken by Australia, which requires that the RIA 'assesses feasible options and include a cost–benefit, impact and risk analysis of each option' (ORR, 1998). The United States requires a broad (soft) 'net benefit' approach: 'In choosing among alternative regulatory approaches, agencies should select approaches that maximize net benefits, including potential economic, environmental, public health and safety, and other advantages; distributive impacts; and equity' (OMB, 2003). Canada's Regulatory Policy is also highly quantitative in that it adopts a 'net benefit' standard to 'ensure that use of the government's regulatory powers results in the greatest net benefit to Canadian society' and it requires that '[a]lternative regulatory solutions must be analyzed to ensure the most effective and efficient is chosen' (Government of Canada, 1999).

The timing of the RIA process is also important to RIA quality in comparing alternatives. This review of experiences in advanced countries suggests that the timing of RIA, perhaps more than the method of RIA, is the most important determinant of how well the assessment of options is done. Surprisingly, many countries do not require that RIA be done before the options are considered and chosen. RIAs that are multistaged seem to encourage earlier use of RIA and lend themselves to better consideration and selection of options. For that reason the discussion above on the early timing of RIA and public consultation is critical to a fuller and more honest appraisal of alternatives.

Partial Analyses

All impacts are not equal. It is perfectly permissible in RIA methods to assign different weights to different kinds of impacts. Analytical methods themselves provide little guidance for assigning different weights and therefore the decision to weigh some impacts more heavily than others is mostly a political decision based on policy priorities and values. Distributional issues have always been difficult to handle within the RIA framework because it is usually analytically difficult to trace the specific effects of a single regulation on specific groups through the complex interactions of society, the environment and the market. Australia's RIA requires that distributional effects be documented from an economy-wide approach rather than zeroing in a priori on specific groups. In Australia, RIAs should document which groups benefit from regulation and which groups pay the direct and indirect costs of implementation. A similar approach is taken in the European Commission and in the United States where emphasis is placed on an integrated approach and overall comparison of benefits and costs rather than on non-transparent weighting of selected impacts. Canada's RIA handles distributional effects similarly.

Yet many countries are requiring that RIA assesses specific effects on gender, regional development and other distributive effects. The implication is that the regulator should avoid placing costs on vulnerable groups or even disproportionate costs and benefits across groups.

On face value this trend seems laudable, but it is problematic in practice. A key assumption of social welfare analysis is that a consistent commitment to better public policy that produces more results at lower cost will, over time, produce better macropolicy and macroeconomic outcomes. For that reason the consistent use of RIA should itself have positive macro impacts that benefit everyone in society. This does not mean however, that macroeconomic impacts for single regulatory interventions can be assessed or managed by regulators. Micro interventions are part of a complex economic system and tracing the marginal effects of a single intervention is usually impossible. What RIAs actually do when they attempt this task is to identify very short-term and static effects on specific industries. Secondary, longer-term and dynamic effects are ignored because they simply cannot be assessed. Hence the practical and unfortunate result of this kind of analysis is to drive policy decisions toward static and short-term results, which often lead to the wrong policy solution.

Another kind of partial analysis is the SME test. Requiring specific tests as part of the RIA demonstrates political commitment to addressing problems facing specific groups, such as competitiveness concerns for the business sector. In this sense, specific RIA tests are often the equivalent of constituency services. SME and business impact tests have always been popular for this reason. This kind of test can boost attention to disproportionate regulatory costs on SMEs but is damaging if it diverts public policy decisions away from those that produce higher net benefits toward those that are less beneficial in general although more beneficial to business or small business interests. In the United States and in the European Union these kinds of tests are explicitly included within the integrated BCA framework and are not considered as a separate or external test.

The most prominent emerging example of partial analysis is the costing of administrative burdens contained in regulations. Reducing administrative burdens has always been a popular element of regulatory reform but it has taken on a disproportionate role in recent years. In 2002, when the Dutch Government committed itself to measuring and reducing the administrative burden on business by 25 per cent using a method called the 'standard cost model' (SCM), which is a bottom-up method of measuring the time needed to comply with administrative requirements and extrapolating from firms to entire economies. Several countries are developing this method for their own use and the SCM is spreading rapidly.[6]

The European Commission decided in October 2005 to develop an EU common methodology based on the SCM and integrate that method into its own RIA guidelines. The analysis will assess net administrative costs (new costs imposed by an act minus costs suppressed by the same act at EU or Member State level). The 'net cost' approach is justified as consistent with the Commission's RIA guidelines and the OECD guiding principles for regulatory quality and performance (CEC, 2005c).

In 2005, the OECD's Red Tape Scoreboard project began developing a method for measuring administrative burden across OECD members using the SCM as a starting point. The danger is that this and other partial analyses will become so dominant that they will overwhelm the integrated analysis that is so important to balance various impacts and benefits with costs. If the administrative burden tests take a disproportionate weight in the RIA it would discourage the use of information and disclosure as alternatives to regulation since these alternatives usually impose relatively high administrative burdens. It would systematically bias decision-making away from regulatory solutions in which administrative requirements are the most efficient solution.

This review strongly suggests that partial analysis strengthens RIA if it reinforces attention to important impacts that have been neglected but only if those impacts are considered within an integrated analytical framework. That is, partial analysis is useful primarily as an input into broader RIA. On the other hand, partial analysis will degrade RIA quality if it is not integrated into a wider analytical framework and therefore is given undue weight in the policy decision. Over-reliance on partial analysis fragments RIA into addressing special interests and renders it useless as a general policy tool.

Risk Assessment and Uncertainty Analysis

Three aspects of risk assessment and uncertainty analysis are included in the RIA programmes of the countries included in this review. The usual and most precise use of the term means the assessment of the probability of an effect due to a specified cause. Here, the purpose of the analysis is to identify that causal probability. The risk assessment is then used to assess the impacts of any particular intervention. The risk assessment does not measure uncertainty but probability. Second, uncertainty analysis projects the likelihood of a range of possible outcomes due to estimation errors. For example, we can determine the worst-case scenario by substituting the most pessimistic estimates for each variable simultaneously and see how much the outcomes change. We can also pinpoint the source of uncertainty by varying each variable one at a time, holding all other variables unchanged, to see which are the most important. Uncertainty analysis is used to provide policy-makers with a more accurate understanding of the likelihood of impacts. Third, a variation of uncertainty analysis is the use of precaution to address unknown risks that are potentially serious and irreversible. The precautionary principle essentially requires that, for certain kinds of impacts and even where uncertainty is very high, worst-case scenarios should be used to justify intervention.

Risk assessment is well elaborated in the RIAs in Australia, the United Kingdom and the United States. In the RIAs in the other countries, risk assessment takes only a minor role and is only briefly mentioned.

Uncertainty analysis is more widely incorporated into RIA guidance in these countries. Almost all of the RIA programmes anticipate that major assumptions will be tested through sensitivity analysis of some kind.

Precaution is not integrated into RIA in these countries. The reason for this is that precaution is not an analytical concept but a policy to react in certain ways under uncertainty. The RIA can produce information to inform the decision to use precaution but the RIA cannot itself demonstrate whether precaution is appropriate.

CONCLUSIONS

This review of current practices in RIA in the most advanced countries confirms that RIA methods supporting environmental, social and economic policies are evolving toward various forms of soft benefit–cost analysis. Countries such as the United States, Australia and also the European Commission are actively seeking ways to improve the rigour and quality of RIA as an integrated framework to deal with the complexity of modern public policy. They are establishing the contemporary benchmark for good RIA. The fact that countries with strong environmental protection standards and records are pushing toward more integrated RIA frameworks, based on soft BCA and stronger emphasis on quantitative measures of impacts, suggests that such a framework is fully consistent with values of social and environmental protection.

The review suggests that governments that are improving or adopting RIAs should base RIA on the integrated analytical framework in which quantitative and qualitative metrics for economic, social and environmental impacts are combined and presented systematically. RIA should become the framework through which trade-offs are identified and benefits are maximized across a range of policy objectives. This framework produces the most rigorous, transparent and consistent information for public policy decisions.

NOTES

1. This definition of RIA as a process rather than as a document was developed by Jacobs and Associates (a consulting firm) in 2005.
2. This point was made in the 2004–05 review by the UK's National Audit Office of UK RIAs. The review found that the RIAs that influenced policy were started early in the process, involved good consultation processes and produced good assessments of the impacts of the policy proposals (NAO, 2005).
3. In 2004–05 full RIAs were required for 7 per cent of new regulations, compared with 13 per cent in 1999–2000.

4. The IIA led to a proliferation of bodies working on better regulation and RIA. This has aroused legitimate fears of lack of coherence and coordination but is also strengthening accountability and monitoring of quality.
5. OMB has pointed out that data quality issues are often confused between inadequate treatment of uncertainty and accuracy of information. Both data problems should be addressed in a data quality strategy.
6. BRTF (2005).

REFERENCES

BRTF (Better Regulation Task Force) (2005), 'Better Regulation – From Design to Delivery, Annual Report 2005' (http://www.brc.gov.uk/publications/designdelivery.asp), Government of the UK.

CEC (Commission of the European Communities) (2005a), 'Impact Assessment Guidelines', SEC (2005) 791, Brussels.

CEC (2005b), 'Better Regulation for Growth and Jobs in the European Union', Communication from the Commission to the Council and the European Parliament, Brussels, 16 March 2005, COM (2005) 97 Final.

CEC (2005c), 'An EU Common Methodology for Assessing Administrative Costs Imposed by Legislation', Communication from the Commission, COM (2005) 518 Final, Brussels.

Government of Canada (1999), 'Regulatory Policy', Privy Council Office.

Jacobs, S. (2006), *Current Trends in Process and Methods of Regulatory Impact Analysis: The Challenges of Mainstreaming RIA into Policy-making*, Washington, DC: Jacobs and Associates Inc. at www.regulatoryreform.com.

NAO (National Audit Office) (2005), 'Evaluation of Regulatory Impact Assessments Compendium Report 2004–05', Report by the Comptroller and Auditor General, HC 341 Session 2004–05, 17 March 2005.

OECD (2002a), *Regulatory Policies in OECD Countries: From Interventionism to Regulatory Governance*, Paris: OECD.

OECD (2002b), 'Government Capacity to Ensure High Quality Regulation', in *Canada: Maintaining Leadership Through Innovation*, Paris: OECD.

OMB (Office of Management and Budget) (2003), 'Circular A-4, Subject: Regulatory Analysis', Washington DC: Government of the US.

ORR (Office of Regulation Review) (1998), *A Guide to Regulation*, Government of Australia, 2nd edn, December.

3. Indicators of regulatory quality

Fabrizio De Francesco and Claudio M. Radaelli

INTRODUCTION

Indicators of regulatory quality, performance measures of regulatory governance and targets for the reduction of paperwork and administrative burdens have become prominent items on the reform agenda of governments and international organizations. The OECD and the World Bank have prioritized regulation in their programmes for 'good governance'. They argue for comprehensive regulatory changes, linking regulatory reforms to performance indicators, covering rules as well as more inclusive and transparent modes of governance. By doing so, these organizations have acknowledged the potential of regulatory reform in terms of governance, participation of the stakeholders and more balanced state–society relations (OECD, 2002; Kaufmann, Kraay and Mastruzzi, 2003, 2005).

In Europe, the European Union (EU) has rapidly emerged as a crucial arena where regulatory policies are defined. With the Lisbon Agenda goal of making the EU the most competitive knowledge-based society, regulatory reform has become a priority for the Member States and the EU institutions. In 2002, the Commission adopted a system of integrated impact assessment to measure a wide range of costs and benefits of proposed legislation, in the context of the goal of sustainable development. In 2003 the European Council, the European Parliament and the Commission signed an 'inter-institutional agreement on better regulation'. In January 2004, the Finance Ministers of Ireland, the Netherlands, Luxembourg and the UK – the Member States in charge of four EU Presidencies over the course of 2004 and 2005 – proposed to coordinate and intensify action on regulatory reform.[1] The Finance Ministers asked the Commission to monitor the process by using 'indicators to measure progress with regulatory quality and reform at European and Member State level'. In December 2004, the Irish, Dutch, Luxembourg, UK, Austrian and Finnish Presidencies of the EU highlighted the issue of tackling the administrative costs of regulation and the need to test the impact of proposed legislation on European competitiveness. They reiterated the invitation to the Commission to develop indicators of regulatory quality. The Competitiveness Council of 24 September

2004 called on the Commission and the Member States to evaluate 'the cumulative impact of existing legislation on the competitiveness of industry and of specific industry sectors' and to develop 'a method for measuring administrative burden on business' (Council, 2004, p. 3). On 25 January 2006, the President of the Commission, Mr Barroso, said that 'every Member State should set up a system to properly measure administrative burdens. The Commission will launch a major exercise of its own to identify and propose how to reduce costs arising from EU rules or their implementation at national level'.[2] In short, in a few years, the EU and its Member States have moved from a discussion of principles of regulatory reform to a debate on indicators of regulatory quality.

In this chapter we review the economic literature and the experience of governments with indicators of regulatory quality, identifying their main advantages and limitations. All too often the academic discussion on indicators has been focused on the technical properties of the measures under consideration and has ended up as an exercise in comparative statistics. By contrast, we look at the political properties of indicators. We shed light on the core stakeholders implicit in different measures. We also draw attention to the relationship between indicators and policy tools that regulators can change, and to the presence or absence of policy processes in which regulatory indicators can operate as an information-rich resource – potentially capable of altering the interaction amongst the actors in charge of policy. In the final part of the chapter, we will show how the analysis of political properties can suggest an original approach to the development of indicators for the EU, drawing on our research in progress.[3]

REGULATORY INDICATORS

The most important advances in the area of regulatory indicators have been achieved by scholars working in partnership with (and in some cases within) the World Bank and the OECD. At the outset it is useful to introduce some important notions, commencing with the difference between simple and composite measures. Typically, a simple measure is an answer to a question in the Yes/No format. These measures do not involve any statistical sophistication, even if in some cases at least, to get a precise number to explain a phenomenon is a complex task. To give an idea of what simple measures are, the number of pages in the Federal Register (Viscusi, Vernon and Harrington, 1995) or the number of regulatory agencies (Gatti, 1981) have often been used as a measure of the extent of regulation. Simple measures will be reviewed in the next section of the chapter dedicated to government initiatives.

Table 3.1 Classification of the main studies with composite measures

Use	Source	
	Subjective	Objective
Subjective	Pryor (2002a, b)	Nicoletti et al. (2000)
Objective	Kaufmann et al. (2003, 2005)	Djankov et al. (2001)

Composite measures are based on the aggregation of individual variables. These measures can be classified according to two dimensions: the source of the data and the type of use. The first dimension is related to the characteristics of primary data on which studies rely. Their source can be either objective (such as an analysis or observation of facts) or subjective (such as a survey of citizens and businesses on their perception of regulatory quality). Typically, subjective measures are constructed by elaborating the responses to questionnaires. The most popular form of questionnaire for subjective measures is the survey of business's views and perceptions of regulation.

The second dimension looks at the use of primary data. Basically, the difference is between a neutral approach to data and a more subjective approach. Some studies rely on aggregation techniques and methods of data analysis that may be considered 'neutral', where personal judgments do not feature. Others contain weights and methods of data analysis that reflect personal judgment of the importance of a particular aspect that composes regulatory quality, for example aggregation conducted through weighted averages. Table 3.1 illustrates the main studies according to these dimensions.

Subjective Indicators

Pryor (2002a, 2002b) and Kaufmann et al. (2003, 2005) have conducted the most important research in this context. Whereas Pryor works on indicators of firms' perceptions, Kaufmann and his associates cover perceptions of a wide spectrum of regulatory stakeholders, including firms, experts or citizens contained in databases produced over the last ten years or so by international organizations, NGOs and think tanks. Pryor derives his index of laissez faire from surveys of business on their perception of different aspects of regulatory quality (Pryor, 2002a). The index enables him to rank countries and thus to compare the perceived overall regulatory quality. However, the index is sensitive to the perception, ideology and political culture of the respondents to the survey, as it is conducted by interviewing exclusively business executives, 'who may be ideologically predisposed to believe that governmental ineffectiveness and the extent of regulation are directly related' (Pryor, 2002a, pp. 300–301). The basis of the index of laissez faire is the firm as the only stakeholder in regulatory policy. Pryor is very careful to address the limitations of his approach, and indeed the major merit of his work is that it produces a clear definition of quality for one specific stakeholder. It should not be stretched to the point of considering the result as being a universal definition of quality.

Let us turn to a study that attempts to overcome some of the limitations of Pryor's approach and looks at a larger pool of stakeholders. In a study commissioned by the World Bank, Kaufmann et al. (2003, 2005) start from governance and situate regulatory policy therein. In particular they identify six dimensions of governance, that is, voice and accountability, policy stability, government effectiveness, rule of law, control of corruption and regulatory quality. For each of these dimensions an overall index has been developed in order to rank, over five time periods (years: 1996, 1998, 2000, 2002 and 2004) 209 countries according to the performance of their governance system.

The main aim of the study by Kaufmann and associates is to develop a system of indicators named 'best measure of quality of governance worldwide', which will allow cross-country comparisons to be made. Turning to regulatory quality, this dimension of governance 'includes measures of the incidence of market-unfriendly policies such as price control or inadequate bank supervision, as well as perception of the burdens imposed by excessive regulation in areas such as foreign trade and business development' (Kaufmann et al., 2003, p. 3). Regulatory quality variables, selected from a huge set of data sources, are aggregated into an overall index. Kaufmann and associates (2003, p. 39) acknowledge that their system of subjective indicators contains margins of substantial errors that should be taken into account in comparing countries. However, they argue that the same margins of errors exist also in objective measures when they are used in order to portray broader concepts such as regulatory quality or the efficiency of governance (Kaufmann et al., 2003, p. 28). On balance their approach provides countries with a tool for comparison and benchmarking – this being the only type of policy process in which these indicators can be used.

Measures Based on Objective Data

Typically, objective variables are based on factual questions such as 'does the government control price in sector X?' or national economic statistics. However, the statistical methodology used to handle primary data can reflect some personal biases. Djankov et al. (2001) draw on a dataset on the regulation of entry of start-up firms in 85 countries. The aim of this study, conducted in association with the World Bank, is to rank countries according to the number of procedures, time and costs necessary to establish a standard firm. To begin with, all procedures required to set a new firm up have been recorded. The accuracy of data collected through government publication and online information has been tested by contacting government agencies and commissioning reports to independent and local law firms. The next step is the computation of the time, expressed in business days and costs, the identifiable official expenses, such as fees, costs of procedures and forms, photocopies, fiscal stamps, legal and notary charges, necessary for the completion of each procedure. Time and official cost are aggregated in a summary 'full cost' measure, 'which adds up the official expenses and an estimate of the value of the entrepreneur's time, valuing his time at the country's per capita income per working day' (Djankov et al., 2001, p. 11). This 'full cost' indicator can be easily related to simplification programmes dealing with the regulation of entry. Regulation of entry however, is just one element of the regulatory environment. To overcome this limitation the World Bank has also developed indicators on other regulatory sectors, namely employment protection law, bankruptcy laws, as well as regulation on access to credit, property registration, protection of investors and contract enforcement (World Bank, 2004a, 2004b). Authors working on OECD data have made considerable progress on indicators of regulatory governance and statistical analysis. The economic department of the OECD has developed a database on objective indicators of product market regulation, covering both economic and administrative types of regulation. This database is designed to produce an overall indicator that measures the extent of regulation. The aim is to assess the relative friendliness of regulation to market mechanisms across countries and to show the interrelation among certain types of indicators and clusters of countries, covering several regulatory areas (Conway, Janod and Nicoletti, 2005). Specifically, the OECD dataset covers the following areas: state control over business enterprises; barriers to entrepreneurship; and barriers to international trade and investment (Conway et al., 2005, p. 8).[4] Another important aim in this approach is the explicit orientation towards policy-relevant recommendations.

OECD product market indicators cover an important sector of regulation and can be related to specific policy instruments, such as simplification programmes. However, other important types of regulation are kept out of the database, such as environmental regulation, health and safety and the regulation of utilities. Moreover, the meaning of regulatory quality is relatively narrow – the emphasis is on markets, not on governance.

An Assessment of Composite Measures

Studies that develop indicators with subjective measures draw on a comprehensive perception of the quality of regulations. However, this comprehensiveness makes it difficult to assess the success of a specific policy instrument, such as regulatory impact assessment, consultation or simplification programmes. The indexes proposed by Kaufmann and Pryor may not inform policy-makers adequately on the key variables they can actually control. In other words, indexes (and variables upon which indexes are built) are not directly related to specific instruments of regulatory reform that can be changed by policy-makers.

Objective measures are also characterized by certain limitations and disadvantages. For instance, in some cases the methodology used to handle primary data relies on personal assessment. OECD data is collected via questionnaires sent to governments. While most of the questions in the OECD questionnaire used by Nicoletti ask for factual information, these 'facts' are reported to the OECD by government officers. Some projects under way have chosen to collect the data by using teams of researchers to avoid this limitation.[5]

The other limitation is that studies developing objective measures are confined to specific regulatory sectors. They do not inform on the overall quality of the regulatory environment.[6]

It is worth noting that all studies providing subjective and objective measures focus on the extent of regulation.[7] The approach of these studies tends to reflect the narrow economic precept that governments should do less. This is a problem for those who think that quantity cannot be considered a direct (albeit crude) measure of quality. Less regulation can mean good regulation for some stakeholders or actors, but not for all.

THE MEASURES USED BY GOVERNMENTS

In this section we review the experience of measuring regulatory quality within government. The review is limited to the measures and tools used in eight countries, namely, Australia, Belgium, Denmark, Canada, the Netherlands, Sweden, the UK and the USA.

Set of Indicators

There is only one case of use of a coherent set of simple indicators of regulatory quality. In Australia, departments and agencies are required to compile every year a set of 'regulatory performance indicators'. The Office of Small Business (OSB) has developed nine regulatory performance indicators (RPIs) (see Table 3.2). Indicators are inspired by the six objectives of regulatory policy. The explicit link between what the country wants from regulatory reform (the six objectives) and the indicators is an element of strength of this approach. The Australian indicators are rich in information, easy to understand and are monitored by the government. Indicators are therefore inserted 'organically' into regulatory reform.

Regulatory Budgets

The regulatory budget is a document containing estimates of regulatory costs imposed by the various regulatory programmes or agencies' departments. It is a tool that monitors the growth of regulatory costs. The regulatory budget generally takes the form of a report to the parliament – thus enhancing accountability.

The international experience shows two different approaches to regulatory budgets. The holistic approach accounts for all regulatory costs and compares them to the regulatory benefits, whereas the minimalist approach focuses on a single component of the total regulatory costs, such as compliance costs or administrative burdens. The US government has chosen to follow the former approach, estimating the net benefit. Several European countries (i.e. the Netherlands, Belgium and Denmark) estimate the total cost of administrative burdens. Both the net benefit and the total cost are simple measures of regulatory quality.

In the USA, the Office for Information and Regulatory Affairs (OIRA) – within the White House's Office for Management and Budget (OMB)[8] – is required to assess the benefits and costs of existing federal regulatory programmes and to recommend specific regulations for reform or elimination. Congress receives a report issued by OMB-OIRA annually on the results of regulatory impact assessment (RIA), alongside the estimate of the total annual regulatory costs and benefits – in aggregate, by agency and programme and by major rule. Several indicators are considered. One is the sum of costs and benefits of regulations in a year, calculated via RIA. The report adds up the results of the last ten years to provide an estimate of the total impact of regulations over the decade. Another indicator is the overall impact of regulation on the public sector.

The OMB indicators are a compilation of RIAs. The measures of costs and benefits derived from RIAs cannot be treated as measures of the actual impact of regulations. RIAs are prepared before a regulation enters the statute book and is enforced. Consequently, the costs and benefits included in an RIA are estimates. Actual costs and benefits can only be measured

Table 3.2 Regulatory performance indicators in Australia

Key Objective	Regulatory Performance Indicator
To ensure that all new or a revised regulation confers a net benefit to the community	1. Proportion of regulations for which the regulatory impact statement (RIS) adequately addressed the net benefit to the community
To achieve essential regulatory objectives without unduly restricting business in the way in which these objectives are achieved	2. Proportion of regulations for which the RIS adequately justified the compliance burden on business 3. Proportion of regulations that provide businesses and stakeholders with some appropriate flexibility (as defined) to determine the most cost-effective means of achieving regulatory objectives A regulation would be regarded as providing flexibility if it had one or more of the following attributes: – it set a performance or outcome-based standard without prescribing in detail steps that business must take in order to comply; or – it included provision for business to seek acceptance of an alternative compliance mechanism to that prescribed in regulation; or – it used a market-based mechanism such as tradable permits to allow businesses flexibility in determining a compliance strategy; or – it incorporated other means to ensure that businesses have flexibility in deciding what steps to take to comply with regulation
To ensure that regulatory decision-making processes are transparent and lead to fair outcomes	4. Proportion of cases in which external review of decisions (as defined) led to a decision being reversed or overturned External review for these purposes is limited to processes with the following characteristics: – review is carried out by a judicial body or any other review body that is either separate from the department or agency that made the decision or is set up by legislation and has a function of reviewing decisions made by the department or agency; – the review body is empowered to reverse or overturn the decision; and – the department or agency is a party to the review 5. Proportion of regulatory agencies whose mechanisms for internal review of decisions meet standards for complaints handling outlined in 'Principles for Developing a Service Charter', published by the Department of Finance and Administration

Table 3.2 (continued)

Key Objective	Regulatory Performance Indicator
To ensure that information and details on regulation and how to comply with it are accessible and understood by business	6. Proportion of regulatory agencies having communications strategies for regulation, or formal consultative channels for communicating information about regulation: – guidelines for this purpose should be documented
To create a predictable regulatory environment so business can make decisions with some surety of future environment	7. Proportion of regulatory agencies publishing an adequate forward plan for introduction and review of regulation An adequate forward plan for regulation should include the following elements: – it should be published in a way that makes it readily accessible to the business community; for example in an annual report, on the Internet, or by distribution to relevant business organizations; – it should outline planned or likely regulatory activity (as detailed below) expected to occur within a specified period, and should be published before that period starts; – it should include information about reviews of legislation to be undertaken in the relevant period, including reviews under way at the beginning of the period; – it should include information about policy development processes that will be taking place during the relevant period that could affect business regulation, where information about those processes is publicly available; – it should include information about government decisions to develop or implement legislation during the relevant period to the extent where those decisions have been publicly announced
To ensure that consultation processes are accessible and responsive to business and the community	8. Proportion of regulation for which the RIS included an adequate statement of consultation 9. Proportion of regulatory agencies with organizational guidelines outlining consultation processes, procedures and standards

Source: Office of Small Business (2003), *Regulatory Performance Indicators: A Guide for Department and Agencies*, Canberra, Australia: Department of Industry Tourism Resources.

once the regulation is enforced. The literature on the accuracy of cost estimates suggests that the difference between a cost estimated in an RIA and the actual cost (as measured once the rule object of the RIA is implemented) can differ markedly (Harrington, Morgenstern and Nelson, 2000). As Parker (2003, p. 1367) argues, confusing ex ante estimations with the actual regulatory costs and benefits is a mistake, similar to confusing a pre-game guess with the actual score of the game (see also McGarity and Ruttenberg, 2002).

In Europe, several countries follow an approach based on administrative burdens. Interestingly, Belgium, Denmark and the Netherlands have established the same policy goal, that is, to reduce regulatory burdens by 25 per cent in a specific period of time. The EU and the UK are adopting the same approach.[9,10] The strategy to reduce administrative burdens targets the stock of existing regulations, as well as the flow of new regulations. In both cases these governments use a specific tool, the so-called 'standard cost model' (SCM). This 'accounting system' was created in the Netherlands and then adapted by other European countries.

The methodology to quantify administrative burdens involved in a single regulation is common to all countries that have adopted this approach. There are two steps. In the first step, costs per administrative action are quantified. They are composed of three variables: the single cost of action, the number of times a firm has to provide specific information in a year (the so-called 'frequency') and the number of businesses affected by regulation. The single cost of an action is given by the hourly labour cost and the time spent dealing with a specific information obligation per regulation. Time can be estimated through business surveys or alternatively through a simulation of an administrative action taken by a 'model firm' complying with a regulatory provision (Legislative Burden Department, 2003, pp. 21–2).

The experience of European countries with SCM provides an interesting approach to total measures of administrative burdens. In terms of communicability, measures such as the total administrative burden created by, say, transport regulation score well and are easy to link to targets. However, the standard cost model has some limitations. It is based on the unrealistic assumption that there is a total compliance with administrative requirements. Second, point estimates are often less informative than probabilistic ranges. Third and more importantly, administrative burdens are only one component of direct costs. The other important component is compliance cost. The risk is one of focusing the public debate on a limited type of regulatory costs. Finally, there is the political risk of tilting regulatory reform towards only one stakeholder, that is, the firm.

Scorecards

This tool is widely used to assess the quality of RIA. Economists (Hahn et al., 2000; Hahn, Malik and Dudley, 2004) and more generally academics (Lee and Kirkpatrick, 2004; Opuku and Jordan, 2004) think tanks (IEEP, 2004; Vibert, 2004, 2005) and stakeholders rely on this tool to evaluate the state of the art of RIA programmes in the USA, the UK and at the European level. Scorecards are composed of a series of Yes/No questions that generate simple measures. A feature of these measures is that they can be weighted and aggregated to create an overall composite indicator. This differentiates scorecards from the checklists. The latter are usually a set of single measures that are not aggregated.

The USA provides an interesting example of scorecard aimed at ex post evaluation. The Program Assessment Rating Tool (PART) is 'a diagnostic tool meant to provide a consistent approach to evaluating federal programs as part of the executive budget formulation process' (GAO, 2004, pp. 2–3). It systematizes OMB performance measurement, achieving transparency and accountability in the formulation of the budget.

PART's questions on regulatory programmes, monitored by OMB, 'are written in a Yes/No format and require the user to provide a brief narrative explanation of the answer, including any relevant evidence to substantiate the answer. Responses should be evidence based and not rely on impressions or generalities' (OMB, 2002, p. 2). As a result these performance indicators are categorical and designed to be objective. They provide 'a consistent approach to rating federal programs', paying particular attention to the individual programme results (GAO, 2004, pp. 9). Indeed, the principle guiding the rating exercise is that regulatory programmes are appropriate and deserve funding when they show clear evidence of effectiveness and are capable of maximizing the benefits to society.

Scorecards are also common across stakeholders. The British Chambers of Commerce (Ambler et al., 2004) has collected information on simple measures of output, such as percentages of RIAs that present a summary of consultations; illustrate how proposed regulations have changed in response to consultation; consider non-regulatory options; include sunset clauses; quantify costs, on business, environment, citizens and government; quantify benefits, on business, environment, citizens and government; quantify net benefits; and report measures of compliance costs for SMEs.

Review by Auditing Bodies

The review of regulatory policy instruments such as RIA by auditing bodies is a common practice. Less common is the use of indicators. In the

USA the General Audit Office (GAO) produces several reports on the effectiveness of regulation in the context of the executive's general auditing activity. In the UK the role of the National Audit Office (NAO) in the quality assurance process has become more important since 2001. In that year NAO produced a report on good RIA practice, drawing some lessons from a review of a sample of 23 RIAs. NAO has also covered the quality of RIA guidance. One interesting feature of the work conducted by the NAO is that desk analysis of specific RIAs is accompanied by semi-structured interviews within the departments and at the Better Regulation Executive.

In Canada the Auditor General of Canada has formulated recommendations to enhance the regulatory quality of health and safety regulation, without proposing any indicator to measure it, however. Although Canada and other countries do not use external review to propose indicators, these exercises provide standards and checklists.

Regulatory Process Standards and Checklists

In Canada the oversight body, the Regulatory Affairs and Orders in the Council Secretariat within the Privy Council Office, has the responsibility to review regulatory proposals and to ensure that there has been proper analysis, using credible methodologies. The Regulatory Affairs and Orders is also in charge of assuring compliance with the federal regulatory process management standards. These standards provide checklists for each stage of the regulatory process. In particular the quality assurance process terminates with regular internal self-assessments of performance and policy compliance.

In Sweden the SimpLex team is the oversight body that should be involved at an early stage of the law-making process. The team reviews and approves RIAs of legislative proposals. In doing so it draws on a checklist based on the OECD reference checklist for regulatory decision-making. The Board of Swedish Industry and Commerce for Better Regulation (NNR) has developed 11 'quality indicators' on the basis of the three documents on RIA standards (ordinances) (NNR, 2002, 2003).

Surveys

There are two types of surveys to assess the quality of regulation: business surveys and surveys of regulators. The USA provides an example of a business survey that measures the cumulative impact of regulation, that is, the Pollution Abatement Costs and Expenditures (PACE) Survey. The survey collects data on pollution abatement and prevention, capital expenditures and on operating costs for air, water, solid waste and multimedia. The survey also collects data on disposal, recycling, site cleanup, habitat protection, environmental monitoring and testing and administrative costs, as well as other payments, such as permits, fees, fines, penalties and tradable permits bought or sold.

The Danish business surveys revolve around a collection of business administrative cost estimations in each regulatory sector, the aim of which is to select a regulatory sector in which simplification can yield the most efficient results. The selection relies on information gathered by business surveys, the so-called 'model companies'. This model is based on a random sample of 1000 firms. These are then surveyed on how the stock of regulation affects the daily administration of a company, providing a quantification of the total administrative burdens. The model considers the representative sample according to business sectors and the size of the firm. In Belgium, business surveys capture the administrative burdens created by existing regulations.

The accuracy of survey results depends on the intrinsic quality of the questionnaire and on the presence of mechanisms that validate the information provided by businesses. However, ex ante survey methods can have disadvantages too. First, they often rely on subjective data stemming from a typical regulated party: the business. Businesses tend to over-estimate regulatory costs and ex ante, there will be limited mechanism to validate their claims. Hence 'regulatory bias' can affect the outcomes of surveys, especially when this bias has the potential to be large due to predicted outcomes being assessed rather than observed outcomes. In the absence of ex post assessment, predicted outcomes cannot be validated against observed outcomes to allow for correction in the bias. Second, experience shows that all too often, survey data are not compared with – and connected to – other research or sources that use different methodologies (SQW, 2005).

Turning to surveys of regulators, in Canada, interviews of a sample of regulators have measured the change in their perception of the usefulness of RIA (in the context of a systematic external evaluation of regulatory impact assessment; Regulatory Consulting Group Inc. and Delphi Group, 2000, pp. 48–50). Canada shows how structured interviews can be usefully employed to look 'inside' government rather than 'outside'. The reliability of these indicators increases with the repetition of surveys across time. The result provides a possible approach to the measurement of cultural change.

An Assessment

On balance, the cross-national experience shows that setting quantitative targets is a popular option, at least in Europe, to encourage public administration to implement measurement systems. Some countries have gone further than that, by introducing measures of quality and/or systematic reviews and monitoring tools based on quantifiable variables.

The number of countries with measurement initiatives is increasing. The OECD (2003, p. 10) lists nine Member States with some experiences in the evaluation of RIA output. Moreover, in 2004, a specific OECD questionnaire on 'ex post evaluation on regulatory tools and institutions' was sent to the national directors of or experts on better regulation. The results of this self-assessed questionnaire are interesting: eight out of 22 OECD Member States have 'an explicit and current policy/strategy on ex post evaluation of regulatory tools and institutions'; a further three countries reported that this policy/strategy is in preparation (OECD, 2004).

One striking fact is that even European countries with information that can be potentially turned into systems of indicators (as opposed to the use of a single target) are not aware of this potential or, if aware, they have not started activity along these lines. There is no evidence of the use of aggregate measures. Even the simplest among the indexes, that is, time and costs to comply with regulation of entry (Djankov et al., 2001), is not currently used (with the single exception of Belgium). Countries that have focused on the reduction of administrative burdens rely on simple measures, such as the time spent to deal with information requests and hourly costs. Considering that most EU Member States are targeting red tape and that the literature has discussed several indexes, there is considerable potential for a closer dialogue between policy-makers and social scientists.

Quality assurance systems seek to change the culture of regulators. Canada provides an example of using interviews to measure changes in the attitudes of civil servants towards regulation. One can see how indicators of quality can be developed along these lines by replicating interviews and even surveys over time. The countries reviewed in this section can be divided into two groups according to how they approach RIA and its evaluation: those targeting administrative burdens and those seeking measurement of quality across a broader range of issues. Indeed, there is an interesting correlation between the approach to RIA and quality assurance structures. Australia, Canada, the UK and the USA have a robust network of quality assurance and also look at RIA beyond the issue of red tape – with some qualifications regarding the recent political enthusiasm for the reduction of administrative burdens in the UK.[11] By contrast, Belgium, Denmark and the Netherlands focus on administrative burdens and are characterized by a simpler system of monitoring.

THE EU LEVEL

What is the role of the EU in the political discussion about indicators? To answer this question, one needs to know what the EU wants from regulatory reform and whether progress across the Member States is uneven or not. Previous work (Radaelli and De Francesco, 2007) has shown that there are multiple goals attributed to regulatory indicators. The Lisbon Agenda has prioritized regulatory reform, but at the same time it has contributed to the proliferation of objectives and goals (including competitiveness, the completion of the single markets and participatory-transparent governance) attached to terms such as 'better regulation'.

Turning to diversity and convergence, there is clustered convergence on measuring regulatory performance. Within the EU there is a cluster of Member States working on measures of regulatory quality across tools of better regulation in the context of sophisticated quality assurance processes and the pivotal role of RIA. Another cluster adopts some indicators and targets in the context of a lean quality assurance process – with emphasis on administrative burdens and simplification. Finally, there is a third cluster of Member States with no systematic experience of indicators of quality, limited investment in quality assurance and a basic approach to RIA.

Considering the ambiguities of regulatory reform at the EU level and the process of clustered convergence, it is useful to think of possible EU-level indicators in terms of three systems. At the basic level, all Member States and the Commission can adopt a first system of indicators based on the quality of institutional design, written guidance and ex ante analysis of RIA, simplification, consultation and reforms to increase the transparency of the regulatory process. At a more sophisticated level indicators can examine and measure ex post the quality of impact assessment and other tools. This second system would also include indicators of real-world outcome (that is, indicators that show what has been achieved via RIA, consultation, etc.) and some use of surveys of regulators and stakeholders (to measure the impact on regulators and culture change). The system can be used by Member States in which consultation, simplification and the measurement of administrative burdens are already well embedded. The major obstacle to the adoption of most of system 2 indicators across the EU is not data-gathering but the fact that RIA and consultation are not used on a routine basis in policy formulation and consequently are not embedded in the law-making process.

The third system is applicable to the Commission and to governments with sophisticated quality assurance mechanisms. It provides a bridge between measurement of regulatory quality and the evaluation of regulatory reform. This should be the level where comprehensive and systematic evaluation takes place. No matter how sophisticated, indicators are just a component of quality assurance. The latter is a complex process involving strategic and operational management, specific structures and dedicated tools. One important element of quality assurance is external evaluation. External evaluation is not based exclusively on indicators. Case studies, qualitative reviews, formative appraisals and other instruments are also needed. However, indicators can perform a useful role in the context of evaluation. At the same time external evaluation is the place where the indicators used in systems 1 and 2 can be assessed on a technical basis.

Indicators however, should be designed with a precise idea of how they should be used. For this reason it is important that the Council has discussed the coordinates of a possible process of facilitated coordination in which regulatory indicators should be chosen and implemented by the Member States and the Commission (see Radaelli and De Francesco, 2007, Chapter 7). To illustrate, the policy officers in charge of better regulation could usefully discuss why they are proposing to widen or limit the range of indicators and the implications for the institutionalization of better regulation in their own countries and at the common EU policy level. In this context (which is not a league table context), a policy conversation on what sort of convergence is being produced by coordination at the EU level could usefully take place. Indicators could be used to articulate the preferences of the Member States in terms of regulatory reform, and coordination at the EU level to facilitate the re-definition of preferences and gradual convergence on major commitments.[12]

CONCLUSIONS

The policy process is a system of interaction. Different actors (such as regulators, politicians, firms and civil society organizations) interact in the formulation of regulatory policy by using a set of resources comprising information, time, legal resources, political legitimacy and money. Indicators are one type of information. By introducing indicators in the policy process, one changes the information set used by the actors and potentially can modify the system of interaction.

In a possible market for indicators there is a supply and a demand. These vary by country, institutional setting, legacies and other factors. The supply covers the production of indicators, the demand covers the reasons for indicators and information needs of different actors. This chapter has exposed the main limitation of the work done so far, that is, a disproportionate emphasis on the supply. Technical properties have been discussed at length by those who supply measures of regulatory quality. However, the discussion on why actors need indicators, how the demand should affect the production of measures and the design of specific policy processes linking knowledge to its utilization has only just begun. The agenda for the future therefore, points towards a more integrated analysis of the demand for and supply of regulatory indicators.

NOTES

1. Ministry of Finance of the Republic of Ireland, 'Joint Initiative on Regulatory Reform', 26 January 2004.
2. See http://europa.eu.int/rapid/pressReleasesAction.do?reference=SPEECH/06/37&format=HTML&aged=O&language=EN&guiLanguage=en.
3. We gratefully acknowledge the support of the European Commission, DG Enterprise, for having funded our research project on indicators of regulatory quality in 2004 (tender ENTR/03/053) and the ESRC grant No. RES 000-23-1284 on regulatory impact assessment in comparative perspective.
4. The study is built on previous work conducted by OECD economists. In 1999, Nicoletti, Scarpetta and Boylaud (2000, p. 9) built the so-called 'International Regulation Database'.
5. See the European Network for Better Regulation project, funded by the European Commission (http://www.enbr.org).
6. The World Bank's *Doing Business 2005* (World Bank, 2004b) includes other sectors of regulation affecting the economic performance of a firm.
7. The difference between subjective and objective measures is relevant, but it should not be exaggerated. Nicoletti and Pryor (2001) have found that indicators contained in three different studies – conducted by Kaufmann et al. (2000) (subjective), Pyror et al. (2002a, 2002b) (subjective), and Nicoletti et al. (1999) (objective) – converge. This should not be taken as an argument for convergence of every type of subjective or objective measure. However, convergence is still remarkable because it relates to some of the most sophisticated studies ever conducted.
8. The Office for Management and Budget's predominant mission is to assist the President of the USA in overseeing and coordinating the preparation of the federal budget, the administration's procurement and financial management, and information and regulatory policies.
9. In December 2005 the European Council welcomed the Commission's methodology to quantify administrative burdens. The Council invited the Commission to start measuring administrative burdens on a consistent basis and in line with transparent criteria, as part of integrated impact assessments. The Council also stressed the important contribution this method could play in identifying legislation in need of simplification and invited the Commission to explore options for establishing measurable targets in specific sectors for reducing administrative burdens.
10. The British government announced on 15 September 2005 that the measurement of administrative burdens had begun: 'After completion of the measurement exercise the baseline will be published and targets for reductions in the administrative burden will be set' (www.cabinetoffice.gov.uk/regulation/). Meanwhile, a target to reduce administrative burdens by 25 per cent had already been announced for three departments that impose significant burdens on the stakeholder: namely the Department for Trade and Industry (DTI), the Department for the Environment, Food and Rural Affairs (DEFRA), and The Health and Safety Executive (HSE).
11. See Radaelli and De Francesco (2006) for details on the UK.
12. Charles Sabel defined discussion as 'the process by which parties come to reinterpret themselves and their relation to each other by elaborating a common understanding of the world' (Sabel, 1994, p. 138).

REFERENCES

Ambler, T., F. Chittenden and M. Obodovski (2004), 'Are Regulators Raising Their Game? UK Regulatory Impact Assessment in 2002/3', London: British Chambers of Commerce, www.chamberonline.co.uk/policy/issues/red-tape/redtape2004.pdf.

Conway, P., V. Janod and G. Nicoletti (2005), 'Product Market Regulation in OECD Countries: 1998 to 2003', Economic Department Working Papers, No. 419, ECO/WKP (2005), 6 April, Paris: OECD.

Council of the European Union (2004), 'Outcome of Proceedings of the Competitiveness Council on 24 September 2004 – Council Conclusions', Doc. 12898/04, Brussels, 30 September 2004.

Djankov, S., R. La Porta, F. Lopez de Silanes and A. Shleifer (2001), 'The Regulation of Entry', CEPR Discussion Paper No. 2953, http://ssrn.com/ abstract=283839.

GAO (General Accounting Office) (2004), 'Performance Budgeting – Observation on the Use of OMB's Program Assessment Rating Tool for the Fiscal Year 2004 Budget', January, Washington DC: USA General Accounting Office.

Gatti, J.F. (1981), 'An Overview of the Problem of Government Regulation', in J.F. Gatti (ed.), *The Limits of Government Regulation*, New York: Academic Press.

Hahn, R.W., R.P. Malik and M. Dudley (2004), 'Reviewing the Government's Numbers on Regulation', AEI-Brooking Joint Center for Regulatory Studies Working Paper, No. 04-03, January, Washington DC, www.aei-brookings.org/admin/authorpdfs/page.php?id=321.

Hahn, R.W., J.K. Burnett, Y.H.I. Chan, E.A. Mader and P.R. Moyle (2000), 'Assessing the Quality of Regulatory Impact Analyses', *Harvard Journal of Law and Public Policy*, **23** (3), Summer, 859–85.

Harrington, W., R.D. Morgenstern and P. Nelson (2000), 'On the Accuracy of Regulatory Cost Estimates', *Journal of Policy Analysis and Management*, **19** (2), 297–322.

IEEP (Institute for European Environmental Policy) (2004), 'Sustainable Development in the European Commission's Integrated Impact Assessment for 2003', Final Report, April.

Kaufmann, D., A. Kraay and P. Zoldo-Lobatón (2000), 'Governance Matters: From Measurement to Action', *Finance and Development*, **37**, 2.

Kaufmann, D., A. Kraay and M. Mastruzzi (2003), 'Governance Matters III: Governance Indicators for 1996–2002', World Bank Policy Research Working Paper, No. 3106, 30 June, www.worldbank.org/wbi/governance/govdata.

Kaufmann, D., A. Kraay and M. Mastruzzi (2005), 'Governance Matters IV: Governance Indicators for 1996–2004', World Bank Policy Research Working Paper, No. 3630, 9 May, www.worldbank.org/wbi/governance/govdata.

Lee, N. and C. Kirkpatrick (2004), 'A Pilot Study on the Quality of European Commission Extended Impact Assessment', Impact Assessment Research Centre, Institute for Development Policy and Management, University of Manchester, 21 June.

Legislative Burden Department (2003), *Focus on Burden!*, The Hague: Ministry of Finance, December.

McGarity, T.O. and R. Ruttenberg (2002), 'Counting the Cost of Health, Safety, and Environmental Regulation', *Texas Law Review*, **80** (7), 2017.

Nicoletti, G., S. Scarpetta and O. Boylaud (1999), 'Summary Indicators of Product Market Regulation with an Extension to Employment Protection Legislation', OECD Economics 24, Department Working Papers 237, Paris: OECD.

Nicoletti, G. and F.L. Pryor (2001), 'Subjective and Objective Measure of the Extent of Governmental Regulation', AEI-Brooking Joint Center for Regulatory Studies Working Paper, Washington DC, www.aei-brookings.org/admin/authorpdfs/page.php?id-424.

Nicoletti, G., S. Scarpetta and O. Boylaud (2000), 'Summary Indicators of Product Market Regulation with an Extension to Employment Protection Legislation', Economics Department Working Paper, No. 226, Paris: OECD, 11 February.

NNR (Board of Swedish Industry and Commerce for Better Regulation) (2002), *How High is the Quality of the Swedish Central Government's Regulatory Impact Analysis (RIAs) in the Business Sector? The NNR Regulation Indicator for 2002*, Stockholm: NNR, June, www.nnr.se.

NNR (Board of Swedish Industry and Commerce for Better Regulation) (2003), *How High is the Quality of the Swedish Central Government's Regulatory Impact Analysis (RIAs) in the Business Sector? The NNR Regulation Indicator for 2003*, Stockholm: NNR, June, www.nnr.se.

OECD (2002), *Regulatory Policies in OECD Countries: From Interventionism to Regulatory Governance*, Paris: OECD.

OECD (2003), 'Proceedings From the OECD Expert Meeting on Regulatory Performance: Ex Post Evaluation of Regulatory Policies', Paris: OECD, 22 September.

OECD (2004), 'Regulatory Performance: Ex Post Evaluation of Regulatory Tools and Institutions', Draft Report by Working Party on Regulatory Management and Reform, Paris: OECD, October.

OMB (Office for Management and Budget) (2002), *Program Assessment Rating Tool – Instructions for PART Worksheets, Fiscal Year 2004*.

Opoku, C. and A. Jordan (2004), 'Impact Assessment in the EU: A Global Sustainable Development Perspective', Paper presented at the conference on the *Human Dimension of Global Environmental Change*, Berlin, 3–4 December.

Parker, R.W. (2003), 'Grading the Government', *The University of Chicago Law Review*, **70**, 1345–486.

Pryor, F.L. (2002a), *The Future of U.S. Capitalism*, Cambridge: Cambridge University Press.

Pryor, F.L. (2002b), 'Quantitative Notes on the Extent of Governmental Regulations in Various OECD Nations', *International Journal of Industrial Organization*, **20**, 693–714.

Radaelli, C.M. and F. De Francesco (2007), *Regulatory Quality in Europe: Concepts, Measures, and Policy Processes*, Manchester: Manchester University Press.

Regulatory Consulting Group Inc. and Delphi Group (2000), *Assessing the Contribution of Regulatory Impact Analysis on Decision Making and the Development of Regulation*, Ottawa, Canada, 31 August.

Sabel, C.F. (1994), 'Learning by Monitoring: The Institutions of Economic Development', in Neil Smelser and Richard Swedberg (eds), *Handbook of Economic Sociology*, Princeton: Princeton University Press and Russell Sage Foundation, pp. 137–65.

SQW (2005), 'Evaluating the Impact of Regulation: Developing a Methodology', Report for the Department of Trade and Industry, London: SQW Limited, http://www.dti.gov.uk/files/file22009.pdf.

Vibert, F. (2004), *The EU's New System of Regulatory Impact Assessment – A Scorecard*, London: European Policy Forum, March.

Vibert, F. (2005), *The Itch to Regulate: Confirmation Bias and the European Commission's New System of Impact Assessment*, London: European Policy Forum.

Viscusi, W.K., J. Vernon and J.E. Harrington (1995), *Economics of Regulation and Antitrust*, 2nd edn, Cambridge: MIT Press.

World Bank (2004a), *Doing Business in 2004: Understanding Regulation*, Washington DC: The World Bank and Oxford University Press.

World Bank (2004b), *Doing Business in 2005: Removing Obstacles to Growth*, Washington DC: The World Bank and Oxford University Press, September.

4. Measuring RIA quality and performance[1]

Peter Ladegaard

INTRODUCTION

Regulation has become a fundamental tool of government in managing more complex and diverse societies. The importance of regulation is reinforced in developing countries undergoing a general transition from state-led to market-led growth. Markets and investors put a premium on business regulation that is predictable, transparent, low-cost and low-risk.

Regulatory impact assessment (RIA) is widely recognized as an important mechanism for governments to promote regulatory quality and to assess expected impacts of proposed regulation. Most OECD economies have already adopted RIA programmes. An increasing number of developing and transition countries are in the process, although with variations in scope and detail.

RIA design and implementation is not a straightforward task. It can be resource-demanding and technically difficult. Successful RIA systems require considerable political capital and support and have implications for the allocation of sometimes scarce administrative resources. So far there has been only ad hoc and somewhat unsystematic attempts to evaluate RIA as well as other regulatory tools and institutions.[2] This has partially to do with the relative novelty of RIA as well with methodological challenges.

Better tools to measure and monitor RIA quality and performance are needed. Evaluation techniques can help in targeting RIAs and in facilitating comparisons, gradual adaptations and improvements of RIA systems.

This chapter presents a framework for RIA evaluation.[3] It suggests a number of tests that governments, donors and other stakeholders can apply to get better information about the performance of RIA. A framework for RIA evaluation can help organize our knowledge about existing practices and help enhance the comparability between different approaches.

The evaluation framework and associated tests are not meant to be exhaustive of the possible approaches to evaluating RIA quality and performance. The possibilities to link credibly regulatory process reforms – such as RIA – to economic outcomes such as competitiveness and growth are gradually improving as more and better comparable data become available.[4] The framework and suggested tests present a starting point to think about RIA evaluation and introduces strategies and tools that governments can apply to know more about the performance and quality of RIA.

The chapter suggests a three-part taxonomy of RIA evaluation tests:

- *compliance tests*, which focus on formal compliance with procedural requirements for RIA as set out in laws, policies or guidelines;
- *performance tests*, which go beyond the question of formal compliance and look at the quality of analysis and the actual application of RIA; and
- *function tests*, which evaluate the actual effect of RIA on regulatory quality and outcomes.

The chapter argues that simple compliance tests should be favoured in the early stages of RIA implementation. Performance and function tests should increasingly be favoured as experience and expertise with RIA is developed.

COMPLIANCE (PROCESS) TESTS

Compliance tests usually focus on formal conformity with RIA requirements as set out in laws or official policies and guidelines. Although RIA guidelines and requirements vary between countries, reflecting differences in policy priorities and the scope of RIA, there is a high degree of observed commonality (Box 4.1). These kinds of detailed obligations can provide a simple benchmark for use in compliance testing.

Examples of basic RIA requirements evaluated in compliance tests are the obligation to quantify costs, to consult with stakeholders and to justify the rationale for government intervention.

Compliance tests do not focus on the quality of, for example, the quantification of costs or the consultation with stakeholders but merely if it was undertaken or not. This 'checklist' or 'scoring' approach has the advantage of providing a transparent, easily comparable and efficient check-up on how RIA is implemented. It is the most readily available indicator for measuring the 'administrative success' of RIA.

RIA compliance tests are of high value. First, they are probably the least expensive and methodologically demanding of evaluations. Conducted in

BOX 4.1 COMMON CHARACTERISTICS OF RIA

1. *Statement of problem*. Is government intervention both necessary and desirable? Is the problem or condition unlikely to be resolved by the intervention of private actors?
2. *Definition of alternative remedies*. These include different approaches, such as the use of economic incentives or voluntary approaches.
3. *Determination of physical effects of each alternative, including potential unintended consequences*. The net should be cast wide. Generally speaking, regulations or investments in many areas of public policy can have environmental implications that must be kept in mind.
4. *Estimation of benefits and costs of each alternative*. Benefits should be quantified and where possible monetized. Costs should be true opportunity costs, not simply expenditures.
5. *Assessment of other economic impacts*. Including effects on competition, effects on small firms, international trade implications.
6. *Identification of winners and losers*. Those in the community who stand to gain and lose from each alternative and if possible, the extent of their gains and losses.
7. *Communication with the interested public*. Including the following activities: notification of intent to regulate, request for compliance cost and other data, public disclosure of regulatory proposals and supporting analysis, and consideration of and response to public comments.
8. *A clear choice of the preferred alternative*. Plus a statement defending that choice.
9. *Provision of a plan for ex post analysis of regulatory outcomes*. It is important, for example, to establish current conditions to have a benchmark to measure performance against. Planning is needed to ensure that procedures are in place for the collection of data.

a range of countries, compliance tests have highlighted non-compliance with RIA requirements, thereby triggering efforts to improve and adapt RIA systems. Compliance tests can be useful not only in focusing efforts by regulatory reform authorities to enhance compliance levels but also in measuring improvements over time. Box 4.2 lists a number of questions that could be used in basic RIA compliance tests.

The low-tech and low-cost nature of compliance tests allows them to be conducted by many different stakeholders, not only well-resourced government or audit offices. Compliance tests conducted by non-governmental stakeholders may focus on compliance with RIA standards that are not specified in government guidelines but that other stakeholders believe should be covered by the RIA. Simple compliance tests conducted by business organizations have often attracted media attention.[5]

BOX 4.2 EXAMPLES OF RIA COMPLIANCE TEST QUESTIONS

- Was an RIA prepared prior to the decision to endorse, reject or modify a draft regulation?
- Did the RIA include a summary of the regulatory proposal and expected impacts?
- Did the RIA include an assessment of expected costs of the regulation?
- Were costs quantified and expressed in monetary terms?
- Did the RIA include an assessment of expected benefits of the regulation?
- Were benefits quantified and expressed in monetary terms?
- Did the RIA present a range of viable regulatory alternatives, including no government action? Were regulatory alternatives quantified and expressed in monetary terms?
- Is there a specific assessment of the impact on (i) public finances; (ii) private sector compliance costs; (iii) competitiveness; (iv) international obligations?
- Has formal consultation with affected stakeholders and the public been carried out?
- Did the RIA include an outline of how the regulation would be implemented and enforced?
- Did the RIA include an outline of how the regulation and its impacts are to be measured and monitored?
- Was the RIA posted on the Internet?

Note: Countries' RIA guidelines and requirements often require an explicit statement of anticipated effects on specific groups or policy areas. The most frequently focused areas of concern are impacts on public finances, small business, administrative burdens in general and competitiveness.

Compliance tests can be and are undertaken ex post as well as contemporaneously with the development of RIA and new regulations. Review by central regulatory review units of line ministries' compliance with RIA is often an integral part of the RIA process for developing regulations. Formally speaking, approval of the RIA document by these bodies is often a pre-condition for the regulatory process to proceed.

In many cases results of compliance tests indicate widespread non-compliance as illustrated in Box 4.3.

How can the apparently low level of compliance with basic RIA requirements be explained? One suggestion made by Harrington and Morgenstern (2003) is that more rigorous, higher-quality RIAs are correlated with the more important and far-reaching regulatory proposals. Thus it is plausible that while there is a relatively low level of compliance with guidelines

BOX 4.3 EXAMPLES OF RIA COMPLIANCE TESTS

United States. Hahn et al. (2000) have undertaken a series of RIA evaluations in the United States over a number of years based on benchmarking the content of actual RIAs against published guidance material. In a review of 48 RIAs completed between 1996 and 1999, they found that many RIAs failed to conform to the relevant RIA guidelines (issued by the Office of Management and Budget). Whereas 90 per cent of RIA monetized costs, only 50 per cent monetized benefits and only 29 per cent calculated net benefits.

United Kingdom. An extensive survey of British RIAs (Ambler, Chittenden and Shamutkova, 2003) showed similar results. A comparison of results across different periods (2002–03 vs. 1998–2002) indicates limited progress in achieving enhanced compliance over time. Costs were reported in 58 per cent of cases in 2002–03, compared with 55 in the earlier period. Benefits were reported in only 9 per cent of cases (6 per cent in the earlier period). The report found improvements over the earlier period in the consideration of alternative regulatory approaches. The proportion of RIAs mentioning non-regulatory alternatives doubled, from 11 to 23 per cent.

Sweden. Since 2001 the Swedish Board of Industry and Commerce for Better Regulation (NNR) has published an annual report on the compliance of the Swedish government with 11 RIA 'quality factors'. Most of the quality factors are identical to the requirements laid down in government guidelines. As the above-mentioned tests in the United Kingdom and the United States, the NNR test benchmarks actual RIA content against the 11 quality factors. The NNR test has become an efficient tool to monitor the quality of the government's RIAs. The recent studies have shown gradual improvements, although from a low base. The 2003 study, for example, showed that only one-half of the RIAs complied with statutory requirement to draw up a special RIA for small and medium-sized enterprises (SMEs) (NNR, 2003).

overall, there is a higher level of compliance with regard to major RIAs. Another reason may be the widely acknowledged difficulties in quantifying and monetizing regulatory costs. Finally, sometimes there may be strong political pressures on reform bodies to avoid stalling the regulatory process by insisting on full compliance with RIA processes – particularly where regulatory agencies are unresponsive and may have delayed the commencement of RIA activity until relatively late in the regulatory process.

A key element in the use of compliance testing is clearly that of determining the reasons for non-compliance. RIA is predicated on the need to achieve a long-term cultural change in the approach taken to regulatory activity. Non-compliance, particularly in the early stages of implementation, may denote a lack of motivation to comply, indicating that the cultural change has not been achieved. The appropriate response may in part be to adopt a more rigorous scrutiny and enforcement regime in the short term. Practical limitations on the extent to which compliance is possible may also be important as noted above. Non-compliance may also reflect a lack of appropriate skills and expertise, which can be addressed directly by the central regulatory reform institution.

The compliance with basic RIA criteria is clearly a necessary but not sufficient condition for a good RIA. The value of compliance tests is based on the assumption that compliance with government guidelines is necessary and supportive for regulatory quality. But compliance with such requirements is not sufficient for regulatory quality.

An RIA may not be of high quality even if it satisfies the guideline checklist. For this reason, performance tests have been developed and applied to RIA. The nature and findings of these tests are reviewed in the following section.

PERFORMANCE (OUTPUT) TESTS

Performance tests move beyond the threshold question of compliance tests. A compliance test might judge an RIA as meeting quality standards if a recommended costing methodology has been applied. But a performance test may regard an incorrect adoption, or the use of another unacceptable methodology as representing a failure to meet the standards. Performance tests focus on RIA application; they are concerned with the quality of the various elements that make up the RIA and with their internal consistency rather than simply the question of whether the elements required are actually present.

Some performance tests can be carried out both ex ante and ex post. A test carried out ex ante can focus on whether methodological elements are correctly (or at least defensibly) applied at the time of writing. At the most basic level, this sort of analysis examines whether the RIA avoids egregious errors, confusion of costs and expenditures, improper definitions of benefits, and so on. Examples of questions addressed in RIA performance tests are given in Box 4.4.

An example of a performance test is in Hahn et al. (2000), who – in addition to the compliance tests discussed in the previous section – assessed whether RIAs were internally consistent, that is, if the same assumptions were used throughout. The authors' operational test was the treatment of

BOX 4.4 EXAMPLES OF QUESTIONS ADDRESSED IN RIA PERFORMANCE TESTS

- Did the RIA clearly state what is the fundamental problem being addressed and why government action is needed?
- Was the analysis of costs and benefits adequate, thorough and realistic? Was the methodology robust? Did the RIA clarify underlying assumptions, uncertainties and strength of evidence, avoid double counting errors; use a plausible discount rate; adjust for the effects of taxes, subsidies and other distortions and so on?
- Was the analysis of compliance adequate? Did the RIA consider the level and pattern of compliance to ensure a proper targeting of the regulation?
- Was consultation effective? Did the consultation documentation provide appropriate information and data to interested parties? Were response times adequate? Have the views of those consulted been articulated, including substantial disagreements?
- Was the analysis of monitoring and evaluation adequate? Did the RIA contain realistic procedures for monitoring and evaluation?
- When in the regulatory process (early, late, or at all?) was the RIA changed/revised based on input from stakeholders and/or additional analysis by the regulator?
- Was the RIA capable of predicting the actual benefits and costs imposed by the regulation?

the discount rate. Hahn et al. found that 86 per cent of RIAs used the officially specified discount rate throughout.

Another critical performance dimension that could be subject to evaluative tests is timing. Many case studies have documented the critical importance of timing to the usefulness of RIA. If RIA is not initiated until after the regulatory process is well under way, it obviously has difficulty being influential in the policy process. A more qualitative approach to performance tests could therefore focus on the timing of the incurred changes, working on the general assumption that the effects of changes in RIA as early as possible in the regulatory process have a much more significant effect than 'add-ons' at the very final stages.

Performance tests can also focus on the predictive ability of RIA by comparing actual regulatory impacts with those predicted in the RIA. At a basic level this form of testing appears conceptually fairly simple and unambiguous: to the extent that clear predictions of regulatory impacts are made ex ante, the task is simply to compare them with observed reality.

A study by Morgenstern, Harrington and Nelson from 2000 compared ex ante estimates with ex post outcomes of 12 environmental regulatory programmes in the United States. The findings indicated that ex ante estimates tended to exceed actual costs, mainly due to difficulties in defining baselines and estimating (incomplete) compliance costs.[6]

Unfortunately such tests are rare. One reason is data problems – information on ex post regulatory performance is rarely (readily) available and may require substantial resources to generate. Another is the lack of incentives. Some regulators may not see benefits in highlighting their RIA performance whether positive or negative. A negative result will tend to undermine their credibility when proposing new regulation – supported by RIA analysis – while a positive result does no more than provide a confirmation of the benefits of a policy that has already been implemented and in which the agency already believes.

An important potential benefit of this test is that it can lead to the identification of systemic factors that are reducing RIA quality. In turn this can lead to mitigating actions to improve RIA guidance and the scrutiny exercised by regulatory review units. A strong result in terms of ex post performance testing does not necessarily lead to the conclusion that RIA is having real, substantial and positive effects on regulatory quality outcomes. Lack of 'outcome' performance can be the result of a failure to integrate high-quality regulatory tools and institutions with the policy decision-making process. Identifying this problem of linkage and providing the tools to analyse it is the role of function, or outcome tests, considered next.

FUNCTION (OUTCOME) TESTS

The compliance and performance tests cited above can tell us much about the quality of RIA but they say little of its impact on policy and actual regulatory quality outcomes. Function tests are concerned with the effect of RIA on regulatory outcomes, whether the application of RIA contributes to improving the quality and performance of regulations in practice and the quality of the regulatory decision-making process. Tests of this sort are fundamental to answering the question of whether RIAs are delivering on their promise of improving the effectiveness, efficiency and accountability of government regulatory actions.

Theoretically, a wide range of policy impacts and regulatory outcomes can be linked to RIA and more broadly to other aspects of the regulatory process and regulatory institutions. Ultimately, RIA should contribute to improving many aspects of good governance, competitiveness and economic growth. However, to establish a direct causality between, say, specific aspects of RIA practices and economic growth would be methodologically challenging and uncertain at best.

This chapter identifies three categories of RIA function tests that can be more directly linked to the RIA process itself. These are tests focusing on:

- changes in the proposed policy;
- changes in administrative/regulatory culture; and
- changes in stakeholder perceptions of regulatory quality.

Changes in the Proposed Policy

One of the main objectives of RIA is to inform the policy process. As the RIA is prepared, developed and nuanced, analysis and views from stakeholders may lead to revisions in the proposed policy, ranging from minor refinements to radical changes. Three different tests can be applied to grasp RIA's impact on the proposed policy.

Frequency tests

A basic function test for RIA is the collection of data on the frequency with which initial regulatory proposals are either modified or abandoned as they progress through the RIA process. Recorded changes may tell us something about the RIA process's learning curve. Where developed and applied in practice, results show wide variability in terms of the recorded frequency of changes. Experiences from the United States, Australia and the Netherlands show variations in the number of regulations amended during the RIA process from 9 to 60 per cent.[7] This may be a result of definitional and methodological differences but could also reflect differences in the quality of RIA requirements and their application in practice.

Applying this test assumes that the modifications made are wholly or largely attributable to the impact of the RIA process in bringing rigour and transparency to the analysis. Other influences on the policy process are of course also likely to have influence so that RIA will constitute only a part of the reason for any observed changes. In countries where RIA is brought to bear on most or all substantial regulatory proposals, other factors may be expected to intervene less frequently. Moreover, a part of the impact of RIA is likely to be unobservable in practice: regulators may in some cases not put forward regulatory proposals because they are conscious that they are unlikely to survive the scrutiny that an RIA process will bring to bear (anticipated reaction). The impact of RIA in preventing poor regulations at the earliest stages of development may well be highly significant but is difficult, if not impossible, to observe directly.

Audit trails

The 'audit trail' approach can be seen as a variant of measuring the frequency of changes in initial proposals. It is one that avoids the vulnerability of the simple measure of the frequency of changes. It focuses specifically on the responsiveness to suggested changes to the regulatory proposal made by stakeholders during the RIA process. Yarrow (2004) argues that there is likely to be a systematic bias against newly raised options brought forward during the RIA consultation process:

> In some ways, regulatory policy development is like an R&D process. There may be a number of ideas and options at the outset, but cost considerations lead to the sequential 'closing out' of what look like less attractive options, in order to devote more resources to the development of other, favoured options. Ideas and evidence introduced in other than the very early stages may have difficulty getting a hearing, because, for example, they point in directions that might already have been closed down.

It is because of the likely existence of such a bias that the adoption of audit trails can be expected to be productive: they increase the pressure on regulators to deal openly with such proposals and require them to be able to justify their treatment of them. Yarrow notes that such approaches are likely to be resource-intensive but argues that, if sufficiently narrowly specified (e.g., being focused solely on the treatment of discrete new options raised during consultation on RIA documents), they can feasibly be used as a supplement to other evaluation methods.

The incidence of changes in response to information obtained via RIA (and the associated consultation process) is a relatively easily measurable form of function test. It is reasonable to expect that regulatory organizations should be able to provide relatively detailed examples of ways in which third party inputs into RIA or consultation processes have materially influenced decision-making. Explicitly recognizing examples of responsiveness in a positive light may also have the desirable property that it acts to counter any potential tendency in regulatory agencies to treat such responsiveness as a signal or admission of prior failings.

As for having a 'frequency test', incidences of policy changes in response to options and comments provided by stakeholders during the regulatory process can be misleading. A low incidence of change can suggest a non-responsive policy apparatus. But it may also suggest one that is functioning at a high level with initial policy proposals so well researched and articulated that they do not require major change at later stages of development. Only a deeper review of the broader question of responsiveness is likely to show conclusively which effect is predominant.

Cost/benefit differences

Tests of the rate of modification of regulatory proposals may constitute good basic indicators that RIA is affecting outcomes. But they cannot provide data on the importance of these changes in practice. A more ambitious approach is to measure the differences between initial regulatory proposals and final regulations in benefit/cost terms. This, at least theoretically, allows a monetized estimate of the impact of RIA to be generated. A fundamental difficulty with this kind of functional test is that the baseline or 'counterfactual' is difficult to conceptualize. Even in the absence of formal RIA requirements it is highly likely that some analysis of the effects of regulation would be undertaken. Put another way, a simple measurement of the difference between the regulatory proposal initially advanced and the final outcome does not constitute an accurate measure of the impact of RIA since the initial proposal is, in any case, likely to be subjected to modification in the course of its development. Moreover, even in the presence of RIA, other aspects of the policy development process may also be said to have played an important role in shaping the final regulation, leading to questions as to the 'attribution' of the changes to RIA or to other elements. In this respect an analysis comparing initial proposals with final regulations risks overstating the impact of RIA.

Perhaps as a result of the difficulties of attributing changes to initial proposals to the RIA process, there has been remarkably little analysis of the effect of RIA characteristics on regulatory outcomes to date despite the extensive use of RIA in many OECD countries over an extended period. Where such studies have been undertaken they have differed substantially in their approach and scope. An early example was a study of 15 regulations for which RIA were prepared, undertaken by the Environment Protection Agency (EPA) in the United States.[8] This study reported highly quantified results: the EPA concluded that the costs of its proposed rules had been reduced overall by $1 billion as a result of the RIA conducted. The cost of the conduct of RIA on these 15 regulations was reported as $10 million, implying a benefit/cost ratio of the RIA itself of 1000:1. Thus it was concluded that RIA had been highly effective in relation to this sample.

Changes in Administrative/Regulatory Culture

A second broad category of function tests focuses on the effects of the RIA system on the administrative/regulatory culture. Underlying the use of RIA is the assumption that it is only when the fundamental logic of the process is fully accepted and adopted in practice by regulators that its full benefits will be attained. It is generally assumed that this is a process of cultural change that will necessarily be achieved only in the medium to long term.

Thus this type of function test can be seen as measuring directly the extent to which this long-term change is occurring in practice. Such a test is perhaps the most important form of functional test.

Although tests of RIAs' impact on the administrative/regulatory culture are rarely the sole objective of RIA evaluations, broad and open survey-based evaluations have often been able to detect and investigate such changes. A review of the Canadian RIA system, published in 2000, concluded that RIA requirements had changed the decision-making process in Canada:

> More attention is paid to alternatives and costs and benefits than appeared to exist when the requirements were instituted fifteen years ago. Officials were sensitive to RIA requirements and departments had systems in place to consider regulatory options and costs and benefits. Resources were being devoted to these activities and a core of expertise was available in several departments. (Delphi Group, 2000)

Similarly, in a review of its regulatory impact statement (RIS) system, New Zealand noted that the introduction of an RIA framework had begun to change the structures and practices involved in the development of regulatory proposals, for instance by encouraging departments to use the RIA framework as a policy development tool rather than seeing it as a retrospective transparency tool.[9]

This type of function test is necessarily largely qualitative in nature and subjectively applied. However, while these factors pose difficulties in terms of interpretation of results and the comparability of results over time and between different areas, the test is potentially more fruitful than other function tests in that it is a more direct measure of the extent to which some of the fundamental goals of RIA are being achieved.

Changes in Stakeholder Perceptions of Regulatory Quality

Finally, changes in stakeholder perceptions of regulatory quality could be indicative of the success and relevance of RIA. Stakeholder perceptions could be captured in surveys targeting various elements of the RIA process such as consultations, plain drafting of legal texts, quantification of impacts, and so on, as well as stakeholders' general perceptions of regulatory quality.

Needless to say, changes in stakeholder perceptions of regulatory quality can also be attributable to sources other than RIA, for example, overhauls of the stock of existing regulation, specific regulatory exemptions, and so on. However, if well designed, surveys of stakeholder perceptions should as a minimum be able to detect views on the influence of RIA in bringing rigour and transparency to the regulatory process.

RIA EVALUATION STRATEGIES

The previous sections looked at a range of tests to assess the quality and efficiency of RIA. Little has so far been said about the strategy guiding these tests. Who should carry out RIA evaluations? What exactly should the tests evaluate? And how can RIA evaluations become an integral part of the RIA process itself? This section tries to answer these questions.

Who Evaluates?

Country practices show variation in terms of who carries out RIA evaluations. Evaluations are carried out by line ministries, dedicated evaluation agencies/units, regulatory review units, national audit offices, independent researchers and business organizations. Each of these modes offers particular advantages. Line ministries and regulatory reform institutions in particular are informed by a clear understanding of RIA and the importance of the tool within the wider regulatory quality context.[10] The key advantage of external bodies carrying out reviews is the transparency of the review activity and the degree of pressure placed on governments to respond adequately to criticisms and identified shortcomings. Where broader audit and review bodies are involved, the evaluation of RIA can be placed in a broader evaluation context with a link to the wider audit and review functions of government.

In most countries however, RIA evaluation has active participation from a centre-of-government regulatory reform unit charged with promoting regulatory quality and with supporting and reviewing RIAs on a daily basis. The practice of charging or actively involving the central regulatory review units in RIA evaluation is sensible since it brings the feedback loop from RIA evaluations directly to the units normally charged with improving and adapting the RIA system. Transparency in the process and publication of RIAs allow other parties to check and balance the RIA evaluations carried out by the regulatory review units.

What to Evaluate?

Each of the three tests suggested in this chapter – compliance, performance and function tests – is intended to evaluate RIA according to different and progressively more demanding criteria. Compliance tests essentially measure whether RIA is taken seriously by regulators. Their concern is with the inputs to the regulatory quality requirement. Performance tests link the inputs with the outputs and ask whether RIA is functioning adequately. Function tests also include the link between RIA and the policy process itself and focus on whether RIA is being used effectively in the sense of contributing to improved policy outcomes. The focus in applying different kinds of evaluation tests should arguably shift with the gradual development of RIA. In early stages of RIA implementation, a key focus must be on achieving a high level of formal compliance, while in a more mature RIA system the focus should shift toward the question of what effects on policy outcomes were observable.[11] An integration of the different kinds of RIA evaluations could generate important benefits and provide a strategic framework for RIA evaluation. In particular, if conducted over a period of time, the integration of RIA evaluations could allow links to be drawn between different aspects of RIA, for example, the observed degree of formal compliance with RIA requirements and RIA's impact on policy outcomes.

CONCLUSION

Regulatory impact assessment (RIA) is an increasingly applied and central tool used to assure regulatory quality. Given the important role RIA is assuming within the rule-making processes of most OECD countries and some developing countries, the relatively low level of RIA evaluation is likely to constitute a barrier to the dynamic development of the RIA tool.

In line with previous work undertaken by the OECD, this chapter has suggested an analytical framework for RIA evaluations based on a three-part taxonomy. This comprises: 1) compliance tests, which measure formal compliance with the specific standards and requirements of RIA as set out in laws or policy guidelines; 2) performance tests, which measure the quality of the analysis and actual application of RIA; and 3) function tests, which evaluate the actual effect of RIA on regulatory quality and outcomes.

There should be a correlation between the kinds of tests employed and the sophistication/experience of the regulatory framework in which the country finds itself. Relatively simple compliance tests should be favoured in the early stages of implementation of RIA. Performance tests should increasingly be favoured as expertise in the application of RIA is developed and where there is a greater concern with the quality of their application rather than simply to ensure that they are applied at all. Function tests should be used to test whether a functioning RIA system is in fact, having the predicted effect of increasing regulatory quality.

The analytical framework suggested here is considered valuable because it can be used by regulatory reform authorities as the basis for organizing RIA evaluations and timing the application of the different tests and approaches.

Countries face a number of challenges in evaluating regulatory RIAs, most notably related to data collection strategies, institutional constraints and cultural barriers. Many of these challenges can be addressed through changes to the regulatory process itself. RIA evaluation could become an integral part of the regulatory process by making appropriate revisions to existing RIA procedures. Regulators and regulatory review units could, for example, be obliged to carry out annual evaluations of a pre-selected number or group of the preceding year's RIAs.

NOTES

1. This chapter is based upon and draws extensively on the report 'Ex post Evaluation of Regulatory Policies' principally prepared by the author in 2004 while working for the OECD. See www.oecd.org/gov. The 2004 report was based on partial contributions from Winston Harrington, Richard Morgenstern, George Yarrow and Rex Deighton-Smith. This chapter is published with permission of the OECD.
2. OECD (2004, Chapter 2).
3. The chapter does not focus on the design and establishment of RIA systems. It assumes that an RIA system is already in place. For an overview of the discussion of relevance, design and implementation of RIA systems in developing countries, see Ladegaard (2005).
4. Databases such as OECD's 'Indicators for Product Market Regulation' and the World Bank's 'Doing Business' project may enable better analysis of the relation/causality between specific regulatory policy efforts (such as RIA) with indicators of economic performance such as competitiveness and economic growth.
5. The regulatory quality indicator developed by the Board of Swedish Industry and Commerce for Better Regulation is a notable example.
6. The study also showed that unit cost estimates were often accurate, although for rules that use economic incentives, unit costs were consistently overestimated. Findings of the study also indicated that benefits may be overestimated. In cases of unit-cost overestimation, Morgenstern et al. argue that unanticipated technological innovation appeared to be an important factor, especially for economic incentive rules. Morgenstern et al.'s findings support the view of some proponents of regulation that RIA tends systematically to overestimate regulatory costs. A key reason advanced for this view is that it tends to adopt a static approach and ignore the often crucial effect of technological innovation in reducing actual costs. Another argument often put forward to support the view that RIAs often overestimate costs is that economies of scale will be reaped in the production of whatever product or service is required due to a regulatory standard and that this will result in often substantial reductions in both real costs and market prices.
7. Regulatory reform country reviews by the OECD have noted that in the United States in 1999, 60 per cent of draft regulations were amended during the process of RIA-based review by the Office of Management and Budget; in the Netherlands in 1995/96 some 17 per cent of proposals subjected to RIA were either modified or abandoned; and in the Australian State of New South Wales 9 per cent of regulations were modified or abandoned during the RIA process. A similar review in the state of Victoria had earlier shown a rate of around 20 per cent (www.oecd.org/regreform section entitled 'background reports by country').
8. OECD (1998).
9. OECD (2004).
10. Examples of regulatory reform units or institutions include the Office for Information and Regulatory Affairs in the United States (located in the Office of Budget and

Management), the Better Regulation Executive in the United Kingdom (located in the Cabinet Office), the Regulatory Affairs and Orders in the Council Secretariat in Canada (located in the Privy Council Office), and COFEMER (Federal Commission for Better Regulation) in Mexico.

11. Somewhat surprisingly, practices show no clear pattern of movement towards more sophisticated RIA evaluations as experience with RIA accumulates. Instead of focusing on basic compliance with RIA requirements, countries with limited RIA experience sometimes attempt to implement much more advanced tests, without first obtaining a sound understanding of basic compliance issues (OECD, 2004, pp. 6, 68).

REFERENCES

Ambler, T., F. Chittenden and M. Shamutkova (2003), *Do Regulators Play by the Rules?*, London: The British Chambers of Commerce.

Delphi Group (2000), *Assessing the Contribution of Regulatory Impact Analysis on Decision Making and the Development of Regulations*, Ottawa, Canada.

Hahn, R.W. et al. (2000), 'Assessing Regulatory Impact Analysis: The Failure of Agencies to Comply with Executive Order 12,866', *Harvard Journal of Law and Public Policy*, **23** (3).

Harrington, W. and R.D. Morgenstern (2003), 'Evaluating Regulatory Impact Analyses', Paper prepared for the OECD project on Ex Post Evaluation of Regulatory Tools and Institutions, Paris: OECD.

Ladegaard, P. (2005), 'Improving Business Environments through Regulatory Impact Analysis – Opportunities and Challenges for Developing Countries', Paper prepared for the *International Conference on Reforming the Business Environment*, Cairo, Egypt, 29 November to 1 December 2005.

Morgenstern, R.D., W. Harrington and P. Nelson (2000), 'On the Accuracy of Regulatory Cost Estimates', *Journal of Public Policy and Management*, **19** (3).

NNR (Board of Swedish Industry and Commerce for Better Regulation) (2003), *How High is the Quality of the Swedish Central Government's Regulatory Impact Analysis (RIA) in the Business Sector?*, Stockholm: NNR.

OECD (1998), *Regulatory Reform in the United States*, Paris: OECD.

OECD (2004), *Regulatory Performance: Ex Post Evaluation of Regulatory Tools and Institutions*, Paris: OECD.

Yarrow, G. (2004), 'Evaluation of Regulatory Communication and Consultation Mechanisms: Approaches, Methodologies and Some Guiding Principles', Paper prepared for the OECD project on Ex Post Evaluation of Regulatory Tools and Institutions, Paris: OECD.

5. Better regulation and impact assessment in the European Commission

Lorenzo Allio[1]

INTRODUCTION

The European Union (EU) is called upon to meet ambitious challenges by the end of this decade. It clearly faces a trade-off. On the one hand the single internal market must be completed in all sectors and the so-called 'Lisbon objectives' must be pursued to ensure that the European economy becomes more dynamic, competitive and knowledge-based.[2] On the other hand a democratic and sustainable 'European economic and social model' must be developed to advance the welfare of European citizens, ensure a high level of protection of public health and the environment as well as social standards. This is in the broader context of polls that show low levels of public confidence and support for the EU, business is affected by excessive administrative burden caused by over-regulation, and non-governmental organizations (NGOs) and civil society are concerned about a perceived liberalization of European society as well as the persistent 'democratic deficit' of the EU. The French and Dutch votes on the ratification of the Constitutional Treaty are but the most recent expression of this malaise.

Regulation supports a two-fold objective: it constitutes the fundamental basis for guaranteeing adequate standards for social, environmental and health protection; and it provides legal certainty for consumers and companies in the process of developing, buying and selling products and services. But at the same time, regulation may cause social and individual costs both to economic actors and to consumers. Low-quality regulation in particular undermines the competitiveness of companies (by reducing entrepreneurship and innovation and increasing costs), restricts economic growth and inhibits the creation of jobs.

As a majority of all new regulation applicable in the EU Member States originates in the EU decision-making process, it is essential to improve and optimize regulatory quality at the EU level. Many governments have developed processes, structures and tools to prepare new regulation and to review and reform existing ones. Regulatory impact assessment (RIA) is one of the most widely used of these tools. This chapter outlines the evolution of 'better regulation' (BR) in general and of impact assessment (IA) in particular at the level of the EU. The next section identifies key factors that help explain the increased interest in BR practices within governmental institutions at the EU level. It seeks to answer the questions of why is there a drive for regulatory reform at the EU level and why is it pursued now? The third section outlines the major steps recently undertaken by EU institutions to improve regulatory instruments and outcomes. The subsequent section outlines the main characteristics of the IA process in the European Commission and assesses the early experience. The final section provides the conclusions and identifies areas for further improvement.

THE RISE OF 'BETTER REGULATION' AT THE EU LEVEL

Reforms and initiatives to improve the quality of law-making are a phenomenon that is as widespread as it is varied. There is no single definition of what 'better regulation' (BR) is. In Europe the term usually encompasses the overall attempt to rationalize and simplify both existing and new legislation. Rather than seeking 'deregulation', a priori, BR seeks to ensure that decision-making meets the needs and expectations of citizens, economic agents and stakeholders in the most legitimate, proportionate and cost-effective manner and keeps the impact of unexpected/unintended consequences to an accepted minimum.

The development of BR measures at the EU level has been slow compared with many other EU policies and with equivalent practices in some Organisation for Economic Co-operation and Development (OECD) countries. Regulatory reform has ranked high on the EU agenda for more than a decade – but until very recently the EU institutions have lacked a comprehensive, consistent and fully fledged strategy for improving the quality of the legislative/regulatory processes and their outcomes (primary and secondary EU legislation). This section identifies six factors that may explain the rise in importance and visibility of BR initiatives at the EU level since the early 1990s.

The International Context

Evidence shows that towards the end of the twentieth century, countries with different institutional and constitutional settings have embarked on reform programmes with the similar objective of better structuring the management of regulatory processes to increase the effectiveness and reduce the costs of regulation (OECD, 2002). Globalization and trade liberalization were a strong incentive for such initiatives, since markets have become more integrated across macro-regions. Western and European countries have increasingly evolved from manufacturing to service economies while competition in world markets has been triggered by the so-called New Economy and the diffusion of new technologies. The boundaries of regulatory activity by the state had to be reconsidered because of the de facto interdependence of markets. Not only did any normal regulatory activity have implications beyond the remit of national states but financial and macro-economic phenomena had very similar impacts on different economies.[3] In addition, the establishment of a 'network and information society' has provided fertile ground for the emergence and proliferation of new social actors (such as social movements and NGOs) that complement and in certain cases replace governmental agents. This phenomenon has produced a significant change in consumer demand for information, consultation and participation in decision-making. The interdependence and higher competition of economies, the greater involvement of non-governmental actors in decision-making and the increasingly intrusive character of regulation into business operations clearly propelled decision-makers to new regulatory agendas.

Policy Diffusion

Since the early 1990s the OECD has played a fundamental role in stimulating the diffusion of regulatory policies at the international level. The development of checklists and recommendations, the setting of international standards for good practices as well as the use of peer reviews and country reports served as a catalyst, filter and diffuser of BR principles and practices.[4] This led not only to convergence of practices among states that had pioneering experiences with regulatory reform,[5] but it also gradually promoted the conceptual linkage between the notion of 'good government' and economic performance. The OECD has contributed to the broad recognition that good governance principles and effective regulatory frameworks are fundamental elements for modern decision-making.

The Role of the State

A third factor was the change of the role of the state in the last 15 years. Regulatory inflation has been a general phenomenon in all Western countries since the Second World War. The concept of the 'regulatory state' has emerged to describe a state activity that has shifted its focus from macro-economic stabilization and redistributive policies towards the improvement of economic efficiency in case of market failures, often developing a network of governing entities.[6] Modern regulatory regimes consist of layers of decision-making bodies added over time. Regulation can now be the result of activity in separate, parallel offices in various ministries; horizontal structures and agencies (created to cope with across-ministry issues such the environment, corporate governance and public health); independent (extra-governmental) regulators; and it has to comply with international regulatory standards set by the World Trade Organization (WTO), the World Health Organization (WHO) and other bodies. This complex institutional and regulatory net has contributed to a reduction in transparency and access to regulation; increased risks of regulatory capture; and a reduction in the capacity of governments to comply with their own political programmes in an effective manner. Also, at the EU level there was a perceived need for public sector reform, New Public Management policies and evidence-based policy-making to help remove these shortcomings. The specific context of the resignation of the Santer Commission due to allegations of maladministration and favouritism at end of the 1990s accentuated the pressure for internal evaluation and opened the door to wider organizational and procedural reforms with the aim of increasing the legitimacy and credibility of the institution's activity (Dimitrakopoulos, 2004).

The EU Internal Market Project

Focusing more specifically on the European integration process, the 1990s represented a fundamental turning point in the nature of regulatory activity at the EU level. As the main objective of the Treaty of Rome (1957) was the creation of a single internal market, the original remit of EU decision-making was primarily the harmonization of existing national legislation and the regulation of broad (economic) sectors by setting minimum standards. With the '1992 Project' consolidated in the Treaty of Maastricht, the focus of EU regulatory activity progressively shifted to regulating areas where no national legislation was in place; that were subject to rapid technological development and progress; and that addressed the specific demands from citizens for security and prosperity. The EU institutions produced new public health and environmental regulation. In addition there has been a quantum leap in the amount and degree of technical details required in EU legislation, which has become more wide-ranging, complex and voluminous.[7] This created new challenges for regulators and made it more urgent to achieve higher levels of regulatory quality.

The European Risk Management Process

Directly linked to the general evolution of the role of the state in modern society as well as to the specific EU regulatory environment, the fifth factor refers to changes in the European risk regulatory models. From the 1990s onward a number of societal and ethically controversial scientific issues (such as genetically modified organisms [GMOs] and stem cells) came to the forefront. In Europe, a series of regulatory failures (e.g., the BSE crisis in the UK and France; the dioxin scandal in Belgium; and the tainted blood scandal in France, among others) confirmed the increased difficulties for governments to manage this new form of risk. A 'risk society' has developed whereby technological progress and human activity produce collateral risks that increasingly require specialized expertise to recognize, assess and manage. Risks are now collective and global and their consequences are irreversible and thus potentially catastrophic (Beck, 1992). As a consequence, risk is increasingly emerging as a key organizing concept for regulatory regimes, characterizing a wider range of policy areas than the traditional environmental, public health and safety policies. The European public tend to distrust authorities and to demand greater risk aversion, while developing a culture of 'managing everything' (Power, 2004). Concern by regulators to intervene increasingly in so-called 'lifestyle risks' is an example of such a trend.[8] According to Hood et al. (2001) societal interaction is determined by the definition and distribution of risks among various groups – including the regulators – and by how risk regulation regimes are shaped and function. Because of the generalization and amplification of risks, regulators are 'under growing pressure to justify their action as bureaucratically rational and defensible in the face of political, executive and judicial scrutiny' (Rothstein et al., 2006, p. 96).[9] Whereas the 'old' risk management model consisted of consensual risk assessment decisions taken by experts behind closed doors, on the basis of technical-probabilistic estimates as well as cost–benefit analyses, new risk management models have sought to produce more evidence-based regulation coupled with greater attention to public perception and public trust.[10] Put in other words, society no longer contents itself with 'being told' but requires to 'be shown' how risk management options are chosen and are likely to have impact (Rothstein et al., 2006, p. 96). As a result, ensuring the highest quality possible for the scientific evidence underpinning regulatory activity has become much more important and BR can contribute to achieving this goal.

The Finalité Politique of the EU

Since at least its formalization in the Declaration attached to the Laecken European Council Conclusions in 2001,[11] the discourse on the finalité politique of the EU has highlighted the contribution that BR can make to enhance 'good governance'. Carried forward by the European Convention on the Future of the European Union and made explicit in the subsequent 'Draft Treaty establishing a Constitution for Europe',[12] the process included reflection on the allocation of competencies and responsibilities both between the supranational and the Member States level and among institutions. It also addressed the revision of processes and mechanisms for decision-making as well as the development of technical tools and instruments to improve regulatory quality. There was a general recognition that regulatory reform helps strengthen both the so-called 'input legitimacy' of the EU (i.e., the legitimacy related to the democratic and participation rationale) and the 'output legitimacy' (linked to the performance rationale). More generally, the aim was to re-design decision-making processes to ensure more intelligent and better performing EU policy-making.

In summary, the BR agenda at the EU level has been driven by three sets of issues. First, the accumulating evidence that regulation does not always achieve its declared societal goal. Second, the recognition that regulatory processes have become increasingly important for good governance on the one hand and economic performance on the other. Third, the recurrent tendency to compare and benchmark existing regulatory frameworks with good practice.[13]

MILESTONES IN BETTER REGULATION AT THE EU LEVEL

The relevance of regulatory reform was acknowledged since the mid-1990s at least. However, initiatives by the EU institutions had remained partial and sectoral. There had been no structured and substantial translation of the political will into a consequently structured 'EU public policy for better regulation'; and there had been insufficient pressure from external stakeholders to trigger reform. It was not until 2000 that a fully fledged BR agenda was conceived at the EU level and enjoyed widespread political visibility.

The EU institutions pursued three overriding objectives[14] that went beyond mere efficiency (cost–benefit) rationales.[15] The first objective was the modernization of the European economies and a boost to their international competitiveness. To this end the European Council launched the so-called 'Lisbon Strategy' in March 2000. This sought to establish 'a strategy for further coordinated action to simplify the regulatory environment, including the performance of public administration' and to rationalize the transposition of Community legislation.[16] The second objective was the pursuit of sustainable development, formalized in the 'Sustainable Development Strategy' agreed in Göteborg in 2001.[17] The third objective was the improvement of 'good governance' to achieve better legitimacy, efficiency and credibility of Community action. Further to the Laeken Declaration,[18] BR was therefore included as an integral part of the European Commission's 'White Paper on European Governance' (EC, 2001).[19]

A number of intergovernmental initiatives were also launched, the most important of these being the establishment by the European Ministers of Public Administration in November 2000 of an expert group chaired by the French Dieudonné Mandelkern, a former Member of the Conseil d'Etat. The mandate of the Mandelkern Group was to identify ways of improving the quality of new and existing EU legislation and to promote the collaboration between Member States. The Group's report[20] (Mandelkern Group, 2001) had a fundamental impact on the subsequent work by the European Commission because for the first time all Member States agreed a significant BR agenda. In the Mandelkern Report, core principles were consistently converted into action for EU Member States and the EU institutions. Recommendations covered key areas such as impact assessment (IA); consultation; simplification; organizational structures for BR; alternatives to regulation; access to regulation and national implementation of EU legislation.

Another important inter-governmental initiative was the creation of the Ad Hoc Group of Directors and Experts on Better Regulation (DEBR). DEBR is an informal inter-governmental group of senior officials responsible for BR at the Member State level. It still exists and is being progressively formalized. The overall mandate of DEBR is to promote and monitor progress on BR amongst Member States; share experience and best practice (with the new Member States in particular); and monitor the implementation of recommendations by the Mandelkern Report and the Commission BR Action Plan (DEBR, 2003). The DEBR meets twice a year and is usually chaired by the State holding the Presidency of the EU. The Secretariat-General formally represents the European Commission but other Commission services are invited to participate in DEBR meetings. In 2001 a Medium Term Programme for the Cooperation in Public Administrations was approved in Uppsala. That programme was updated in the following year at a meeting of the ministers responsible for public administration in La Rioja (May, 2002). It received final political backing under the Italian Presidency.[21]

Actions at the Community level developed equally rapidly and from 2002 onwards the EU institutions have more systematically addressed BR. However, at present there is no clear and formal description of how BR is organized within the EU. Roles and responsibilities are not clearly defined and many initiatives and processes overlap. The most comprehensive picture is probably provided by an informal working document produced by the Secretariat-General of the Commission in the summer of 2004. The document not only lists the actors and groups involved but sketches organizational mechanisms.[22] The following paragraphs summarize the most important initiatives launched by the EU institutions.

The European Commission's Action Plan on Better Law-making

The first comprehensive measure undertaken in the new framework was the Commission 'Action Plan on Better Law-making' of June 2002 (EC, 2002a). This document aimed at developing a new common legislative culture in Europe by improving current procedures; widening the breadth of policy tools employed; and simplifying existing legislation. Directly stemming from the Action Plan, eight communications on specific actions were issued by the Commission (see Box 5.1). In addition, websites of the Commission, the Parliament and the Council were upgraded to include measures taken to enhance the transparency of the institutions and widen

BOX 5.1 KEY COMMUNICATIONS RELATED TO THE COMMISSION ACTION PLAN ON BETTER LAW-MAKING

- general principles and minimum standards for consultation (COM (2002) 704 final) (EC, 2002e);
- the collection and use expertise (COM (2002) 713 final) (EC, 2002f);
- impact assessment (COM (2002) 276 final), including internal guidelines (EC, 2002b);
- simplifying and improving the regulatory environment (COM (2002) 278 final) (EC, 2002c);
- the proposal for a new comitology decision (COM (2002) 719 final);
- the operating framework for the European Regulatory Agencies (COM (2002) 718 final) (EC, 2002g);
- a framework for target-based tripartite contracts (COM (2002) 709 final);
- better monitoring of the application of community law (COM (2002) 725 final).

Note: In its Communication 'Updating and Simplifying the Community *Acquis*' (COM (2003) 71 final), the Commission provided a framework for the consolidation and codification of the *acquis* with the specific goal of reducing the volume of the existing text by at least 25 per cent by January 2005. See EC, 'Communication on Simplifying and Improving the Regulatory Environment', COM (2001) 726 final, p. 5.

the access to EU documents published in this policy area. Requirements have also been introduced to improve the quality of regulation drafting.[23]

The Inter-institutional Agreement on Better Law-making

Regulatory reform depends on strong and continued political commitment. While the Commission bears responsibility for the preparatory, policy management and implementing stages, the European Parliament and the Council are responsible for deliberating, amending and adopting proposals in an efficient way. Since mid-2003 the focus of the Commission has shifted from the formulation of principles and tools to the implementation of the new procedures and practices in collaboration with the other institutions. It became clear that in order to be effective and encompass all stages of EU decision-making, BR initiatives had to be coordinated among and implemented by all EU institutions. The 'Inter-institutional Agreement (IIA) on Better Law-making' of 2003[24] served as a catalyst in this respect.

Negotiations of the agreement were not without difficulties because of institutional sensitivities and prerogatives on the one hand and the need to preserve the existing inter-institutional balance on the other. The European Parliament for example, proposed to be more closely involved in the '*comitology*' procedures[25] and the joint multi-annual legislative programming. On the other hand, provisions covering alternative methods to regulation (notably co- and self-regulation) were the object of contentious negotiations, with Parliament fearing a loss of democratic control over EU decision-making. Overall, the final agreement was in line with the Commission's 2002 'Action Plan on Better Law-making' and it includes a number of positive provisions (see Box 5.2).

Before 2003 the BR process at the EU level was not structured and no calendar for common action was agreed. The IIA constituted a major step towards consolidating the political commitment and the inter-institutional cooperation that are necessary to carry out regulatory reform successfully. For the first time all major aspects of the BR agenda were consolidated in a single political statement. However, the final text fails to provide sufficient impetus to the reform process. The IIA does not go beyond the current status quo on several topical aspects. For instance, the obligation for the Commission to provide an account of the results of the impact assessments in the explanatory memorandum is stated again. But regrettably the IIA does not require minimum standards for the quality of the explanations given in the explanatory memorandum. Moreover, no particular mention is made to assessing legislation involving risk-related issues. A particularly sensitive issue refers to the possibility of the two branches of the legislative of having further impact assessments carried out on 'substantive

BOX 5.2 HIGHLIGHTS OF THE INTER-INSTITUTIONAL AGREEMENT (IIA) ON BETTER LAW-MAKING

The IIA:

- calls for better coordination in the programming of legislation and the mutual sharing of information at all stages of the decision-making process;
- calls for enhancing transparency and accessibility of documents (information, publication and broadcasting);
- invites the Council and the Commission to attend European Parliament plenary sessions and committee meetings;
- frames the use of co- and self-regulation where appropriate, specifying that recourse to these instruments should be made only when 'fundamental rights or important political options are at stake or in situations where the rules must be applied in a uniform fashion in all Member States' (Paragraph 17).
- promotes the use of consistent IA practices;
- calls for better transposition, implementation and enforcement of EU law (for instance, by introducing a binding deadline for the transposition of directives);
- calls for a simplification of the EU legislation and a reduction in its volume;
- envisages the provision of more resources and additional staff.

amendments' (Paragraph 30). This possibility poses major procedural questions however, which the IIA does not solve. The real impact of the IIA will depend as much on the political willingness of the institutions to implement its provisions and monitor progress, as on its procedural feasibility. A High-Level Technical Group on Inter-institutional Cooperation, which is responsible for this task, will need to ensure that a number of short-term provisions are implemented. These include agreement on the criteria and procedures for carrying out IAs on substantive amendments; and modifications in the working methods of the European Parliament and the Council with particular emphasis on the procedures for the adoption of simplification proposals.[26]

The Draft Treaty Establishing a Constitution for Europe

A further arena for BR has been the Convention on the Future of Europe. The 'Draft Treaty Establishing a Constitution for Europe' presented in July 2003 contained a series of provisions that would, if implemented, help improve the quality of the EU regulatory process. These included the clarification of the allocation of competences between the Union and the Member States and a simplification of the legislative procedures; the introduction of a clear hierarchy of legal instruments and a considerable reduction in their number (from 15 to 6); a reform of the monitoring process on the application of subsidiarity; the consolidation of the principles of participatory democracy, transparency and openness, notably through the formal recognition of the role of the social partners; positive signals for political commitment to undertake IAs and wide pre-legislative consultation; and the introduction of a simplified procedure to ensure compliance with EU laws, including a faster and more effective procedure for applying sanctions.[27]

International Dimension

Improving the quality of EU regulation also means enhancing regulatory convergence at the international level. The European Commission has facilitated cooperation both on a multilateral basis and bilaterally. Bilaterally, particular emphasis has been given to the transatlantic dimension. 'EU–US Guidelines on Regulatory Cooperation and Transparency'[28] were, for instance, agreed in April 2002. Improved regulatory cooperation is also one of the key elements in the Transatlantic Economic Partnership (TEP). Similarly, the EU launched a 'Joint Action Plan Canada–EU Regulatory Dialogue and Cooperation'[29] with the Canadian Government in Spring 2003. Moreover, the Commission supports bilateral dialogue on regulatory cooperation with a number of countries including Japan and China. Discussions are also taking place on a multilateral basis, in particular within the OECD. Finally, regulatory cooperation is considered a priority in most of the business roundtables and dialogues.[30]

The Political Turning Point of 2004

Simultaneous to these institutional and administrative steps, there has been in the recent past a strong acceleration of the political discourse around regulatory reform in the EU. 'Better regulation' has become one of the most fashionable terms circulating in the corridors in Brussels. European leaders have made political statements about the need for high levels of regulatory quality especially from the Seville European Summit in 2002 onwards[31] and systematically, at each year's Spring European Summit in Brussels.[32] Equally importantly, the Irish, Dutch, Luxembourg and UK Presidencies launched a 'Joint Initiative on Regulatory Reform' in January 2004[33] with the aim of boosting and prioritizing regulatory reform. The same commitment was renewed one year later when the subsequent two Presidencies of the EU (Austria and Finland) joined the group common statement for the period 2005–06.[34] In the broad context of the mid-term review of the Lisbon Process in 2005, it became apparent that economic performance in the EU continued to stutter and the reforms expected from the Lisbon Agenda had failed to materialize. BR was clearly seen as a means to relaunch the drive for improved economic performance.

A number of strategic and programmatic documents published by the Commission in 2005 highlighted the increased visibility and relevance attributed to BR. In its *Strategic Objectives 2005–2009*, the Commission specified that:

> Legislation should aim at the highest levels of quality, coherence and effectiveness. Better regulation means that legislation should be well-prepared and as simple as possible. Impact assessment, including on competitiveness, before initiatives are launched and throughout the legislative process, must become second nature. Reviews of legislation in force should be systematically done. Subsidiarity and proportionality must be applied in full. Better regulation should be a priority also at the Member States' level. (EC, 2005a, p. 4)

Similarly, in its Work Programme for 2005, the Commission stated that 'high standards in EU governance and regulation are essential for the EU policy delivery to be both credible and legitimate. In particular, better regulation and improved quality of legislation contributes directly to stimulating growth, competitiveness and employment, whilst ensuring adequate protection for citizens and the environment' (EC, 2005b, p. 10).

Under the leadership of President Barroso, the Commission seems to have shifted clearly the political significance of BR, moving its emphasis from it being a constitutive element of 'good governance' towards supporting policies that boost competitiveness. This transition culminated in the *Communication to the 2005 European Spring Council: Working Together for Growth and Jobs* (EC, 2005c),[35] and the related Communication on *Better Regulation for Growth and Jobs* of March 2005 (EC, 2005d). Building on and complementing the original 2002 Action Plan, this Communication puts BR in coherence with the relaunching of the Lisbon Agenda and the political priorities of the Barroso Commission. In presenting this Communication, the Commission's Vice-President Günter Verheugen explicitly acknowledged that one of the innovative elements of the new Commission undertaking was its 'political' nature, whereas 'previous attempts were administrative' initiatives.[36]

The March 2005 Communication put forward a number of areas for action. First, as it will be outlined below, mechanisms for IA were substantially improved and revised guidelines and new technical annexes were published in June 2005 (EC, 2005g).[37] Moreover, notably under the thrust of the Dutch Presidency, greater focus was put on reducing the administrative burden and compliance costs imposed on economic operators by regulation.[38] Disproportionate and unnecessary 'red tape' was felt to reduce flexibility significantly, undermine financial viability and divert management time. Particular attention was given to the implications for small and medium-sized enterprises (SMEs) in Europe. The Commission published a Communication on this subject in October 2005 (EC, 2005h) as well as supporting documents.[39]

A second area for action was rationalization and simplification. About 200 proposals by the Commission that were still pending before the European Parliament and the Council were screened to assess whether they were still relevant and justified.[40] At the same time, mechanisms for identifying legislation that requires simplification were reinforced and a three-year programme to repeal, codify, recast or modify 222 basic laws and over 1400 related legal acts was presented in October 2005 (EC, 2005i). The importance of a closer dialogue with the Member States and sub-national authorities was also acknowledged.[41] Finally, the *Better Regulation for Growth and Jobs* (EC, 2005d) Communication put the basis for a structured flow of expertise and advice to the Commission. A group of high-level national regulatory experts is being set up with a view to advise, in particular, on simplification and IA, implementation and enforcement questions. The group will also discuss the development of a coherent set of common indicators to monitor progress as regards the quality of the regulatory environment both at the EU level and in the Member States themselves, as a basis for benchmarking. The Commission will also call on external expertise and advice on technical issues from academics and practitioners from the economic, social and environmental fields.

The renewed thrust towards BR was reflected on a number of other initiatives. At the international level, the Commission intensified cooperation with key economic partners. In particular the progress made in transatlantic relations is striking. Two sets of 'Roadmap for Regulatory Cooperation' were developed for the 2004 and 2005 EU–US Summits, which frame activities aimed at reducing regulatory costs and expand market opportunities both on a sectoral and horizontal basis. Moreover, the Commission has regularized in-depth contacts with the US Office of Management and Budget with a view to sharing experiences and best practices. A High-Level Forum for Regulatory Cooperation takes place twice a year as a gathering of senior officials as well as representatives of business, key stakeholders and think tanks from both sides of the Atlantic. The active involvement of stakeholders is a fundamental precondition for the success of such initiatives.

The Commission is not the only institution promoting this new approach to BR. The European Parliament and the Council have also intensified their commitment. A significant achievement during 2004 was the adoption under the Dutch Presidency of a list of 15 priorities for simplification by the (Competitiveness) Council, selected on the basis of suggestions from Member States following an invitation made by the Irish Presidency.[42] Initiatives more closely related to IA are illustrated in the next section.

THE SPECIAL CASE OF IMPACT ASSESSMENT

Overall, the inputs provided by the Barroso Commission and the Irish, Dutch and UK Presidencies of the EU have accelerated the implementation of the BR agenda in the EU. Impact assessment (IA) features as the cornerstone of this framework because, if well designed and implemented, it serves a number of functions. First, it requires decision-makers to act with much stronger rigour and makes the policy process more accountable and transparent. In particular, IA helps structure the policy-making process; decompose complex reality; identify cause–effect links and likely impacts; select and prioritize policy options; and consider unintended consequences. IA also empowers citizens and responds to their right to know the reasons for political and regulatory choices. Finally, it fosters better programming, integrates policy objectives and enables institutional learning.

Past EU Initiatives on IA[43]

The requirement to carry out IA was progressively formalized in the mid-1990s. A protocol attached to the Amsterdam Treaty in 1996[44] replaced a simple, legally non-binding Declaration annexed to the Treaty of Maastricht.[45] At the same time the President of the European Commission produced Regulatory Policy Guidelines that required the Explanatory Memoranda to include answers to a list of questions related to the likely impacts of the proposed measures.[46] However, those guidelines were general and contained no guidance on the methods or technical assumptions that were to be used when evaluating the impact of any proposal. Hence, each Directorate-General (DG) was responsible for determining how this mandatory requirement was to be satisfied. Some exceptions were budgetary impact; environmental impact (Article 174.3 of the EC Treaty explicitly requires environmental impact assessment to be undertaken);[47] and to a certain extent, business impact.[48] In addition, individual DGs used a range of methods to assess the impact of proposed legislation. These were tailored to meet the specific requirements of each directorate and its policies. As a result these initiatives remained partial and sectoral and they were not backed by the necessary political support. The experience of the Commission with IA throughout the 1990s constituted a valuable practice but with hindsight it proved to be a relatively fragile basis. A new innovative approach was required.

The Commission's Integrated Approach

Set in the framework of the 2002 'Action Plan for Better Law-making', the Commission's new IA approach (EC, 2002a) is 'intended to integrate, reinforce, streamline and replace all the existing separate impact assessment mechanisms for Commission proposals' (EC, 2002b, p. 3). As such it probably constitutes the biggest single innovation in the entire BR framework. An official defined the new IA as the 'crown jewel' of the entire BR package designed by the Commission. Never had an EU institution been so ambitious in this respect, for the approach required an almost revolutionary change in the regulatory habits of Commission officials. In order to assist them, internal 'Guidelines on Impact Assessment' and two technical 'Handbooks' were issued (EC, 2002d). These documents set procedural rules and explained how to conduct the required analysis.

In conceiving the process the Commission set a number of operational principles that made the approach so innovative. First, IAs had to be comprehensive. The new tool was explicitly meant to replace previous single sector IAs (business-based, gender-based, economic, environmental and trade assessments) and establish one approach for all the Commission's services. This should promote simplicity and comparability between sectors and DGs. Second, IAs had to be integrated. They had to be carried out on an integrated, cross-sectoral approach, which covered the economic, social and environmental impacts of all major Commission proposals. This should promote coherence. Third, IAs had to be coordinated. IA had to be associated with the so-called 'planning cycle' (i.e., the Annual Policy Strategy and the Legislative and Work Programmes) of the Commission. This should increase the visibility and transparency of the entire process (since the lists of IAs are published) and enhance accountability (since delivery is monitored and the Commission commits publicly through its Work Programme). Fourth, IA had to be outward-looking. RIAs had to be complemented by improved consultation procedures and the results had to be published. This should increase transparency and enable greater involvement of stakeholders. Finally, IA had to be proportionate. The principle of 'proportional analysis' implied that the depth of analysis should match the efforts in producing an IA to the significance of the likely impacts. Together with an improvement in the collection and use of (scientific) expertise, this should provide evidence-based policy-making.

Besides these innovative points it is important to underscore a common feature that remained from the old IA practices. The Commission confirmed its traditional approach to IA as being not exclusively regulatory impact analysis but covering more broadly 'the major initiatives, i.e. those presented by the Commission in its Annual Policy Strategy or its Work Programme' (EC, 2002b, p. 5). Such initiatives are not only related to legislative proposals (for European directives and regulations), but also to Commission policy papers (so-called White Papers and Action Plans), expenditure programmes, relevant negotiating guidelines for international agreements and legislative amendments.[49] Arguably, this comprehensive approach is the result of the emphasis put by the EU decision-maker on various broad principles of BR in the past 20 years (Cavatorto, 2001). While the principles of 'minimum harmonization' and 'mutual recognition' dominated the political and institutional debate throughout the 1980s (leading to the introduction of the so-called 'New Approach Directives'),[50] from the early 1990s onwards greater attention has been given to the principles of subsidiarity and proportionality. Accordingly, action by the Commission has historically been directed towards a holistic perspective to regulatory reform, primarily addressing the simplification of the overall *acquis*, the access to documents and the general allocation of competences between the national and the Community level. In other words, EU regulatory reform has traditionally encompassed the governance of all policy initiatives undertaken by the Commission and considered less the specificity of regulatory initiatives. This is one explanation why the Commission has never reduced IAs to the strict quantitative application of sector-specific cost–benefit analysis, but it has seen IA as a tool to frame the overall policy-making (Hahn and Litan, 2004).

The work method developed by the Commission in the 2002 Guidelines was based on the following phases (EC, 2002d). First, the analysis of the issue (i.e., the identification of the problem as well as the key players and stakeholders). This should answer the question: what is the problem being addressed? Second, the definition of the objectives (both general and specific), which must be measurable and verifiable. This should answer the question: what are the objectives? Third, the identification of the policy and regulatory options, with special emphasis on the principle of subsidiarity and proportionality. This should answer the question: what policy options are available? Fourth, the measurement and comparison of the economic, social and environmental impacts in qualitative and quantitative terms, where possible also in monetary terms. This should answer the question: what are the impacts of different policy (and regulatory) options? Fifth, consultation, following the minimum standards developed by the Commission. This should answer the question: how do we select the preferred option? And finally, monitoring and evaluation, that is, setting measurable indicators to measure achievement for implementation.

The functioning and scope of the IA procedure were based on two stages, both linked to the Commission's Strategic Programming Planning Cycle. In a first step, short preliminary impact assessments (Pre.IAs) had to be carried out on all proposals included in the Annual Policy Strategy (in February of each year). In the words of the Commission, a Pre.IA should 'give a first overview of the problem identified, possible options and sectors affected. It will serve as a filter to help the College identify the proposals that will be subject to an extended impact assessment' (EC, 2002b, p. 6). In selected cases and based on the former analysis, subsequent extended impact assessments (Ex.IAs), had to be included in the Commission Work and Legislative Programme (in October of the same year). Ex.IAs should serve the double purpose of carrying out 'a more in-depth analysis of the potential impacts on the economy, on society and on the environment', on the one hand and 'consult[ing] with interested parties and relevant experts', on the other (EC, 2002b, p. 7). The critical point in this approach is the junction from Pre.IA to Ex.IA. The procedure outlined in the 2002 Guidelines (EC, 2002d, p. 13) implied that the Secretariat-General collects and reviews all Pre.IAs and identifies whether there are proposals requiring an Ex.IA. The Commission then decides which proposals require an Ex.IA and includes them in its Annual Policy Strategy and Work Programme. The decision whether to carry out an Ex.IA depends on whether legislative proposals and policy-defining initiatives are likely to have substantial economic, environmental or social impacts; would have a major impact on one or more groups in society; or introduce major change or policy reform.[51] However, no further indication was given as to which criteria should apply to make such a decision.

The Lead DG[52] remained responsible and accountable for both leading the policy design process and carrying out and reporting. Other DGs and the Secretariat-General were given a more or less formalized co-responsibility in the case of major cross-Commission initiatives. Reports on IA has to be attached to every proposal sent for inter-service consultation: 'All relevant information' has be made available to all services and 'a summary and/or the result of [the IA] must appear in the explanatory memorandum' (EC, 2002d, pp. 14–16). The final Ex.IA report has to be attached to the proposal as a working document of the services for the final adoption. After adoption by the Commission, the Ex.IA has to be sent to the Council and the European Parliament along with the proposal and made available on the Web. However, the Lead DG can organize its Ex.IA at its own discretion, provided that it follows the underlying 'guiding principles' (EC, 2002d, pp. 10–11). It can set up an 'inter-departmental group' (including the Secretariat-General and other DGs) and it has the ultimate authority to decide if, which and when stakeholders should be consulted.

First Experiences (2003–04)

The first year of implementation of the new system was 2003 and it was an ambitious first trial year. The Commission selected 43 key proposals for Ex.IA from the Work Programme 2003, which represented one-fifth of the total number of proposals (more than 200). But DGs could complete less than the half by the end of the year. In 2004 only 30 Ex.IAs were carried out of 70 initially planned.[53]

First experience with the IAs suggests mixed results. The tool is generally viewed positively by officials, as it provides a good framework for horizontal thinking. It forces officials to 'think outside the box' and to consider policy coherence and it strengthens consultation with stakeholders. It also appears clear that IA promotes a multidisciplinary approach and has substantially contributed to increasing the political visibility of BR in EU decision-making. Overall, however, the quality of IAs has remained below expectations. A number of studies and scoreboards indicate that IAs were more structured but most lacked good quantification of the costs and the benefits and in-depth assessment.[54]

To address these weaknesses, the Commission set up an inter-service Impact Assessment Working Group (IAWG) in April 2004 with the mandate of ensuring better coordination and to make recommendations for improvement. In its report of October 2004 (EC, 2004),[55] the Working Group argued that the overall quality of the IAs had increased considerably. There had been a steady increase in the capacity to carry out more and better IAs, which proved that the Commission services were responding positively to the new requirements. Moreover, the scope of what must be considered in an IA had widened significantly. Finally, there had been a broad and rapid diffusion of best practices within the Commission. Nonetheless, the report acknowledged a number of deficits. In an internal note it was deplored that:

> in many cases, the IAs remain an ex post justification of an already decided proposal and are not used effectively in the preparation of the proposal; the assessment of policy options is often artificially done; several IAs still focus too much on the issue and do not adequately cover the three dimensions (economic, social, environment); both the qualitative and quantitative analysis of impacts remain weak in many cases; subsidiarity and proportionality aspects are not always addressed; and the structure and presentation of several of the IAs are poor.[56]

The Current Commission System (2005)

As a result of this internal stock-taking exercise and following the renewed political input provided by President Barroso (see above), the Commission modified its approach to IA. IA was confirmed as the pivotal element for improving the preparation of EU legislation; but it had to be more focused, objective, precise and proportionate (EC, 2005b, p. 10). Accordingly, the Commission intervened at a number of levels:

Programming and scope

The Annual Policy Strategy for 2005 simplifies the selection process for IA, but in overall terms, the scope of the IA system remains unchanged. From 2005 all major policy-defining and pre-legislative documents as well as all major legislative proposals in the Work Programme have now to undergo IA.[57]

Procedures

The revised approach transforms the Pre.IA into a 'roadmap' addressed to other services and the public. Roadmaps inform on the planned proposal; the policy options and likely impacts identified; and the consultation to be undertaken and its timing. In this respect they do not substantially differ from Pre.IAs. Roadmaps are automatically made for all legislative and non-legislative proposals. They are published with the Commission's Legislative and Work Programme and made available for public comments at an earlier stage.[58] This should foster inter-service dialogue and coordination, improve consultation and enhance transparency, as all roadmaps are promptly published on the Internet. Alongside this, Ex.IAs are replaced by impact assessments, with the term better reflecting the principle of 'proportionate analysis' and the fact that certain IAs may remain relatively limited in the scope and depth of their assessment.[59]

Organization

The process is structured on a system of internal checks and balances. In particular, there is a relative centralization of the political responsibility of the process. A greater role for instance is attributed to the Competitiveness Council Commissioners Group (CCCG), chaired by one of the Commission's Vice-Presidents. The CCCG is the body politically responsible for all aspects of the proposals related to competitiveness. Lead operational DGs remain responsible for the quality and content of their proposals. DGs are invited to set up internal mechanisms and specific units to achieve good regulatory standards. DGs are also responsible for providing adequate training to their officials involved in producing IAs and drafting the proposals.[60] The coordination and monitoring role of the Secretariat-General is strengthened as is its mandate to promote administrative and regulatory reform. Moreover, the Secretariat-General is now empowered to consider the quality of the IA report as part of the formal Inter-Service Consultation procedure (ISC) that occurs at the end of the process. If the IA report subjected to ISC does not reach a satisfactory level of quality, a suspended or unfavourable opinion may be issued. This is designed to enhance the oversight powers of the Secretariat-General. Finally, the Secretariat-General represents the Commission externally on matters related to regulatory reform.

Administrative capacity and expertise

One of the IAWG recommendations indicated that 'the main shortcomings of the Commission's IAs currently stem from a lack of compliance and systematic application of the existing method, rather than from the method itself'.[61] Corrective measures were the development of inter-service coordination (including the use of ad hoc inter-departmental steering groups); increasing the overall resources devoted to IAs; and improving the pooling and spreading of information through the Commission's intranet. In particular, the new process requires an 'inter-service steering group' to be established for each proposal. If this is not required, the sponsoring DG must provide valid reasons. A further compulsory requirement is the need to include in each roadmap an external consultation plan (EC, 2005d, p. 10).

Work method

A new, formal policy-making model replaces the previous, less structured approach. The six-step framework of the final IA (problem identification; definition of objectives; development of options; analysis of the impacts of options; comparison of options; and ideas for monitoring and evaluation) is described more thoroughly and made compulsory so that each of the stages of the framework must be covered.[62]

Actions at the Level of EU Institutions

The Council and the European Parliament also addressed IA-related internal issues. Overall, initiatives undertaken by the Council to implement the 2003 inter-institutional agreement have remained timid. The Council confirmed that the IAs produced by the Commission are 'an important element of the negotiations and the decision-making process . . . and should be used systematically' and that 'they should be the basis for any Council impact assessment'.[63] As a pilot experiment under the Dutch Presidency, the Council decided to carry out an assessment of substantive amendments tabled by Member States to the proposed Directive on batteries and accumulators.[64] While it did not cause major procedural complications or delays, the experience has showed the difficulties for the Council in ensuring high-quality assessments. Collaboration with the Commission, especially in sharing methodologies and information, also proved to be less smooth than expected. However, to date, this is the only concrete initiative undertaken by the Council on IA and further evidence is needed to gauge the capability of the institution to best assess amendments.

The European Parliament has been more active. A number of reports on BR include proposals to implement systematically the IIA provisions on IAs on the one hand, as well as general contributions to improving the quality of Commission IAs on the other. At the Plenary Session in May 2006 for instance, no less than four reports were discussed on BR-related issues, including IAs, simplification and transposition and implementation of Community law.[65] Reports generally highlight the need for the quality of Commission IAs to be reviewed by an independent agency; recommend that comitology decisions should also be subject to IAs; and call upon the Commission to better inform the Parliament. Besides discussions on institutional competences and procedures the Parliament has experimented with ways to carry out IAs on amendments. The Internal Market Committee in particular was the first committee to commission its own IA for amendments on the 'Toubon Report' on 'Nominal quantities for prepacked products' in November 2005.[66] Similar case studies are currently being undertaken on Commission proposals on legal protection designs (so-called car spare parts), pyrotechnics and public procurement.

Trilateral cooperation between the EU institutions has led to the agreement of an inter-institutional 'Common Approach to Impact Assessment' in November 2005.[67] The agreement covers four key areas, ranging from general principles; the roles and responsibilities of each institution; inter-institutional collaboration; and review. The Common Approach contributes to the development of a more cohesive approach to IA at the EU level. It provides a common definition of the purpose, coverage and nature of IA, and establishes a shared awareness of the importance of transparent and open assessment processes. However, it remains below expectations on a number of key issues. Specifically, the concept of 'substantive amendment' (on which IAs should be carried out) is not defined and it is accepted that the European Parliament and Council are to develop their own separate definitions. This clearly reduces the transparency, certainty, predictability and consistency of the process. Second, the Common Approach makes it clear that the Council and Parliament will only carry out assessments on a substantive amendment if they consider it 'appropriate and necessary'. Again, neither of these criteria is defined, potentially dramatically limiting the commitment of these two institutions to the use of IAs.

CONCLUSIONS AND FUTURE PERSPECTIVES

Regulation and poor quality legislation in particular causes costs that are not only of an economic nature or related to clearly quantifiable factors. These costs affect the overall legitimacy of decision-making since poor-quality legislation jeopardizes the capacity of regulators to meet societal expectations and achieve agreed goals. Moreover, unintended consequences are more likely to emerge if legislative quality remains suboptimal. For instance, complex economic costs (such as changes in the employment and innovation rate) might push economic actors to choose more costly production patterns and divert investments, and consumers might face higher product prices because of legislative requirements. Ultimately, fundamental values are concerned because of restrictions in individual or collective freedoms and personal choice. Such costs are more likely to be reduced by working on the quality rather than the quantity of legislation. The basic approach to BR embraced by the EU institutions has not been indiscriminate deregulation but improving regulatory design along rational lines. While already multifaceted at the national level, this type of reform is even more complex at the EU level, where three independent institutions (the Council, the European Parliament and the Commission) need to take account of different regulatory cultures and institutional settings while contending for institutional prerogatives. Moreover, many officials in the EU institutions still fear that BR is an impediment to legislation. The success of a Directorate-General has historically been measured in terms of the quantity of regulatory outcome and activity produced rather than its quality. In particular, there is no incentive mechanism (promotion, reward system) to stimulate compliance. The reform requires a great deal of political goodwill, sound processes and a cultural change in decision-making.

Since 2002 the European Commission has focused on IA as the key element for its BR agenda. Its three-fold IA system based on balanced consideration of the economic, social and environmental impacts constitutes a significant improvement compared with previous practice. IA is linked to the preparatory stage of policy-setting and decision-making on the one hand, and the revision of the *acquis communautaire*, on the other. This reflects the peculiar nature of EU decision-making where the Commission is not a proper legislator (despite being the initiator of the legislative process), and there is not guaranteed coherence between political preferences in the legislature and the executive. The integrated approach takes into account the political and organizational sensitivities of the various institutions and the necessity to underline the trade-offs involved in the proposed policy choices. Nonetheless, only practice will tell whether the tool can guarantee a robust balance between all three dimensions. The danger is real. Interpreting the new political emphasis put on BR by President Barroso for instance, Commission Vice-President Verheugen explained at a highly publicized press conference in March 2005 that:

> Better regulation at all levels constitutes a central component in the Commission's proposal for revitalising the Lisbon process. The equation is simple: Less red tape = more growth and jobs. Today we have presented a specific package of measures for cutting down on red tape with a view of improving the environment for business and industry and hence strengthening the competitiveness of the EU economy.[68]

Strikingly, no mention can be found of sustainable development, the social dimension or good governance measures in that important speech.

With the shift away from the partial and sectoral initiatives of the 1990s, the Commission's current approach clearly brings the EU more into line with the 'good practices' identified by the OECD. It is for instance, good practice that close collaboration exists between the Commission service responsible for developing the proposal and the team in charge of producing the IA. There should however, be formalized checks and balances. Greater leadership and responsibility should be given to central quality control and oversight units both within the Commission's Secretariat-General (for the supervision of the content and quality of the single assessments) and externally (to oversee the IA process). In particular, a formal power to 'return' IAs that do not meet the quality standards set by the institution should be entrusted to the Secretariat-General.[69] A further important area for improvement is making the process more open. Other Commission services and the Member States should have a formal opportunity to input to draft IAs and stakeholders should be allowed to comment on the basis of a peer-review system. The 'Scoping Paper' issued by the Health and Consumer Protection (SANCO) DG paves the way in the right direction but it applies to the Health and Consumer Protection DG only and on preliminary, relatively 'quick and dirty' assessments.[70] Finally, annual reports on the functioning of the system should be submitted to the European Parliament.[71]

Conceptually the new approach has so far failed on three fronts. First, as illustrated in this chapter, one of the most important functions of modern governments is management of both technological and, increasingly, lifestyle risks. Hence, regulatory quality tools addressing the likely impacts of regulation should be designed to allow decision-makers to identify and understand specific aspects related to clearly defined policy areas. The Commission's integrated approach remains a 'policy-making' tool that cannot offer the same depth of analysis provided by more elaborate and tailored IA systems. The Commission IA guidelines are weak especially on the 'problem definition' stage. They do not focus for example, on the need to recognize the characteristics of different types of risk and require scientific risk assessments; to identify causal links between hazards, risks, policy options and benefits; to revise decisions when significant new (scientific) information becomes available; to use precaution only in certain defined circumstances; and to focus on 'risk–risk'. This gap should be filled (the guidelines should be complemented), especially if we consider that the most prolific Commission DGs are also those addressing sector-specific issues in general and risk-related issues in particular.[72] Second, the new approach has failed to create and formalize an 'outside-in' logic that balances responsibilities for the provision of expertise and monitoring between Commission services and external actors. In addition, the mechanisms are weak for linking IA procedures to other BR tools like consultation, for the collection of scientific advice and for ex post evaluation. More formal arrangements for transparent and inclusive consultation and involvement of stakeholders should, for instance, be introduced at an early stage. Roundtable and platform-type consultations should be promoted alongside the current broad, open approach. Their ultimate aim should be to increase the capability of the EU institutions to understand complex societal and economic costs and how economic actors respond to regulation and changes in the regulatory environment. Third, the scope of the Commission IA is confined to only part of the process. Two important phases are not covered, notably, implementation ('comitology' decisions are still excluded from the IA process, despite their importance) and ex post evaluation, so that there is no full feedback loop on the complete policy-making cycle.

The roles of the Council and the European Parliament in the IA process are still uncertain and little has so far been done by these institutions to implement the Inter-institutional Agreement of 2003. The European Parliament and the Council should play their respective roles in implementing BR at the EU level especially by assessing the impacts of their 'substantive amendments'.[73] One major operational complication as mentioned above remains the definition of when an amendment should be considered to be 'substantive'. To date neither institution has developed clear definitions or criteria on this matter. The Council merely notes that:

> the final decision, if agreement has not been reached in the Working Party, on whether a Council amendment is to be considered as 'substantive' . . . should be taken by the Permanent Representatives Committee on a proposal from the Presidency, taking into account the level of support for producing an impact assessment.[74]

The European Parliament has not gone further than the suggestion that:

> amendments by Parliament that will have an impact on the environment, society and industry will be submitted for cost-assessment to an audit set up with whatever reasonable means Parliament has at its disposal. If it transpires that the amendment exceeds the cost threshold [above which the EU institutions have decided that an extended impact assessment should be carried out] . . . the audit will carry out an impact assessment on the amendment.[75]

This notwithstanding, the European Parliament has been working towards granting specific budgets to its audit Committee, which may be used at the Committee's discretion to commission external studies, including IAs, through calls for tender procedures. Yet responsibility for BR is not confined only to the EU institutions. Member States should also become more active in driving the agenda forward, notably by working more closely with the Commission in the preparation of IA and better implementing legislation (Allio and Fandel, 2006). Industry, NGOs and other stakeholders have their role to play.

More generally there is no clear picture of the entire IA process: roles and responsibilities are not clearly allocated and the process is not based on formal, accountable procedures. Indicators for benchmarking progress should be clearly defined and applied to outcomes of BR policies rather than single outputs.[76] Also, the new approach has, in many cases, failed to identify the fundamental nature of the problem and its root causes. The coverage provided of the different types of impacts has not always been balanced and better mechanisms for the collection and use of data need to be established to ensure that the best data available are correctly processed in public decision-making. More efforts also need to be made to identify all possible policy options (including alternatives to traditional regulation and the so-called 'no action option') and to justify the choice of the preferred option.[77] Moreover, the same rigour that is applied to the analysis (and quantification) of the likely costs should be applied to the benefits associated with a specific policy option. Nor has the system systematically addressed the need for specialized training for regulators. In addition, a disconnection between political priorities and budget and financial resources remains. High-quality human resources are needed to support the new regulatory environment and should be better allocated both internally and on a case by case basis through outsourcing. Finally, the Commission's internal reward and promotion structure should be revisited to create attractive incentives for officials to comply with the reformed system and instil a new regulatory and evaluation culture.

Introduced in 2003, and revised in 2005, the new IA approach still needs to be tested and assimilated by the Commission's services. So far the

Commission has focused particularly on designing techniques and tools. This must now be combined with an appropriate and timely use of these instruments. It is necessary to go beyond the technical approach and make regulatory reform both more visible and palatable to regulators and economic operators. There is a need in the EU for incentives to apply the techniques and make them work well in practice, with the use of appropriate sanctions for non-compliance. A 'sense of urgency' needs to be conveyed. The capacity of the European institutions to integrate regulatory reform into their modus operandi will be one of the keys for achieving success.

BR has enjoyed clear political backing at the EU level and it has gained both in relevance and visibility. Unprecedented progress has been made by the EU institutions in recent years. However, the risk is that the increased political salience attached to BR hijacks the discourse to the field of partisan political interplays. BR might easily become a surrogate for broader political debate about the role of the state and the extent of accepted regulatory intervention in contemporary society. The statements by Commission President Barroso in April 2006 about the necessity to set up an impartial and independent mechanism, under the direct authority of the President of the Commission, to support and control the quality of individual IAs, gives hope that the way chosen will be primarily to strive for the best possible management of regulatory processes.[78] To this end it remains critically important that this approach is sustained and that external stakeholders make sure that political backing is continued. The objective is ultimately to create a participatory society that advances the prosperity and welfare of European citizens.

NOTES

1. The author has been a Policy Analyst at the European Policy Centre (Brussels), where he has been responsible for the EPC Better Regulation Programme from 2002 to 2006. He is a PhD student at King's College London. The author would like to thank particularly Richard Meads and Jacopo Torriti for the constructive discussions had during the drafting of this chapter.
2. Presidency Conclusions, Lisbon European Council, 23–24 March 2000.
3. The South East Asian economic crisis in 1997–98 and the Mexican crisis in 2000, for instance, illustrate this evolution.
4. See in particular the work done by the OECD Directorate for Public Governance and Territorial Development at www.oecd.org, in particular OECD (1995, 1997a,b, 2000) and Gonenc, Maher and Nicoletti (2000).
5. On the concept of 'policy diffusion' in relation to RIA in Europe, see Radaelli (2002, 2004a, 2005b). More generally, see Bush, Jörgens and Tews (2004) and Stone, Maxwell and Keating (2001).
6. See Majone (1996, 1997, 1999) and Schneider (2002).
7. The total volume of the *Official Journal of the EU* (OJEC) is estimated to be more than 80 000 pages.

8. Unlike risks related to technological progress, 'lifestyle risks' occur because of the everyday actions and behaviour of individuals. They are primarily the result of voluntary decisions to accept risks linked to activities such as drinking, eating, driving, smoking and leisure. Recently, the European Commission has undertaken initiatives addressing obesity and alcohol consumption.
9. Moreover, significant unintended negative consequences arose from regulatory activity: the so-called 'risk–risk paradox' potentially bore much greater consequences. The paradox can be simplistically referred to as the possibility that decisions taken to manage one single risk may create other countervailing risks (Graham and Weiner, 1995).
10. See Ballantine (2003, 2005); Löfstedt (2004); Löfstedt and Vogel (2001), and Vogel (2003).
11. Laecken Declaration on the Future of the Union, Presidency Conclusions, Laecken European Council, 15–16 December 2001.
12. See http://europa.eu.int/constitution/futurum/constitution/index_en.htm.
13. For Europe, the typical yardstick throughout the 1990s has been the United States.
14. The three drivers – competitiveness, sustainability and governance – have always been considered as being closely intertwined and complementary. See, for instance, Williams, MacDonald and Kind (2002) and Löfstedt (2004). Only recently, the general discourse about BR appears to give priority to the competitiveness aspects (see below).
15. See Hahn and Litan (2004) and Radaelli (2005a).
16. Presidency Conclusions, Lisbon European Council, 23–24 March 2000, Point 17.
17. Presidency Conclusions, Göteborg European Council, 15–16 June 2001.
18. See note 11 above.
19. See also http://www.europa.eu.int/comm/governance/governance_eu/index_en.htm.
20. The report was endorsed by the Laeken European Council in December 2001.
21. http://www.funzionepubblica.it/docs_pdf/MTP%20final%20ing.pdf.
22. The Commission working document entitled 'Who is doing what on better regulation at EU level – organization chart' was compiled by the Secretariat General TFAU-2 (Task Force Avenir de I'Union – Unité Gouvernance et affaires institutionnelles) and refers to the situation as of 1 July 2004.
23. Following the Inter-Institutional Agreement on 'Common Guidelines for the Quality of Drafting of Community Legislation' (OJ C 73, 17 March 1999, p. 1), a 'Joint Practical Guide' (http://europa.eu.int/eur-lex/en/about/techleg/guide/index_en.htm) was issued and the Commission's Legal Service is entitled to make drafting suggestions at an early stage of the legislative process. The Commission has also organized training in legal drafting and joint seminars with Member States. See, for instance, http://ec.europa.eu/transparency/index_en.htm. The Commission published a progress report in January 2004 (COM (2004) 45 final). Statistics show that the number of requests for access to documents has doubled since the introduction in December 2001 of EU Regulation 1049/2001.
24. OJ C 321, 31 December 2003, p. 1.
25. The term 'comitology' refers to the system of committee mechanisms that control and assist the European Commission in the exercise of its implementation duties (further to Article 202 of the Treaty Establishing the European Community). These committees are composed of representatives of the Member States and are chaired by the Commission. 'Comitology' procedures are governed by the Council Decision 1999/468/EC.
26. For a more detailed analysis of the IIA, see Allio, Ballantine and Hudig (2004).
27. Given the 'pause of reflection' imposed by the double negative vote in the French and Dutch referenda in May 2005, it is difficult to assess fully at this stage the implication that a revision of the constitutional and institutional setting of the EU decision-making process will have on better regulation. Crossick and Allio (2003) provide a general assessment of the impacts of the Draft Constitutional Treaty on business.
28. http://europa.eu.int/comm/enterprise/enterprise_policy/gov_relations/interntl_regul_coop_eu_us/regul_coop_guide.htm.
29. http://www.europa.eu.int/comm/enterprise/enterprise_policy/gov_relations/canada/joint_action_plan.htm.

30. For an overview of the international regulatory cooperation, see http://www.europa.eu.int/comm/enterprise/enterprise_policy/index.htm.
31. Presidency Conclusions, Seville European Council, 21–22 June 2002, Point 9.
32. See, for instance, Presidency Conclusions, Brussels European Council, 25–26 March 2004, Point 23; or Presidency Conclusions, Brussels European Council, 22–23 March 2005, Points 20 and 24.
33. 'Joint Initiative of Regulatory Reform', an initiative of the Irish, Dutch, Luxembourg and UK Presidencies of the European Union, 26 January 2004.
34. 'Advancing Regulatory Reform in Europe, A Joint Statement of the Irish, Dutch, Luxembourg, UK, Austrian and Finnish Presidencies of the European Union', 7 December 2004, at http://www.hm-treasury.gov.uk/media/B39/14/advancing_regulatory_reform_in_europe.pdf.
35. See also the Commission's website http://europa.eu.int/growthandjobs/index_en.htm.
36. Günter Verheugen at the Press Conference 'Better Regulation' of 16 March 2005 in Brussels, quoted from http://www.euractiv.com/Article?tcmuri=tcm:29-136893-16&type=News.
37. See http://www.europa.eu.int/comm/governance/impact/index_en.htm.
38. The Six EU Presidencies Joint Statement restates the mandate given to the Commission by the ECOFIN Council to develop a common European methodology to measure the administrative burden of EU legislation and regulation. The initiative includes assessing administrative burden for all new directives before the end of 2005; using the new methodology also when developing new simplification proposals; and annually reviewing, within the Council and on the basis of Commission reports, changes in the administrative burden of EU regulation. A brief assessment of the Dutch contribution to the Better Regulation agenda of the EU institutions is given by Allio (2005).
39. See http://ec.europa.eu/governance/impact/key_en.htm.
40. The Commission decided to withdraw 68 proposals that were either inconsistent with the Lisbon objectives; did not meet BR standards; were not advancing the legislative process; or were simply outdated. See http://europa.eu.int/comm/enterprise/regulation/better_regulation/index_en.htm#with.
41. On the role of regions in the EU BR agenda, see for instance Burrows et al. (2004).
42. See Council document 15017/04 (COMPET 194) of 23 November 2004.
43. This section does not seek fully to describe EU experiences with IA in the past. Summaries and analyses are provided by Cavatorto (2001) and Pelkmans, Labory and Majone (2000).
44. 'Protocol on the Application of the Principles of Subsidiarity and Proportionality', OJ C 340 of 10 November 1997.
45. Declaration No. 18 of the Maastricht Treaty on estimated costs under Commission proposals, whereby the Inter-Governmental Conference 'notes that the Commission undertakes, by basing itself where appropriate on any consultations it considers necessary and by strengthening its system for evaluating Community legislation, to take account in its legislative proposals of costs and benefits to the Member States' public authorities and all the parties concerned'.
46. European Commission, 'Regulatory Policy Guidelines', internal document, 1996.
47. On the use of IA by the Commission in the environmental field, see among others, Lee (1995); Canter (1996); Barker and Wood (2001).
48. See EC (DG Enterprise) (2002).
49. Significantly, however, 'comitology' decisions are excluded from the scope of the 2002 IA guidelines.
50. The 'New Approach' was launched in 1985 and sought to 'the fixing of minimum standards, mutual recognition and monitoring by the country of origin' (European Council Conclusions, Milan, 28–29 June 1985, Point 1.2.5(2)).
51. Exceptions to this principle are Green Papers, periodic decisions and proposals that follow directly from international obligations, implementing decision and technical updates.

52. The 'Lead DG' is the Directorate-General that is officially entrusted with the preparation of a Commission proposal.
53. For a comparison, the number of completed Ex.IAs at the end of May 2006 totalled 129, distributed as follows: 21 (2003); 30 (2004); 72 (2005) and 6 (2006). See http://ec.europa.eu/governance/impact/practice_en.htm.
54. See, for instance, Allio et al. (2004); Lee and Kirkpatrick (2004); IEEP (2004); Mather and Vibert (2005); Vibert (2004); Renda (2006) and Torriti (2005 and forthcoming).
55. See EC (2005e, g).
56. European Commission internal note, unpublished.
57. In particular, decisions made through the 'comitology' process are still excluded, although the Commission may, on a case by case basis, decide to carry out an impact assessment on a proposal that does not appear on its Work Programme.
58. See the Secretariat-General website http://ec.europa.eu/governance/impact/practice_en.htm.
59. According to this principle, the depths and scope of the analysis will be proportional to the expected significance of the likely impacts of the proposed action (see EC, 2005h).
60. In particular, DG SANCO issued a document in June 2005 complementing and strengthening the minimum requirements set in the Secretariat-General's Guidelines of June 2005. The so-called 'SANCO Scoping Paper' (EC (DG SANCO) (2005)) applies to the DG only. It describes internal processes for developing legislative proposals, including early consultation mechanisms; consideration of alternatives to regulation; integration of policy objectives; and training. The paper was presented to the public at a conference organized in October 2005 in Brussels (see http://ec.europa.eu/dgs/health_consumer/events/impact_assessment_en.htm).
61. European Commission internal note, unpublished.
62. Further important changes include: indirect and unintended impacts of legislation; alternatives to 'command and control' regulation; early consultation; comparison of policy options; and new technical annexes.
63. Council document 10862/05 (COMPET 152) of 5 July 2005, Annex B, pp. 6–7.
64. See Council document 14372/04 (ENV 605, ENT 144, CODEC 1212) of 9 November 2004.
65. The reports (by Frassoni, McCarthy, Doorn, Gargani and Kaufmann, MEPs) and the debate can be found at the Press Room of the EP website, at http://www.europarl.europa.eu/news/expert/briefing_page/7648-129-05-19-20060426BRI07646-09-05-2006-2006/default_p001c005_en.htm.
66. See http://www.europal.europa.eu/comparl/imco/studies/0511_study_prepackedproducts_en.pdf.
67. See http://ec.europa.eu/governance/impact/docs/ii_common_approach_to_ia.pdf.
68. Günter Verheugen, Speech at the Press Conference 'Better Regulation' of 16 March 2005 in Brussels, at http://europa.eu/rapid/pressReleasesAction.do?reference=SPEECH/05/178&format=HTML&aged=0&language=EN&guiLanguage=en.
69. This is an important right conferred to the Office for Management and Budget in the US system.
70. The paper represents DG SANCO internal guidelines that complement the Commission-wide document. For an assessment of this initiative, see European Policy Centre's contribution at www.theepc.be/en/iwp.asp?TYP=TEWN&LV=187&see=y&t=&PG=TEWN/EN/detail_g&l=1&AI=507.
71. These recommendations draw from Allio et al. (2004) and Ballantine (2001).
72. Again, the DG SANCO Scoping Paper represents a first initiative in this regard, but fails to tailor specifically the Commission-wide policy framework for IA to best accommodate public health and food safety needs.
73. 'Inter-Institutional Agreement on Better Law-making', Paragraph 30.
74. Council document 10862/05 (COMPET 152) of 5 July 2005, Annex B, p. 6.
75. European Parliament, 'Report on Assessment of the Impact of Community Legislation and the Consultation Procedure' (Doorn Report), A5-0221/2004 of 24 March 2004, p. 6.

76. DG Enterprise commissioned a study on quality indicators in 2004 (Radaelli, 2004b). The recommendations of the study were well received but so far no formal internal document of the Commission defines criteria for evaluating the effectiveness of BR tools.
77. See UK BRTF (2005).
78. José-Manuel Barroso, 'Delivering Quality in European Regulation', Speech at the European Parliament Plenary debate on Better Regulation, 4 April 2006, Strasbourg, at http://europa.eu/rapid/pressReleasesAction.do?reference=SPEECH/06/221&format=HTML&aged=0&language=FR&guiLanguage=en.

REFERENCES

Ad Hoc Group of Directors and Experts on Better Regulation (DEBR) (2003), 'Report to the Ministers Responsible for Public Administration in the EU Member States on the Progress of the Implementation of the Mandelkern Report's Action Plan on Better Regulation', Athens.

Allio, L. (2005), 'What colour for the future "Better Regulation policy" of the EU?', *Challenge Europe*, **13**, online journal, http://www.epc.eu/en/ce.asp?TYP=CE&LV=177&see=y&t=42&PG=CE/EN/detail&1=3&AI=432

Allio, L. and M.H. Fandel (2006), 'Making Europe Work: Improving the Transposition, Implementation and Enforcement of EU Legislation', EPC Working Paper No. 25 (June), European Policy Centre, Brussels.

Allio, L., B. Ballantine and D. Hudig (2004), 'Achieving a New Regulatory Culture in the European Union: An Action Plan', EPC Working Paper No. 10 (April), European Policy Centre, Brussels.

Ballantine, B. (2001), 'Regulatory Impact Analysis: Improving the Quality of EU Regulatory Activity', EPC Occasional Paper (September), European Policy Centre, Brussels.

Ballantine, B. (2003), 'Improving the Quality of Risk Management in the European Union: Risk Communication', EPC Working Paper (June), European Policy Centre, Brussels.

Ballantine, B. (2005), 'Enhancing the Role of Science in the Decision-making of the European Union', EPC Working Paper No. 17 (March), European Policy Centre.

Barker A. and C.M. Wood (2001), 'Environmental assessment in the European Union: Perspectives, past present and strategic', *European Planning Studies*, **9**, 243–54.

Beck, U. (1992), *Risk Society*, Sage.

Burrows, N. et al. (2004), 'The Better Regulation Strategy', Discussion Paper prepared for the Sub Rosa meeting of 22 October 2004 in Brussels.

Bush, P.-O., H. Jörgens and K. Tews (2004), 'The Global Diffusion of Regulatory Instruments: The Making of a New International Environmental Regime', European Integration Online Papers (EIoP), at http://eiop.or.at/eiop/texte/2004-021a.htm.

Canter, L. (1996), *Environmental Impact Assessment*, New York and London: McGraw-Hill.

Cavatorto, S. (2001), 'Unione Europea: molto rumore per nulla?', in C.M. Radaelli (ed.), *L'analisi di Impatto della Regolazione in Prospettiva Comparata*, Rubbettino Editore, Soveria Mannelli, pp. 276–310.

Crossick, S. and L. Allio (2003), 'The Intergovernmental Conference and Business', EPC Issue Paper 16, European Policy Centre, Brussels.

Dimitrakopoulos, D.G. (ed.) (2004), *The Changing European Commission*, Manchester: Manchester University Press.
EC (European Commission) (2001), *White Paper on European Governance*, COM (2001) 428 final of 25 July 2001.
EC (2002a), *Communication on European Governance: Better Law-making*, COM (2002) 275 final of 5 June 2002.
EC (2002b), *Communication from the Commission on Impact Assessment*, COM (2002) 276 final of 5 June 2002.
EC (2002c), *Simplifying and Improving the Regulatory Environment*, COM (2002) 278 final of 5 June 2002.
EC (2002d), *Impact Assessment in the Commission. Internal Guidelines on the New Impact Assessment Procedure Developed for the Commission Service*, October 2002.
EC (2002e), *Consultation Document: Towards a Reinforced Culture of Consultation and Dialogue – Proposal for General Principles and Minimum Standards for Consultation and Minimum Standards of Interested Parties by the Commission*, COM (2002) 704 final of 11 December 2002.
EC (2002f), *A Framework for Target-based Tripartite Contracts and Agreements Between the Community, the States and the Regional and Local Authorities*, COM (2002) 709 final of 11 December 2002.
EC (2002g), '*Improving the Knowledge Base for Better Policies.' Communication on the Collection and Use of Expertise by the Commission: Principles and Guidelines*, COM (2002) 713 final, of 11 December 2002.
EC (2002h), *The Operating Framework for the European Regulatory Agencies*, COM (2002) 718 final, of 11 December 2002.
EC (2002i), *Better Monitoring of the Application of Community Law*, COM (2002) 725 final of 11 December 2002 (as per CORRIGENDUM of 16 May 2003).
EC (2002j), *Proposal for a Council Decision on Amending Decision 1999/468/RC Laying Down the Procedures for the Exercise on Implementing Powers Conferred on the Commission*, COM (2002) 719 final of 11 December 2002).
EC (2004), *Staff Working Document Impact Assessment: Next Steps in Support of Competitiveness and Sustainable Development*, SEC (2004) 1377 of 11 October 2004, at http://ec.europa.eu/governance/impact/docs/key_docs_sec_2004_1377_en.pdf.
EC (2005a), *Strategic Objectives 2005–2009, Europe 2010: A Partnership for European Renewal Prosperity, Solidarity and Security*, COM (2005) 12 final of 26 January 2005.
EC (2005b), *Commission Work Programme for 2005: Communication from the President in Agreement with Vice-President Wallström*, COM (2005) 15 final of 26 January 2005.
EC (2005c), *Communication to the Spring European Council: Working Together for Growth and Jobs – A New Start for the Lisbon Strategy – Communication from President Barroso in Agreement with Vice-President Verheugen*, COM (2005) 24 final of 2 February 2005.
EC (2005d), *Better Regulation for Growth and Jobs in the European Union*, COM (2005) 97 final, of 16 March 2005.
EC (2005e), *Report from the Commission 'Better Lawmaking 2004' Pursuant to Article 9 of the Protocol on the Application of Subsidiarity and Proportionality (12th Report)*, COM (2005) 98 final, of 21 March 2005.

EC (2005f), *Annex to the Report from the Commission 'Better Lawmaking 2004' Pursuant to Article 9 of the Protocol on the Application of Subsidiarity and Proportionality (12th Report)*, SEC (2005) 364 final, of 21 March 2005.
EC (2005g), *Impact Assessment Guidelines*, SEC (2005) 791, of 15 June 2005.
EC (2005h), *Communication on an EU Common Methodology for Assessing Administrative Costs Imposed by Legislation*, COM (2005) 518 final, of 21 October 2005.
EC (2005i), *Implementing the Community Lisbon Programme: A Strategy for the Simplification of the Regulatory Environment*, COM (2005) 535 final, of 25 October 2005.
EC (DG Enterprise) (2002), *Business Impact Assessment Pilot Project. Final Report – Lessons Learned and the Way Forward*, Enterprise Papers No. 9.
EC (DG SANCO) (2005), *Guidelines for the Preparation of a Scoping Paper*, July 2005, at http://www.epc.eu/en/iwp.asp?TYP&TEWN&LV=187&see=y&t=PG=TEWN/EN/detail_get=1&AI=507.
Gonenc, R., M. Maher and G. Nicoletti (2000), *The Implementation and the Effects of Regulatory Reform: Past Experience and Current Issues*, OECDECO/WKP (2000) 24, 29 June 2000.
Graham G. and J. Weiner (1995), *Risk vs. Risk. Tradeoffs in Protecting Health and the Environment*, Cambridge, MA: Harvard University Press.
Hahn, R.W. and R. Litan (2004), *Counting Regulatory Benefits and Costs: Lessons for the US and Europe*, AEI-Brookings Joint Center for Regulatory Studies.
Hood, C., H. Rothstein and R. Baldwin (2001), *The Government of Risk – Understanding Risk Regulation Regimes*, Oxford and New York: Oxford University Press.
IEEP (Institute for European Environmental Policy) (2004), *Sustainable Development in the European Commission's Integrated Impact Assessments for 2003*, London.
Lee, N. (1995), 'Environmental assessment in the European Union: a tenth anniversary', *Project Appraisal*, 10.
Lee, N. and C. Kirkpatrick (2004), 'A Pilot Study on the Quality of European Commission Extended Impact Assessments', Manchester: University of Manchester.
Löfstedt, R.E. (2004), 'The swing of the regulatory pendulum in Europe: From precautionary principle to (regulatory) impact analysis', *Journal of Risk and Uncertainty*, **28** (3), 237–60.
Löfstedt, R.E. and D. Vogel (2001), 'The changing character of regulation: a comparison of Europe and the United States', *Risk Analysis*, **23** (2), 411–21.
Majone, G. (1996), *Regulating Europe*, London and New York: Routledge.
Majone, G. (1997), 'From the positive to the regulatory state', *Journal of Public Policy*, **17** (2), 139–67.
Majone, G. (1999), 'The regulatory state and its legitimacy problems', *West European Politics*, **22**, 1–24.
Mandelkern Group on Better Regulation (2001), *Final Report*, November 2001.
Mather, G. and F. Vibert (2005), *Rebalancing UK and European Regulation*, London: European Policy Forum.
OECD (1995), *Recommendation of the Council of the OECD on Improving the Quality of Government Regulation*, Paris.
OECD (1997a), *Regulatory Impact Analysis: Best Practice in OECD Countries*, Paris.

OECD (1997b), *Report on Regulatory Reform – Thematic Studies*, Paris.

OECD (2000), *Reducing the Risk of Policy Failure: Challenges for Regulatory Compliance*, Paris.

OECD (2002), *Regulatory Policies in OECD Countries. From Interventionism to Regulatory Governance*, Paris.

Pelkmans, J., S. Labory and G. Majone (2000), 'Better EU regulatory quality: assessing current initiatives and new proposals', in G. Galli and J. Pelkmans (eds), *Regulatory Reform and Competitiveness in Europe, Volume 1: Horizontal Issues*, Cheltenham, UK and Northampton, MA, USA: Edward Elgar, pp. 461–526.

Power, M. (2004), *The Risk Management of Everything. Rethinking the Politics of Uncertainty*, London: Demos.

Radaelli C.M. (ed.) (2001), *L'Analisi di Impatto della Regolazione in Prospettiva Comparata*, Dipartimento della Funzione Pubblica, Rubbettino Editore.

Radaelli, C.M. (2002), 'The Politics of Regulatory Impact Analysis in the OECD Countries: Best Practice and Lesson-drawing', Paper delivered to the workshop on *Regulatory Impact Analysis in Comparative Perspective*, CARR, LSE, London, 11 March 2002.

Radaelli, C.M. (2004a), 'Getting to grips with quality in the diffusion of regulatory impact assessment in Europe', *Public Money and Management*, October, 271–6.

Radaelli, C.M. (2004b), 'Project on Indicators of Regulatory Quality. Final Report', European Commission and University of Bradford, 17 December 2004, at http://www.bradford.ac.uk/irq.

Radaelli, C.M. (2005a), *What does Regulatory Impact Assessment mean in Europe?*, Related Publications 05-02 (January), AEI-Brookings Joint Center for Regulatory Studies.

Radaelli, C.M. (2005b), 'Diffusion without convergence: how political context shapes the adoption of regulatory impact assessment', *Journal of European Public Policy*, **12** (5), 924–43.

Renda, A. (2006), *Impact Assessment in the EU. The State of the Art and the Art of the State*, Brussels: CEPS.

Rothstein, H., M. Huber and G. Gaskell (2006), 'A theory of risk colonization: The spiralling regulatory logics of societal and institutional risk', *Economy and Society*, **35** (1), 91–112.

Schneider, V. (2002), 'Regulatory Governance and the Modern Organizational State: The Place of Regulation in Contemporary State Theory', Paper presented at the workshop on *The Politics of Regulation*, 29–30 November 2002, Barcelona.

Stone, D., S. Maxwell and M. Keating (2001), 'Learning Lessons, Policy Transfer and the International Diffusion of Policy Ideas', CSGR Working Paper No. 69/01, University of Warwick, at http://www.warwick.ac.uk/csgr/wpapers/wp6901.pdf.

Torriti, J. (2005), 'Functional Dimension of the European Commission's IAs: Openness, Transparency, and the Extent of Quantification', Paper for EASY-ECO Conference Manchester 15–17 June 2005.

Torriti, J. (forthcoming), 'Regulatory impact assessment in the EU: A tool for better regulation, less regulation or less bad regulation?', *Journal of Risk Research*.

UK BRTF (Better Regulation Task Force) (2005), *Routes to Better Regulation – A Guide to Alternatives to Classic Regulation*, December, London.

Vibert, F. (2004), *The EU's New System of Regulatory Impact Assessment – A Scorecard*, European Policy Forum.

Vogel, D. (2003), 'The hare and the tortoise revisited: The new politics of consumer and environmental regulation in Europe', *British Journal of Political Science*, **33**, 557–80.

Williams, E., K. MacDonald and V. Kind (2002), 'Unravelling the competitiveness debate', *European Environment*, **12** (5), 284–90.

6. The evolution and development of regulatory impact assessment in the UK

Colin Jacobs

INTRODUCTION

This chapter builds on a growing body of literature that documents the UK experience of regulatory impact assessment (RIA). The literature charts the history of RIA in the UK and the current situation puts the UK in the vanguard of countries working effectively with the concept. Overall, very high rates of compliance (96 per cent, personal communication with Head of RIA Unit, 2005) are currently enjoyed, meaning that all bills are accompanied by RIAs signed off by ministers before they reach parliament. However, whilst awareness is growing there remain high variations in quality and effectiveness in terms of the actual use of the RIA within government. After providing a critical account of the ways in which RIA was established in the UK, the emphasis is on how it has evolved, including improvements in method and process.

RIA is a systematic method for assessing the impact (positive and negative) of existing regulations (an ex post RIA) as well as the potential impact of proposed new regulatory measures (an ex ante RIA). Its purpose is to 'explain the objectives of the (regulatory) proposal, the risks to be addressed and the options for delivering the objectives. In doing so it should make transparent the expected costs and benefits of the options for the different bodies involved, such as other parts of government and small businesses, and how compliance with regulatory options would be secured and enforced' (NAO, 2001, p. 1). The appraisal should be multidisciplinary and consider the economic, environmental, social and distributional consequences of a regulatory measure as far as possible.

The rationale for RIAs is thus a mixture of wanting to be sure that a regulation truly contributes to strategic policy goals (internal logic) and ensuring that policy is sufficiently based on consultation with stakeholders and that costs and benefits of options are transparent (external logic). RIA can therefore both oil the wheels of the internal machinery of government and also contribute to better governance and strengthen democracy. It can help reduce inappropriate or ill-informed regulation, which might create unnecessary bureaucracy, inhibit competition, create barriers and generally disadvantage small organizations. Importantly, RIAs should also prevent policies that are unenforceable from being introduced.

In March 1995, the Organisation for Economic Co-operation and Development (OECD, 1995) provided a checklist of ten questions[1] against which all regulations can be assessed. In many respects this still stands as a useful yardstick against which different governments and countries have developed their own national systems.

This chapter has three objectives. First, it assesses the current standing of RIAs based on a brief historical review of the roots of RIA in the UK. Second, it focuses in particular on the issue of RIA quality and considers what is currently being done to improve matters. Third, it tries to predict the future of RIA in the UK: in which direction is it likely to develop, how well prepared is the UK government to use RIAs and what are the benefits and costs of a strongly centralized model?

HISTORY AND STAKEHOLDERS IN THE UK

In the 1980s, governments in the UK and US attempted 'deregulation', which was later refined into a less ideological concern with 'regulatory quality' by the mid-1990s. At the same time, RIAs evolved from a simple concern with cost-compliance assessment to attempts to measure benefits and take risks into account. The main emphasis was on reducing the burden of regulation on small business, which accounts for over 95 per cent of business stock in the UK and employs some 12.5 million people. In 1992, responsibility for overall coordination of regulation was moved from the Department for Trade and Industry (DTI), which focused chiefly on business impact, to the Cabinet Office, which extended the remit to cover the impact on the voluntary sector and public services. RIAs were officially introduced in 1998 and approximately 200 are now undertaken each year. The purpose remains predominantly to limit red tape and bureaucracy interfering in small business performance. However, moving the leadership of RIA to the Cabinet Office has given the process a higher profile and the Prime Minister, Tony Blair, is enthusiastic about its value and the need to roll out the approach across government. Further political support is ensured through the requirement that a minister signs a declaration at the end of each RIA that the relevant department has evaluated the proposed policy and that the benefits of regulation justify the costs.

In 1997, with the change of government in the UK, the methodology of RIA changed with an explicit consideration of benefits in what was called 'regulatory appraisal' and a Regulatory Impact Unit (RIU) was set up within the Cabinet Office. This is well resourced with around 80 staff organized around thematic areas such as scrutiny, Europe, public sector and policy. The work is split between scrutinizing new proposals and reforming the existing body of regulation, and covers both public and private sectors. In addition, each ministry or department has a departmental RIU (DRIU), which provides guidance and support to policy officials drafting RIAs. The units can consist of just one or two staff in a department with little regulation to around eight staff in a major regulatory department such as the DTI or the Department for Food, Environment and Rural Affairs (DEFRA). The DRIUs are the key players at the base of the RIA pyramid and were the main source of first-hand information for the research reported later in this chapter. A Quality Committee made up of RIU staff and DRIU officers undertakes an ex post evaluation of RIAs by reviewing a random selection on a quarterly basis.

Figure 6.1 below shows the various stakeholders in RIA in the UK. The Better Regulation Task Force (BRTF) was set up in 1997 to provide advice to government on regulation and was replaced on 1 January 2006 by the Better Regulation Commission (BRC). The BRC now reviews the government's overall regulatory performance and has taken on new responsibilities for monitoring the regulatory reforms set out in the Chancellor of the Exchequer's 2005 Budget speech, including vetting departmental plans for administration burden reduction. Alongside the BRC, the Better Regulation Executive (BRE) now operates within the Cabinet Office to take forward the government's better regulation agenda. The BRE was created in May 2005. Other players include the National Audit Office (NAO), which reviews a sample of RIAs each year and provides suggestions for improvements. In 2001 it examined regulation across government in the belief that it imposes costs, foreseen or unintended, on businesses, charities and voluntary organizations (NAO, 2001). The report asserts that RIAs can ensure that policy decisions are well informed and do not lead to disproportionate or counterproductive impacts. The NAO's review of RIAs highlighted the need to start at a sufficiently early stage; consult effectively with those affected by the proposal; and analyse appropriately the likely costs and benefits.

In 2002, the House of Commons Public Accounts Committee recommended that the NAO should evaluate a sample of RIAs each year. In 2003 the NAO reviewed ten final RIAs (i.e., approved by the relevant minister) considered to represent examples where quality needed to be improved. The sample was largely made up of RIAs identified by their Better Regulation

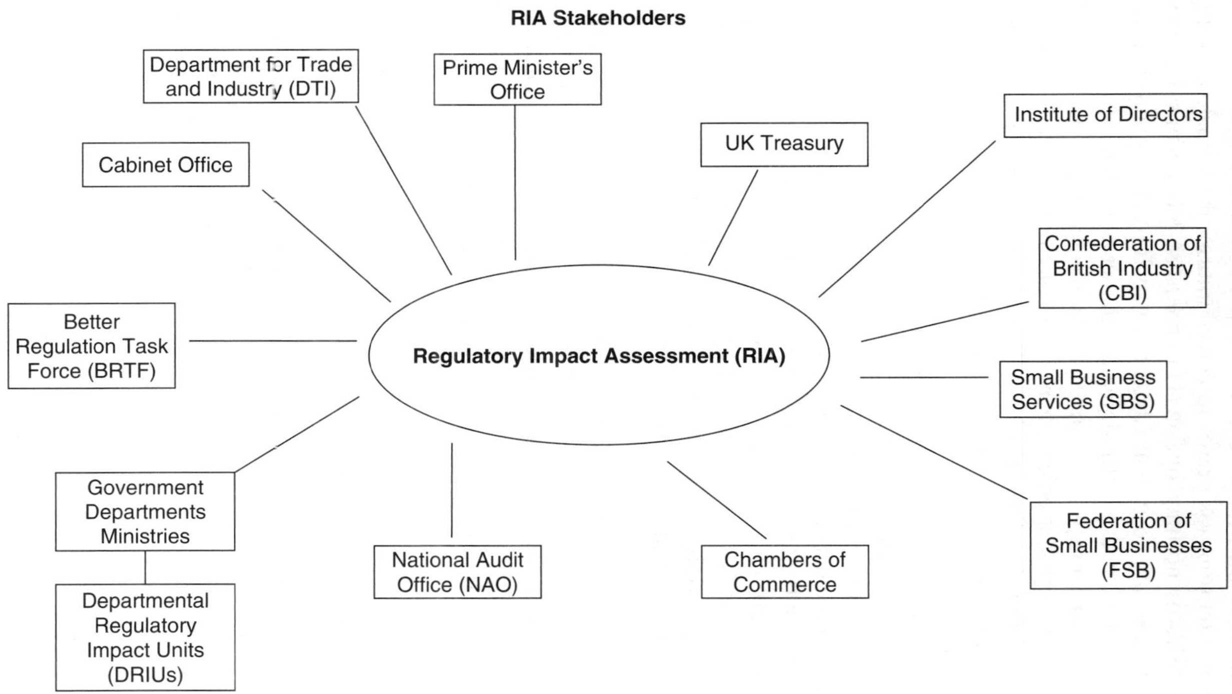

Figure 6.1 Stakeholders in RIA in the UK

Task Force (BRTF). The main findings were that the RIA is now embedded within government as part of the policy-making system but that insufficient attention was drawn to consideration of alternatives to regulation and the 'do nothing' option (Humpherson, 2004). Consultation was found to be a strong positive attribute of many RIAs but quantifying costs and benefits remained a methodological challenge with insufficient attention to information gaps and sources. Perhaps most importantly the RIAs did not always consider enforcement issues or the best means to monitor and evaluate impact. This gap is confirmed by the author's own observations and highlights an issue that is more fully discussed in a later section of the chapter.

The BRTF was set up in 1997 with independent powers to review areas of government action in which its members (business and the voluntary sector) were interested and published a number of articles. Recent reviews included one on independent regulators and the role of the so-called 'arm's length bodies' in the Department of Health (DH). Government has proven responsive to criticism from business and in the BRTF's (2003) report, 'Imaginative Thinking for Better Regulation', encouraged alternative actions to regulation, including, for example, self-regulation by business, the use of directives and voluntary codes of practice. The BRC now continues this agenda.

The BRTF's and now the BRC's mission is to help to raise regulatory quality and spread awareness of best practice. The BRTF developed five principles of good regulation: proportionality, accountability, consistency, transparency and targeting. Proportionality, to ensure that the right balance of costs and benefits is achieved; accountability, so that ministers' decisions are accountable to government, parliament and the people; consistency, so that regulation is equally applied; transparency, in showing that regulation is based on consultation, and targeting, to ensure that interventions are focused and do not have unintended consequences.

The Small Business Service (SBS) of the DTI was set up in April 2000 with the role of interfacing between UK government departments and industry. With 14 staff dealing with regulation, its role is advisory as well as servicing the Small Businesses Council, consisting of entrepreneurs appointed by the Secretary of State for Trade and Industry. The SBS has a wide remit as far as RIAs are concerned and a brief to review those that are likely to have an impact on small businesses. A key contribution is the development of a Small Firms Impact Test (formerly 'litmus test'), which must be part of the RIA where the impact is judged to be significant. The SBS monitors compliance by comparing the statutory instruments (SIs) published every six months against the RIAs. However, it is in its relationship-building and awareness-raising role that the SBS is most valued. Through a database of some 1400 names, it can recommend companies that are keen to be engaged in consultation, which can be by questionnaire or face to face interview. It is increasingly aiming to become involved at an early stage in the regulatory process rather than in a 'tick-box' fashion and claims that businesses for the first time have noted that they feel listened to and are engaged.

On the opposite side there are a range of business interests such as the British Chambers of Commerce (BCC), Confederation of British Industry (CBI) and Federation of Small Businesses (FSB), whose role is explicitly to lobby for the private sector. As such they act as a counterbalance to the government machinery and regularly publish complaints about excessive red tape and bureaucracy. Whilst admitting that in theory RIAs should lead to benefits being greater than costs, their view is that too often the cumulative regulatory burden is discounted and that the dynamic effect on competitiveness and benefits claimed to justify the regulations are seldom quantified (David Frost, Director General, British Chambers of Commerce, 2003 in foreword to Ambler, Chittenden and Shamutkova, 2003). Nor are they adverse to challenging government figures and from a sample of 200 RIAs (28 per cent of all produced and 40 per cent of those available) the BCC found that although 84 per cent claimed that consultation occurred, only 38 per cent noted with whom the discussions took place. In only 6 per cent of cases did they reckon that the net benefits for consumers were adequately considered. Moreover, the option of not regulating was only considered in 11 per cent of RIAs and less than half (44 per cent) quantify all options. The remainder provided a cost/benefit analysis for the preferred option only (31 per cent) or no quantification at all (24 per cent). The report claimed that this makes the decision to adopt, amend or reject a regulation biased and greatly reduces the usefulness of the system' (Ambler et al., 2003).

Failings are ascribed to the Civil Service culture, where civil servants are minded to follow the wish of the minister and there are no incentives (career, financial or otherwise) in delaying, challenging or blocking their political master's policies. In conclusion the BCC report notes that 'overall business is dissatisfied and unconvinced by the RIA process in practice' (Ambler et al., 2003). The report is also disappointed by the lack of internal monitoring, although this has since been strengthened by the NAO role in annually reviewing RIAs. Currently there is no way of knowing what proportion of policies is abandoned or a non-legislative solution found before government moves from the initial stage of an RIA to a partial or full RIA. Proper tracking and records of the number of withdrawals would lend greater confidence.

The presence of business lobbies provides an element of counter-argument to strong government machinery. An adversarial model has advantages and in this case has identified weaknesses in the use of RIA, although the Cabinet Office argues that the examples used in the BCC report are out of date and procedures have since been tightened up. However, the value of a range of stakeholders should not be underestimated and can be the source of creative tension, which at the minimum serves to keep the government on its toes.

The different logics and values behind RIAs are classified by Radaelli (2004), who sees civil servants seeking conformity to rules and standards. In this scenario RIAs are a valued ritual within the government apparatus. By contrast, the private sector will look to minimize costs and maximize profits. However, these polarities are simplistic, in the same way that a simple count of new regulatory burdens as against those removed fails to understand the way in which policy works. The impact of different policies is highly variable and their effect can be quite out of proportion to their number. For example, numerous attempts to drive up standards of hygiene and safety through self-regulation may ultimately be unsuccessful if there are non-compliant companies trying to cut costs and who will only respond to a change in the law. Even then there will be questions over the practicality of enforcing the law.

It should also be remembered that the UK administration is not based on a legalistic model unlike many countries in continental Europe. The Cabinet Office has no legal authority to require ministries or agencies to conduct an RIA. A more subtle form of persuasion and/or coercion ('carrot and stick') is required in these circumstances. The strong central messaging combined with support from a dedicated government unit is the key to the success of this model.

INTERNAL PROCESSES

Figure 6.2 below from the Cabinet Office guidance (2004) illustrates the process through which policy flows from its initial steps to a full parliamentary Bill or Act. RIAs will track the process and be prepared at 'initial', 'partial' and 'full' stages. An initial RIA should be prepared as soon as a policy idea is generated; a partial RIA, which builds upon this, is produced prior to the consultation exercise (which involves a minimum period of 12 weeks) and must accompany the consultation document; and the full RIA is prepared for the post-consultation collective agreement. A final RIA is signed by the minister to confirm that benefits justify costs and is referred to parliament where appropriate. It is also published on the department's website. The guidance goes on to say that the RIA should be proportionate to the likely impact of the proposal and can be quite short if the costs

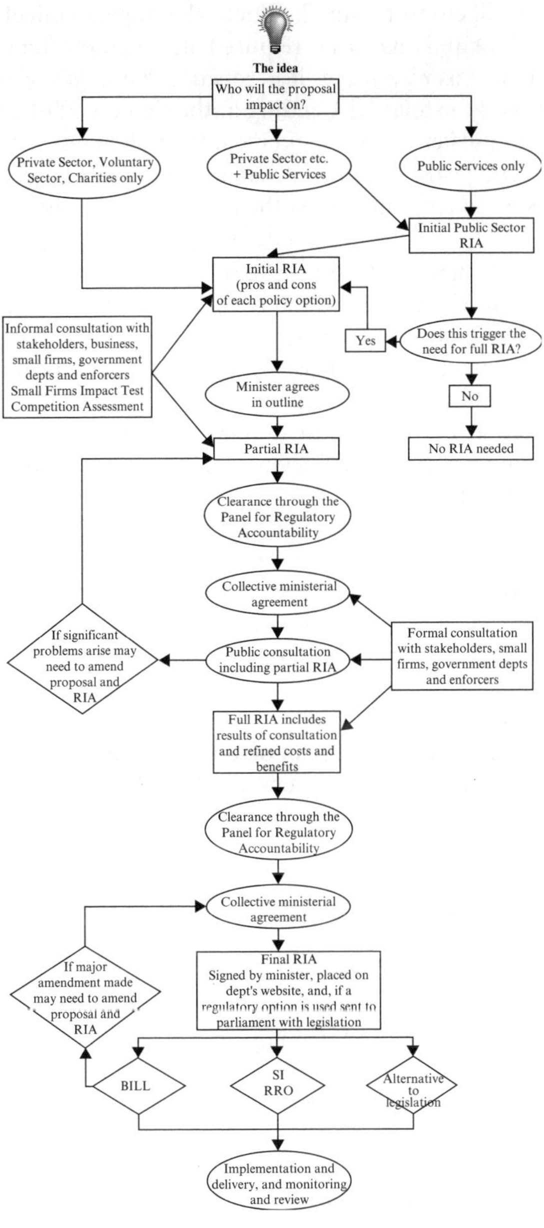

Source: Cabinet Office (2004). Available at www.cabinetoffice.gov.uk/regulation/documents/ria/word/ukflow.doc.

Figure 6.2 The RIA in the policy-making process

and benefits are likely to be small. Where the impact is likely to be substantial, more data and analysis is required although the final RIA should be a succinct report using annexes if necessary. The length of time between an initial RIA and the final RIA ending in the signing off of the document by the relevant minister can vary significantly with major areas of legislation taking several years and minor changes less than 12 months.

Each RIA should contain at least the following elements:

- A clear statement of the objective of the proposal.
- A statement of the background to the measure and the current legislative or regulatory framework.
- Risk assessment: that is, an assessment of the scale of the problem to be addressed by the proposed measure.
- Identification of options, including a 'do nothing' option as well as alternative means of achieving the objective without recourse to regulation or legislation.
- Cost/benefit analysis: identification of sectors affected and where possible. Benefits and costs should be quantified. Costs should include compliance costs as well as environmental and social costs.
- Impact on small firms and/or voluntary sector.
- Impact of each alternative on competition.
- Enforcement.
- Equity and fairness.
- Monitoring: how is the impact of the measure to monitored? Major new regulations have to be reviewed within three years of coming into force.

THE CHALLENGE OF RAISING QUALITY

Top-down Initiatives

The RIA system has developed strongly over the last five years or so in the UK and is now well supported centrally with endorsement by both the Prime Minister and the Chancellor of the Exchequer and through networks across government. Each government department has a minister with responsibility for regulatory reform and a senior official who acts as a board level 'champion' for better regulation. In addition, the Budget 2004 announced that:

> In future, any regulatory proposal likely to impose a major new burden on business will require clearance from the Panel for Regulatory Accountability (PRA),

> chaired by the Prime Minister, based on a thorough impact assessment of the proposal agreed by the Cabinet Office Regulatory Impact Unit, before the proposal is put to wider Ministerial approval. The Panel will consider all such proposals in the context of the Department's previous regulatory performance and the overall burden of regulation across key business sectors. (Personal communication with Head of RIA Unit, 2005)

As a result of the Panel's work, the Department for Trade and Industry (DTI) has undertaken to introduce deregulatory measures to reduce costs to business by more than £1 billion over five years. In addition, the DTI promised to look at simplifying existing regulation in the consumer area to take account of the duty not to trade unfairly, which will be introduced through the EU's Unfair Commercial Practices Directive. The PRA is said to have made officials at all levels more aware of the importance of better regulation as well as working as a further filter through which policy must pass.

Bottom-up Initiatives

There are a variety of bottom-up initiatives, which are designed to drive up regulatory quality. For example:

- The day to day scrutiny of RIAs and capacity-building work of the RIU Scrutiny Team and economists.
- The work that the RIU does with the Departmental Regulatory Impact Unit (DRIU) network, policy officials and others, including training, sharing of best practice, workshops, and so on.
- The current review and revision of the RIA Guidance – a new web-based version will be published shortly to make it more user-friendly.
- Work within departments, for example the DTI where several workshops and pilot demonstrations have been held.
- The NAO annual review of a sample of RIAs and its published report.
- The work of the BRC and BRE to identify good and bad practice and to seek ways to embed and improve the RIA process further.

A FRAMEWORK FOR MONITORING FURTHER IMPROVEMENTS

It is against this background that the author conducted interviews with a sample of DRIUs identifying common areas of concern over the quality of RIAs. These were classified into five broad categories: unclear objectives;

lack of evidence to support conclusions; failure to consider alternatives; weak monitoring and evaluation; and the need for an earlier introduction of RIA. At one of the DRIU quarterly meetings the framework for analysis was presented and there was agreement that these constituted the main challenges facing departments. On this basis, a simple monitoring tool known as goal attainment scaling (GAS) was used to gain an impression of change. GAS compares the level of outcome against the goals. It is particularly useful for the measurement of activities and impacts that do not lend themselves to easy quantification. Leading indicators can be agreed and rankings on a scale between performance very much below expectation (1) to as expected (3) and above expectation (5) can be drawn up.

The results of ten face to face interviews[2] with DRIUs were then recorded. Respondents were asked to record changes over the last 6–12 months on a scale of 1 = significant deterioration to 5 = much better. This showed that all departments were optimistic about the direction of change and on average recorded no less than 3 (no change) and three departments awarded 5s (well above expectation) for aspects of the RIA. The average score was 3.6 and eight of the ten cases gave 4s (slightly better) in some aspects – see Table 6.1 for the full results.

Several points should be borne in mind when interpreting this data. Obviously it is a small sample and the direction of change is more important than the raw score. It is also a piece of self-evaluation that should be triangulated by objective observers. Future NAO reviews are the most likely source for this. However, it should be borne in mind that similar evaluations based on peer review among DRIUs have shown them to be more critical than external evaluators. There is a strong motivation to be impartial, practical and realistic; all traditional attributes of the British Civil Service.

Areas where there was a marked improvement were: in setting clear objectives; providing evidence to support a case; and considering alternatives to regulation. In the area that traditionally has remained most stubborn – introducing RIA earlier in the cycle – DRIUs reported the highest level of improvement overall (average 3.9). Conducting RIAs at the beginning of the policy cycle has a knock-on effect in terms of improving the overall quality of the RIA. The area most often neglected is monitoring and evaluation but again there were exceptions and interesting pilot work is being done at Customs & Excise (which has since merged with the Inland Revenue). A discussion of the main findings against each category now follows.

Setting Clear Objectives

This is the crucial area that frames the policy argument, clarifies its purpose, states why regulation is necessary and explains the need for a careful scrutiny

Table 6.1 Interviewee responses

Question		DEFRA	Treasury	Health	Customs & Excise	Inland Revenue	Work & Pensions	Health & Safety	Home Office	Deputy PM Office	DTI	Total	Average
1	Setting clear objectives	3.5	5	4.5	3*	4	3.5	3	4	4	3	37.5	3.75
2	Lack of evidence	3.5	4	3.5	4	3.5	3	4	4	3	3	35.5	3.55
3	Failure to consider alternatives	4	3	5	3	3	3	4	3	3	3*	34	3.4
4	Weak M&E**	3	3	4	5	3	3	3	3	3	3	33	3.3
5	Early introduction of RIAs	3	4	5	4	5	3	4	3.5	4	3.5	39	3.9
Total		17	19	22	19	18.5	15.5	18	17.5	17	15.5	179	17.9
Ave		3.4	3.8	4.4	3.8	3.7	3.1	3.6	3.5	3.4	3.1	35.8	3.58

Notes:

* In both of these cases the respondent believed that their department had very little influence and therefore did not wish to award a mark. Rather than skew the averages, these responses were awarded a score of 3 = no change.

** M&E = monitoring and evaluation.

of its impact. Needless to say, a poorly formulated policy that is unclear about its objectives at the outset will adversely affect the quality of the overall RIA. That said, civil servants may have to translate political concepts or intentions that have been ambiguously expressed (sometimes deliberately) by ministers who want to 'test the water'. In some cases this may then be written up by a civil servant who is unaware of the full background and has to translate a general intention into a specific objective. There may at times be a mismatch with policy designed towards establishing a general preference or area, whereas the RIA seeks to establish specifics that can be measured and are time bound.

In some departments, such as Customs & Excise and Inland Revenue (now combined), there is less scope for ambiguity as the objectives are driven by tax measures. Or in the case of the Health and Safety Executive or the Food Standards Agency in DEFRA, 60–70 per cent of policy is derived from the European Commission. In this case the department's goal is to influence policy in Brussels through ministers and MEPs being involved at the drafting stage.

It is therefore not surprising to observe that practitioners rate this as an area that has shown only modest improvement (average mark of 3.75) although there are two departments – Health and Treasury – that have recorded scores of 4.5 and 5 respectively. At the Treasury, the DRIU reported that the quality of RIAs had improved a great deal since March 2004 and that the improvement had continued into 2005. With the help of the RIU, policy-makers have taken on board the message that the aim of the intervention must be fully explained and must make sense to readers without financial services knowledge. A similar sense of improvement is evident at the Home Office where a 'no nonsense approach' and sense of purpose at ministerial level was mirrored by clear objectives within the RIAs.

Lack of Evidence to Support Case

RIAs are required to consider a number of options including the 'null hypothesis', that is, doing nothing. A poor RIA will fail to state the assumptions behind its choice of options or the assumptions may be speculative. For example, the RIA for Sewerage Undertakers (Pollution Inventory) direction (Cabinet Office Regulatory Report website, DEFRA, 2001) states that

> the provision of data per se will result in improved knowledge of emissions from sewage treatment works and better public access to information on the environment. Raised awareness of what flows through a sewage treatment works and its origin, including domestic sources, should both assist public understanding and help address the challenge of polluting emissions.

This assertion without a clear causal link based on research or evidence seems questionable.

This may be due in part to a professional weakness. One DRIU commented that 'policy people are fearful of making assumptions whereas economists are more experienced in stating these openly as part of risk assessment'. In this respect the move toward integrating or embedding economists and statisticians within policy streams in some departments is proving extremely valuable and allows a more balanced approach. As a result, departments such as the Inland Revenue report an increasing analytical capability to assemble the basic data and provide competent analyses.

Measuring alternative options remains however, an inexact science and whereas it is more straightforward to estimate costs, there are conceptual difficulties to measuring benefits. Much depends on who is expected to benefit and what weighting should be given. In some areas there is a compelling case. For example, the Tobacco Advertising and Promotion (Sponsorship) Regulations 2003 (Cabinet Office Regulatory Report website, DH, 2003) seek to limit the impact of tobacco advertising in sport and note the findings of one survey that showed that teenage boys who are fans of motor sport are twice as likely to smoke as those who are not. However, despite strong evidence of this kind, it is notable that a final full RIA was only produced in 2004 after the intention was made in a 1998 White Paper, 'Smoking Kills', to follow the EC directive by ending tobacco sponsorship by 2003. The RIA considers three options: 1) to not allow a transitional period for those with existing tobacco sponsorship agreements; 2) to give all those in receipt of tobacco sponsorship the same transitional period to end their arrangements; and 3) to impose a deadline of 30 July 2003 for existing sponsorship agreements but allow exceptional global events longer, subject to clear demonstration of a year on year reduction in the amount of sponsorship and of visible advertising.

The report goes on to justify option 3 not on the basis of objective evidence but because it is line with policy steers provided through the White Paper and subsequent pronouncements on the need to protect business on the basis of fairness and equity. No quantitative measurement is made of options 1 and 2 and the report reads like a post hoc justification for the preferred option 3. The benefits are understandably inexact but could be expressed as percentage reduction in smoking, cost to the NHS and impact on productivity at work. The costs of a delay in reducing smoking as proposed under option 3, has been calculated at around £25 million (range: £12.5–£37.5 million) in lost productivity alone. Despite longwinded discussions and evidence of wide consultation, these sizeable impacts seem to have been over-ridden by the policy arguments.

The difficulty of using a cost/benefit analysis on its own to justify a preferred option is well understood. Benefits are not easily quantified although there is doubtless an increased awareness of their importance. Equally, there may be resource and time constraints to giving a serious consideration to options outside of the minister's objectives. Even if they were costed there is a view that some options could be ruled out for political reasons and not justify the nugatory work. Equally, there are cases where the minister will go straight to consultation (required under a partial or full RIA) and skip the initial phase as they are determined to make strong political statements about for example, tackling crime or anti-social behaviour. In other cases, the rigidity of the Budget and Finance Bill timetable constrains a full consideration of all options.

Some issues seem to lend themselves well to the RIA methodology and consultation has allowed a fuller assessment of costs with implications. Consultation is considered one of the big success areas of RIA both by the Cabinet Office and the NAO and there is evidence that when properly carried out it can lead to good results.[3] For example, the New Chemicals (Hazard Information and Packaging for Supply) Regulations (CHIP 3) (see Cabinet Office website, Regulatory Reports, HSE, 2004) produced a comprehensive costing in 2004 following in-depth formal consultation. A minimum of 12 weeks is stated under a code of good practice for consultations and only reduced where there are urgent national concerns – for example, recent anti-terrorism legislation. This is monitored through a forward look programme issued every six months, which identifies those consultations below the minimum standard.

In the case of CHIP 3, consultation showed that around 3800 firms, representing 267 000 employees – for the most part from small firms with nine or fewer employees – would be adversely affected. Re-labelling or disposing of products already on the market would incur costs in the order of £200 million or around 4 per cent of the paint industry's turnover alone. Additional costs would be attributed to soap, pharmaceutical, agricultural, explosive and cement manufacturers and to costs of upgrading equipment, training and administration. In all cases the assumptions were carefully recorded.

The safety benefits, although difficult to disentangle from the role played by other CHIP regulations in mitigating or preventing incidents, have also been estimated using the approach adopted by Department of the Environment, Transport and the Regions (DETR) to valuing the reduction in risk associated with road traffic fatalities. Other health benefits, the reduced disruption to work, and damage to the environment through an increase in public information are considered impossible to calculate. Nevertheless, assuming costs on 'best case' assumptions are £200 million for a 12-month transition, £400 million for a six-month transition and around £700 million for a three-month transition; and there are potential safety benefits of around £200 million and unquantified health benefits of probably the same order based on previous work by the Health and Safety Executive (HSE) on costs of accidents, the effect of shortening the transition period from 12 months to six months results in costs that would outweigh the potential safety and health benefits of the entire CHIP classification regime for a period of around five to ten years – even given the best case assumptions. Whilst the calculations are not full proof, the evidence gathering and attention in recording the basis of all estimates in this particular case is commendable.

Failure to Consider Alternatives

An explicit goal of the RIA is to encourage the use of alternatives to legislation. These can be in the form of codes of practice, directives and guidance, self-regulation and tax and market mechanisms. The BRTF publication on 'Imaginative Thinking for Better Regulation' in 2003 was explicitly issued with this in mind. It called for a culture change in which policy-makers looked for alternative approaches to implementation as well as considering the unintended consequences of regulatory interventions. The report recognized that it is often a good career move for civil servants to work on a Bill Team and that the system tends to reward those who further the minister's view rather than ask awkward questions or delay implementation through bureaucratic procedures such as the RIA. A variety of instruments are changing the situation, such as increased awareness through training courses, use of annual reports to document good examples of RIAs and wider promotion in parliament and the House of Lords. Perhaps the best advertisement is where leading ministers, for example at the DTI, have used an RIA as a source of information in parliamentary debate.

The BRTF report identified faults with 'classic' regulation, mainly in the form of unintended consequences, such as additional maternity rights, which can cause small-firm employers to avoid hiring women of childbearing age. Or for example, the Animal By-products Regulations, which are designed to deal with the treatment of raw meat and blood but have caused a number of small corner shops to stop selling these products, increase their prices or even close because they cannot fulfil the new requirements. A series of alternatives were considered, including creating competitive markets, price caps and tax credits, subsidies and awards as well as the possibilities of self-regulation and co-regulation. The fact remains however, that alternatives to regulation are heavily circumscribed by the nature of the sector. For example, in areas such as tax there may be few alternatives, assuming that few will willingly police themselves more closely in this area. For departments such as the Inland Revenue there may be little gain in doing nugatory work on options when there is a short window to prepare for legislation between September and the following March budget and consultation can only take place post-budget. In these circumstances the RIA is used as much as an information and education tool rather than devoting scarce resources to costing unrealistic options.

The survey of DRIUs recorded an average mark of 3.4 on considering alternatives, showing only a slight improvement. Nevertheless, some departments such as Health showed a marked improvement (5) and reported more creative brainstorming around options. The HSE was also committed to finding alternatives such that 'legislation is almost the last resort'. This push was reported as being more driven from the top than as a result of written advice or guidance. A good example was in the area of work-related stress. HSE decided on the basis of the available evidence that legislation was inappropriate as it is difficult to prescribe ready-made solutions to stress. Instead, it developed a suite of standards of good management practice to enable employers and employees to work in partnership to address work-related stress at an organizational level. Launched on 3 November 2004, these standards help simplify the risk assessment process for stress and provide the yardstick by which organizations can gauge their performance in tackling its key causes.

Weak Monitoring and Evaluation (M&E)

There was a limited application of M&E, despite the textbook need to review policy and then feed back results into a redesign or new policy. This was both lacking in terms of revisiting the estimates of impact within the RIA, to see if these turned out to be accurate and in terms of the ultimate success of the policy choices. Had regulations, acts and bills achieved what they actually set out to do? Was there demonstrable evidence of achieving targets? In practice the reverse appeared the norm and there was often a complete break between evaluation as an ex ante (formative) activity and an ex post (summative) activity with very limited comment on monitoring arrangements let alone enforcement or implementation. In some cases, periodic review was recommended but without reference as to how information would be collected, by whom and with what purpose.

This was surprising as there are instances where the process has obviously paid dividends in the past. A standard VFM (Value for Money) study by the NAO of the pension system at the Occupational Pensions Regulatory Authority (OPRA), in 2002, showed that OPRA had estimated that the public would want anywhere between 13–30 000 personal reports. Through monitoring the situation carefully, it found after one year that the demand at around 250 000 was in fact much larger. A more accurate risk assessment of the potential demand would have saved resources.

The gap often experienced between design and M&E was explained in several ways. First, the people involved in policy design – the 'Bill Team' – come together for a period of about six months but then disband and have no real interest in following up their work. A second reason is that there are few if any incentives to learn what actually happens when a different group of people write the legislation and finally enact the bill, act or directive. Politicians (and therefore civil servants) are rarely interested in results that may be several years down the line. This short-term and narrow thinking is compounded by a third reason, which is that there are many intervening variables that make it difficult to prove that change is in fact the result of a specific policy or set of policies. The 'attribution problem' is well known to evaluation practitioners but is not in itself an adequate excuse for lack of follow-up. The results – as one astute respondent put it – is that the UK is very good at policy creation but has an inherent bias toward novelty at the expense of consistency and careful monitoring of results.

However, even in this area there were departments prepared to do more. The survey shows that the 'enlightened' few were high performers elsewhere. They were Customs and Excise and the Department of Health, which now have an evaluation committee chaired by the Director-General that is committed to making people start looking at counterfactual information. Did the intervention in fact make any difference? A more concerted effort to monitor is made by requiring clear proof under the spending review that past interventions have recorded successes. This is combined with increasing awareness and a move toward a series of strategic programmes to improve health standards across several indicators.

At Customs and Excise there has been a strong commitment to monitor specific areas of legislation since 2003, such as the simplified schemes for VAT accounting – the Flat Rate Scheme, Annual Accounting and Cash Accounting. The impact of changes are measured through interviewing small businesses, reviewing take-up through internal records and telephone interviews. Eighty-four per cent of respondents felt that their VAT return was easier to make, paying a little tax often put less strain on cash flow, and there were time savings of around four hours in each quarter of the year. Overall take-up has increased considerably. The estimated financial savings to an average company were initially estimated at £1000, but have since been revised down to £600. For the Flat Rate Scheme, savings were estimated at £90 per business per year.

The same department has reported success in other areas, for example in tackling spirit fraud where compliance costs were expected to be high due to the need to set up new systems. In January 2005, the Chancellor announced the adoption of key industry proposals to keep compliance costs to a minimum and significantly reduce the estimated costs. This meant a reduction in start-up costs from £23 million to £7 million and in ongoing costs from £54 million to £5 million. This is a good example of the way in which continuing consultation with industry can pay significant dividends.

At the Inland Revenue there was a similar enthusiasm to measure impact, particularly where there was a large amount of administrative data available, for example on family tax credits. All RIAs since 2001 have been ordered for review. The methodological problems, however, have only begun to be appreciated and there is little evidence base in many areas. For example, there is a concerted effort under the aegis of a Select Committee to look at the administrative costs of tax compliance with a view to meeting a public service agreement (PSA) target to reduce compliance costs. This will require regular monitoring, deemed 'policy maintenance', to check actual costs of compliance against estimates every two years. An initial step will be to agree core elements of compliance costs before surveys of small businesses can be conducted. A particular challenge for the new department of HM Revenue & Customs will be to introduce this level of monitoring without extra funding.

Outside of the major regulatory ministries there seems little likelihood of rapid progress. Change will come more slowly as a result of increased awareness but is unlikely to be widely embraced without a bigger push from the Cabinet Office. In departments facing major downsizing, such as the Department of Work and Pensions, there are likely to be more pressing demands on finite resources, despite evidence (see the examples, above) that sensible monitoring can in fact achieve savings and recover any initial start-up costs.

Early Introduction of RIAs

The early introduction of RIAs is in many ways a first principle by which it is widely agreed that quality improvements can be achieved. If the RIA can be written at an early point – within the first six months – then it is much easier for its value to be accepted as the critical instrument in policy design. This requires departmental regulatory units to be involved from the beginning. Ideally, this will happen as a result of policy advisors involving themselves at the outset. Less satisfactorily they will need to impose themselves or at least monitor forthcoming policies.

A typical regulatory department such as DEFRA notes that despite a lot of encouragement and numerous directives around policy innovation, very few policy initiatives have an initial assessment. Partial RIAs are often only done when staff needs to go to consultation. At another major regulatory department, it was reckoned that in around 50 per cent of cases RIAs were still an after-thought bolted on to policy designs. There is recognition among most players that the key to success is raising the profile of RIAs and that this is best tackled through a multi-pronged strategy, including training, websites, guidance and making an initial RIA compulsory in some cases, for example where there are competing bids for primary legislation. On its own there may be a danger that officers will be overwhelmed by the amount of information, and face to face awareness-raising through seminars is both more popular and successful in bringing about converts. Winning hearts and minds will not come from exhortation alone and there is a need to maintain a sense of proportionality and common sense. A valid initiative in the attempt to popularize regulation is the inclusion of a Better Regulation Award (funded by industry) in the Public Servants of the Year Awards for the most creative solution to a policy objective.

A further piece of best practice that will improve matters is for financial, economic and legal practitioners to be more closely involved with policy workers in future. Traditional barriers that create a policy elite are being gradually broken down in an attempt to improve the current government's service delivery agenda. However, this is by nature a medium to long-term process and it is notable that one DRIU, from a major financial department, still commented that there are cases where draft RIAs are only being received a few days before the ministerial submission is required. It is likely, however, that this problem is limited to less important policy because the iterative nature of the RIA process means that DRIUs in a major department such as the DTI, will see an RIA several times before it has final ministerial approval.

ROLLING OUT THE METHODOLOGY

Since early 2004 the RIA methodology has been extended to public sector policy initiatives in UK central government and various approaches have been brought together in a process of rationalization and simplification. This process is supported by the Scrutiny Team in the Regulatory Impact Unit, which is responsible for working with departments to embed the use of the RIA process and improve the quality of RIAs. The view is that there should be one assessment tool for both private and public sector measures and a more holistic approach should be taken to reducing bureaucracy and red tape. This, in practice, has meant the integration of the Cabinet's existing Policy Effects Framework (PEF) within the RIA process. RIAs are being promoted as a flexible tool for the analysis of economic, social and environmental impacts, which can easily be extended to more proposals from the public sector. It is also a useful communication tool and forms a good basis for consultation with stakeholders. There is a threshold test to differentiate between 'high' and 'low' impact measures with only the high impact measures requiring an RIA.

It is premature to judge the success of this process but there are early indications of good take-up. Departments such as DEFRA, which have well developed environmental impact assessments, have been prepared to place these under the RIA umbrella, which is sufficiently flexible to allow sector-specific instruments within its broad categories. Despite a strong tradition of scientific independence, which might have been expected to be a resistance to the imposition of a standard methodology, resistance has been limited. This can be put down to the power of a centralizing agenda led by reform ministers with representatives in each department but also the basic common sense of the argument, particularly for DEFRA, where over 50 per cent of policy is derived from the EC, which has already adopted the RIA concept. Work is also underway to integrate the RIA with so-called 'gateway programmes', which exist within departments to reduce bureaucracy and encourage policy-makers to think about the implications of new policy proposals at the outset and in working up implementation arrangements.

The result is that an extraordinary range of RIAs are now available covering issues as diverse as: anti-social behaviour and the sale of spray paints to persons aged under 18 in an attempt to limit graffiti (Cabinet Office Regulatory Report [RR] website, Home Office, 2003); legislation to allow local authorities to intervene in neighbour disputes over high hedges (Cabinet Office RR website, Office of the Deputy Prime Minister, 2003); and the modernization of the General Medical Services Contract to provide greater flexibility for medical practitioners and primary care trusts to integrate non-medical staff within their services and thereby improve patient choice. The fact that the issues vary so widely from the original RIA raison d'être of reducing costs for small businesses, does not seem to have hampered the analysis. There is no evidence to suggest that RIAs dealing with the public sector are any better or worse in their quality than those with a private sector focus.

Doubts however have been expressed about the way in which new RIAs handling social issues are being integrated with traditional RIA domains, such as economic and environmental impacts. The difficulty is that the two systems were developed completely separately and the immediate pushing of responsibility on to individual departments for the new system may result in variable results. The original PEF was developed about three years ago and was never mandatory with the result that it was poorly understood and only applied to obvious areas such as schools and hospitals, where frontline services were most obviously affected by excessive bureaucracy. 'Gateways' or evaluation frameworks have therefore been developed in some departments, such as Health, and Education and Skills (DfES), and to a lesser extent elsewhere, for example, in the Department for Transport where there is a small gateway to consider transport demands on local authorities. Future expansion of the RIA process, such as to Work and Pensions, will require much more work in the face of stringent economies.

The danger of over-complicated support systems is nowhere better illustrated than in the proliferation of websites on the subject of policy-making. Although there is some cross-referencing, for example between the Cabinet Office's RIA website (http://www.cabinetoffice.gov.uk/regulation/ria) and the pre-existing Policy Hub (http://www.policytub.gov.uk), the two have been written at different times for very different purposes. The result is an excessive amount of information that cannot be easily or quickly accessed by users. Similar gaps in the provision of training on RIAs are evident between the Cabinet Office RIU and CMPS (Centre for Management and Policy Studies – formerly the Civil Service college) courses on Better Policy-making. Whilst these anomalies are being addressed they require time and resources, which too often are sacrificed when a new and more urgent initiative presents itself to government.

CONCLUSIONS

RIA has enjoyed remarkable success in its nine or so years of existence (in its current form) in the UK. High rates of compliance, the backing of the Prime Minister and senior ministers, Cabinet Office support, and the fostering of closer consultation with the business sector, are all achievements. The overall quality of RIAs has also undoubtedly improved in the view of practitioners who have experienced almost a decade of major improvement. A combination of 'hard' and 'soft' incentives have shaped its development.

Soft measures include copious guidance in the form of instructions, websites, workshops and training, as well as a network of reform ministers and champions to support the work of departmental units. Further technical support has been given by the 80 or so staff within the Cabinet Office, including economists, policy-makers and administrators. Hard measures include rulings that demand RIAs be signed off by the relevant minister and the annual review of a sample of RIAs by the NAO each year. Also, the

Prime Minister's Panel for Regulatory Accountability, which is normally chaired by the PM or the Chancellor of the Exchequer, requires a higher level of scrutiny for policies above a threshold value of £20 million or those areas of policy that might be considered politically sensitive. It is hard to imagine another methodology having the expressed backing and ear of the two most powerful government ministers.

Despite these successes there are weaknesses in the UK model that may prove critical to its long-term survival, at least in its current form. First, there remain stakeholders, particularly in business, that are sceptical of the process. The RIA for them is simply a set of statistics that can be skewed to fit the government's arguments and rarely has sufficient independence. The damage to companies and their market competitiveness of excessive regulation is claimed to be underestimated. For this set of critics, regulation in whatever form is often unwelcome and the demand for further integration with EU law and standards is an infringement.

A closer analysis however, shows that an RIA has in some cases been extremely valuable in highlighting innovative solutions to regulation that would have major negative impacts on British manufacturers. For example, the 140 or so small firms manufacturing chocolate in the UK would have been unable to trade their products in the EU because they failed to meet the minimum cocoa content requirements outlined in the EU's Cocoa and Chocolate Products Regulation of 1993. The recent update of 2003 (see Cabinet Office RR website, Food Standards Agency, 2003) however, allows traditional British milk chocolate, which contains more milk and less cocoa than commonly eaten on the continent, to be sold under the label of 'family milk chocolate'. The relevant RIA estimated that the one-off cost relating to labelling and packaging would be £2.5 million, representing just 0.1 per cent of producers' revenue. On this basis, the option to re-label chocolate in line with EU regulations was not only legally required but had considerable economic benefit to British manufacturers in reaching the wider European market.

Conversion to the RIA methodology among civil servants has been relatively straightforward on the surface and has been in line with prevailing government attitudes to regulation. However, scratch the surface and there is a sense that progress is patchy. The current model is heavily resourced from the centre with a large Cabinet Office unit and additional organizational support from government-funded bodies such as the BRE, BRC and Small Business Services. Leadership has been predominantly 'top-down' and the author's surveys reveal that whilst the Cabinet Office plays a largely positive role, it sometimes lacks real understanding of the limitations of departments struggling without sufficient resources to implement over-ambitious and sometimes contradictory government plans. There is an understandable concern among smaller departments that an over-emphasis on the large regulatory departments will be to their detriment. RIAs in these departments can be few but with a disproportionate importance.

Here there is an interesting comparison with New Zealand where the general discipline of RIA is applied across all policy initiatives, not just regulatory ones, with an equivalent of an RIA required as an accompaniment to all policy submissions. In the view of one respondent this makes for a greater focus on evidence-based policy, greater ease with the use of problem definition, options analysis and quantification of all benefits and costs. A systemic approach of this nature may obviate the need for a special RIA unit or at least reduce the heavily centralized, top-down model, adopted by the UK.

At any rate it is clear that increasing efforts need to be made to redirect energies to supporting (and rewarding) bottom-up activities, in which initiatives are taken by departments and they are able to achieve quality improvements through their own policing and peer networks. In this way a more sustainable model can be achieved. The Cabinet Office recognizes this and is eager that departments take ownership of the agenda.

A second concern is that the roll-out to public sector areas has been too fast and too under-resourced. A methodology that was developed to safeguard against over-regulation of the business and voluntary sectors cannot switch overnight to the much broader social and political issues embraced by the public sector. Increasingly, the RIA process has been asked to encapsulate other forms of impact assessment, including environmental, health, rural proofing (safeguarding rural assets against urban bias) and race equality. Questions should be asked about the flexibility of the system to embrace such widely different issues.

Moreover, extra resourcing is required to support the plethora of approaches. The nightmare of a government creating further bureaucracy in its attempts to limit red tape cannot be too easily dismissed. Already, more is spent by the government in the UK on regulating its own services (between £700 million and around £1 billion) than in regulating the privatized utilities (Hood et al., 1999). This may be a legitimate use of taxpayers' money but the burden must be continuously reviewed.

A fair counterpoint to this argument is that RIAs have in fact saved scarce resources through the integration of a plethora of wide-ranging tools and guidance that exist in priority areas, such as health, sustainable development, delivery of public services and race equality. This simplifies and classifies information available to policy-makers under priority areas while strengthening the RIA brand and reducing the chances of a myriad of competing assessment tools. As RIAs are increasingly used throughout the EU there is value in having a common frame of reference (Jacobs, 2005).

The UK experience of RIA is internationally at the cutting edge. As such, much can be learnt from its impact in making information more widely available and the democratization value of the wide use of consultation and publication of RIAs on the Internet. The limits to the model are still being tested but by and large the picture remains both dynamic and positive. The system that has evolved in the UK with its focus on multiple stakeholders is well tailored to a free market governed by common law.

NOTES

1. The ten questions are: 1) Is the regulatory problem correctly identified? 2) Is government action justified? 3) Is regulation the best form of government action? 4) Is there a legal basis for regulation? 5) What is the appropriate level or levels of government for this action? 6) Do the benefits of regulation justify the costs? 7) Is the distribution of effects across society transparent? 8) Is the regulation clear, consistent, comprehensible and accessible to users? 9) Have all interested parties had the opportunity to present their views? 10) How will compliance be achieved?
2. Representatives (usually from the DRIU) were interviewed at: Department of Trade and Industry (DTI); UK Treasury; Department for Environment, Food and Rural Affairs (DEFRA); Department of Health (DH); Customs and Excise; Work and Pensions (DWP); Health and Safety Executive (HSE); Home Office; Deputy Prime Minister's Office; and Inland Revenue. (Customs & Excise and Inland Revenue have now combined to form HM Revenue & Customs.)
3. See the Cabinet Office publications on codes of practice on consultation published in 2000 and 2004 for details of the approved methodologies.

REFERENCES

Ambler, T., F. Chittenden and M. Shamutkova (2003), *Do Regulators Play by the Rules? An Audit of Regulatory Impact Assessments*, London: British Chambers of Commerce.

BRTF (Better Regulation Task Force) (2001/02), 'Champions of Better Regulation', Annual Report, http://www.brc.gov.uk/downloads/pdf/ar 2002.pdf.

BRTF (2003), Imaginative Thinking for Better Regulation, http:www.brc.gov.uk/downloads/pdf/imaginativeregulation.pdf.

Cabinet Office, Policy Effects Framework website.

Cabinet Office (2005), Regulatory Impact Assessment Guidance, www.cabinetoffice.gov.uk/regulation/ria/ria_guidance/index.asp.

Cabinet Office, Regulatory Report website, www.cabinet-office.gov.uk/regulation/scrutiny/2003regulatory_reporting/index.asp; includes the following reports: DEFRA, The Sewerage Undertakers (Pollution Inventory) Direction 2001; Department of Health, Tobacco Advertising and Promotion (Sponsorship) Transitional Regulations 2003; Food Standards Agency, The Cocoa and Chocolate Products (England) Regulations 2003; Health and Safety Executive, New Chemicals (Hazard Information and Packaging for Supply) Regulations (CHIP 3): RIA (Post consultation) 2004; Home Office, Anti-Social Behaviour

Bill, Restricting the Sale of Spray Paints to Persons Aged Under 18 2003; Office of the Deputy Prime Minister, High Hedges (No. 2) Bill 2003.
Cabinet Office, RIA website, www.cabinetoffice.gov.uk/regulation/ria.
Hood, C., C. Scott, O. James, G. Jones and T. Travers (1999), *Regulation Inside Government: Waste-watchers, Quality Police and Sleaze-busters*, Oxford: Oxford University Press.
Humpherson, E. (2004), 'The NAO's Evaluation of RIAs: Reflections on the Pilot Year', *Public Money and Management*, **24** (5), October, 277–82.
Jacobs, C. (2005), 'The Role of Regulatory Impact Assessment in Democratisation: Selected cases from the transition states of Central and Eastern Europe', Working Paper for the Centre on Regulation and Competition, Manchester University, February.
National Audit Office (NAO) (2001), 'Better Regulation: Making Good Use of Regulatory Impact Assessments', HC 329, London.
NAO (2003), 'Opra: Tackling the Risks to Pension Scheme Members, Report by the Comptroller and Auditor General', HC 1262 Session 2001–02, 6 November 2002, publ. 2003.
NAO (2004), 'Evaluation of Regulatory Impact Assessments Compendium Report 2003–04', HC 358 Session 2003–04, 4 March.
OECD (1995), *Recommendation on Improving the Quality of Government Regulation*, 9 March.
Radaelli, C.M. (2004), 'Getting to Grips with the Notion of Quality in the Diffusion of Regulatory Impact Assessment in Europe', *Public Money and Management*, **24** (5), October, 272–6.

7. Auditing regulatory impact assessment: UK experience

Ed Humpherson[1]

INTRODUCTION

Regulatory impact assessments (RIAs) are increasingly popular across the OECD and elsewhere. The UK government has championed RIAs since 1998, a move that echoed earlier initiatives in the USA, Canada and Australia. The European Commission is also an enthusiastic proponent of impact assessment, regarding it as a formal tool to enable coherent policy resolution of the triangle of impacts on sustainable development: social, environmental and economic. And UK independent regulatory bodies have also been keen to undertake impact assessment with entities such as the Financial Services Authority and the Office of Communications establishing and publicizing impressive regulatory impact assessment (RIA) methodologies and processes.

To many observers RIAs might represent an important step up in the quality of policy-making and policy communication in government. Hence, to those who focus on the quality of public governance they could be a good thing – a tool of 'better regulation'. To others however, they might represent a form of lip service to proportionate policy-making, rarely if ever challenging or substantively altering the presumptions on which policy decisions are made. To yet others they perhaps represent a worrying victory for pro-business interests, a tool for downplaying consumer protection and for seeking reductions in regulatory controls over private sector activity.

As a result, accompanying the popularity of RIAs has been a call for audits on their quality from an external perspective. For example, Mather and Vibert called both for a system of audit in the European context, which echoes the UK system of audit undertaken by the National Audit Office;[2] and for an upgrade to the UK system to become more comprehensive. Others such as the British Chambers of Commerce have echoed this call for systematizing the audit of RIAs.[3] In a letter to the *Financial Times*, Lord Haskins, a former head of the Better Regulation Task Force, suggested that the quality of RIAs undertaken by UK departments is so poor that all departments, and not just a sample as at present, should be referred to the National Audit Office (NAO).[4] This chapter considers the genesis of the UK system of audit by the NAO, highlights the findings of its work and describes how the notion of quality in RIAs is hard to pin down – a problem that means that any external auditor needs to review constantly the basis on which conclusions are reached.

RIAs IN THE CONTEXT OF UK PUBLIC SECTOR AUDIT

At first sight it might seem strange that an external auditor is involved with the examination of a key policy document such as an RIA. Audit is after all in its classic form focused on financial statements aimed at providing assurance to the shareholders, the owners of the business assets, that managers are not squandering these assets. To understand the basis on which the NAO undertakes its work it is necessary first to appreciate the nature of an audit, then to introduce performance audit and the audit of RIAs.

An audit is, in essence, an independent review to assess the performance of an organization or process and to recommend changes to improve performance. A common methodological distinction is between a substantive audit – the detailed testing of individual items – and a controls-based audit (sometimes also called a systems-based approach), which assesses the functioning of whole systems. The concept of *control* – a process within an organization that ensures that the organization achieves its aims at a low level of risk – is integral to an audit. The auditor tests for the presence and operation of these controls.

Another common thread is the retrospective nature of the work. In recent years both public sector and private sector audit has shifted away from a substantive and towards a controls or systems-based approach. While this cluster of concepts is typically employed to provide an opinion on financial statements, it can in principle be used to support many other activities in which a trained, independent observer draws a conclusion on the qualities and reliability of a set of assertions by an individual entity. For this reason there are many non-financial as well as financial environments in which the term audit crops up: from the classic statutory audit of a company's accounts, via compliance audits (e.g., the UK's Office of Fair Trading [OFT] supermarket code)[5] to clinical audits in the healthcare sector.[6]

Performance audit is an important part of the National Audit Office's role.[7] It involves a consideration of the economy, efficiency and effectiveness with which public sector entities have carried out their functions.

Economy and efficiency are fairly straightforward concepts. Put simply, economy relates to the cost at which an activity is carried out. Efficiency considers the relationship between costs and outputs (though the definition of a public sector output is often complex). Effectiveness on the other hand, is very broad indeed. It relates to whether a public body has met the objectives set for it by Parliament and whether it has used the policy tools at its disposal to achieve the broad goals set by Parliament.

These key concepts – controls, substantive testing, retrospectivity and performance audit – will run through the remainder of this chapter.

The audit of RIAs is a form of performance audit – with a particular focus on effectiveness. But before describing this audit it is first important to say a little more on the target of the audit, the RIA itself. Regulatory impact assessments have been used since 1998 and around 200 'final' ones are produced each year. RIAs are required for any form of regulation, including formal legislation, codes of practice or information campaigns, that impact on business, the public sector and voluntary organizations. They allow policy-makers to analyse the likely impacts – economic, social and environmental – of a policy change and the options for implementing it. The UK government considers RIAs to be a key tool in delivering better regulation and supporting its aim of regulating only when necessary. Its Better Regulation Executive provides guidance on when and how to complete RIAs.

The audit of RIAs assesses how well departments have used the tool of RIAs to assess the impacts of proposed policies. There is a strong analogy with the mainstream of audit described above. Under financial audits for example, the focus of the auditor is on the quality of controls in place in an organization. The auditor assesses the existence of these controls, tests how well they are working on a sample basis and draws conclusions about the organization as a whole accordingly. Similarly for regulation the NAO has identified the RIA as the principal control, assessed the quality of RIAs on a sample basis and drawn conclusions. Furthermore, if government has two main ways of achieving policy outcomes – direct fiscal activity and regulation – it would be odd and imbalanced for the government's auditor to focus narrowly only on fiscal expenditure.[8] The NAO is therefore committed to evaluating the way government regulates society and as a result has produced a range of reports on regulatory matters. The audit of RIAs is the most important of these.

FINDINGS OF THE NAO's WORK ON RIAs

This section sets out the scope and findings of the NAO's work on RIAs. It shows how successive reports have embodied a journey from the audit of individual RIAs to the audit of the whole system and culture that produces them.

The 2001 Report[9]

The NAO first explicitly examined RIAs in its report, *Making Good Use of Regulatory Impact Assessments* (2001). It examined the development of the better regulation agenda within government and the use of RIAs by government departments. The report's starting point was that regulation imposes costs, foreseen or unintended on businesses, charities and voluntary organizations but also yields potential benefits. It argued that government departments should consider these costs and benefits (quantitative and qualitative) and other effects during the policy-making process by using the RIA tool. As such, RIAs can ensure that policy decisions are well informed and do not lead to disproportionate or counterproductive impacts. They are also published documents so therefore they can act as a means of communicating the process by which the government has reached a decision on a particular policy proposal.

RIAs that added value tended to be characterized by:

- *Starting at a sufficiently early stage.* RIAs are more likely to add value if they are prepared while policy-makers are still considering options for achieving their policy objectives, so that the analysis in the RIA informs the design and choice of the options. Those being consulted are more likely to respond constructively if they feel that their comments will have an impact on the development of policy. For this to happen consultation needs to start early in the process.
- *Consulting effectively with those affected by the proposal.* Although knowledgeable in their field, policy-makers do not always have practical experience of applying regulation. To ensure that proposals are workable and have minimal side-effects, policy-makers need to draw on the experience of others during policy design. Persuading businesses and other interested parties to comment on the likely impact of something that could happen in the future is a challenge. The judicious use of face-to-face and group methods may add value to paper-based approaches to consultation.[10]
- *Analysing appropriately the likely costs and benefits of the proposal.* A key purpose of the RIA process is to help examine whether the benefits justify the costs. Comparing costs with benefits of policy options can add value.

The 2004 Report[11]

The 2001 Labour Party General Election Manifesto included a proposal that an external body, possibly the NAO, should take on a more systematic and ongoing role in auditing RIAs. In April 2002 the parliamentary Public Accounts Committee (PAC) also recommended that the NAO should audit a sample of RIAs each year. In response, the Cabinet Office held discussions with the NAO and in December 2002, the Cabinet Secretary formally invited the Comptroller and Auditor General to audit a sample of RIAs each year. As explained below, the NAO's second RIA audit examined the thoroughness and quality of a sample of ten final RIAs (final RIAs are those that have been approved by the relevant minister), thereby preserving the principle of retrospectivity identified in the opening section above on the audit context.

The resulting second report from the NAO published in 2004, focused to a greater extent than the first on the technical content of RIAs. It found that perhaps unsurprisingly, there are a wide range of practices and approaches used across government departments. But from within this spectrum the following general messages were discernible:

- RIA was becoming embedded within government as part of the policy-making system. All new regulations are subject to RIAs and, in the NAO's view, departments should always produce RIAs even where it may appear to them to be unnecessary (for example, for policies that are voluntary and impose no obligations on the private or voluntary sectors of the economy).
- Within the sample there was an insufficient degree of attention paid to the generation of alternative options, including alternatives to regulation where appropriate and to the analysis of these options. In most cases the RIAs did not even consider a 'do nothing' option, which in the NAO's view is an essential starting point for counterfactual analysis of the sort required for RIAs and allows departments to assess and demonstrate the expected net impacts of the proposals.
- By contrast, consultation was the strongest element of the sample. It seems that Cabinet Office guidance has enabled departments to improve the form, content and timing of consultations, though departments could do more to show how they have integrated consultation responses into the final version of the RIA. Under this guidance each department is required to have a consultation coordinator to disseminate best practice.
- Quantifying costs and benefits remains a methodological challenge for departments. The sample contained some attempts at quantification,

especially of the risks or hazards that regulation is designed to reduce but rarely were the benefits quantified. The NAO also noted that RIAs often rightly acknowledged information deficiencies but failed to reflect the consequent uncertainties in quantified estimates of impacts. For example, there was a tendency towards excessive accuracy in quoted figures, rather than using ranges or sensitivity tests to show inherent uncertainties.
- The RIA sample did not show a strong predisposition to consider the enforcement, sanctions or evaluation of the RIAs. In other words, departments may be able to strengthen their consideration of how the proposed regulation will impact on behaviour over time and how behavioural changes such as increasing non-compliance will be monitored and evaluated.

The 2005 Report[12]

The third report again considered a sample of ten RIAs based on the suggestions of the Cabinet Office Better Regulation Task Force. But while the previous reports identified the wide range of technical issues that arise in RIAs and the wide range of solutions that different government departments have adopted, the third report sought to diagnose the characteristics of good RIAs and bad RIAs. It proposed that the technical quality of an RIA was a product of the way a departmental policy-making team approach the challenge of writing it.

The report identified three approaches to preparing RIAs, differentiated in terms of their technical quality and their influence on policy-making:

- *Pro-forma RIAs*. These have no impact on policy and are produced merely because there is an obligation on departments to do so. They may be started after the decision has been made. This tends to lead to RIAs that are inadequately resourced and produced too quickly.
- *Informative RIAs*. These have limited impact on policy. These RIAs are not integrated into the policy-making process; for example, they may have been started fairly late. Although the RIA will have only limited relevance, a department can still produce a high-quality RIA that clearly outlines the expected impacts and it is therefore a useful communication tool.
- *Integrated RIAs*. These inform and challenge policy-making. These RIAs are started early and are properly resourced, which allows for better gathering and analysis of evidence. In these cases, the RIA can help shape the policy-making process and communicate the reasons

for the department's decision to regulate in the chosen way. In some cases the role of the RIA in challenging policy-makers will lead them to a non-regulatory response.

The 2006 Report[13]

The most recent report, published in June 2006, concentrates to a greater extent on departmental culture than the first three reports.[14] It seeks to explain the different types of RIA identified in 2005 – pro-forma; informative; or integrated – by reference to the culture and process of a department. It therefore goes beyond simply identifying culture and process but shows in what way context matters, focusing on the regulatory work of four large departments: the Department of Trade and Industry; the Home Office; the Department for Culture, Media and Sport; and the Department for Transport, and asking a range of questions focusing on the link between RIAs and departmental management decisions. For example, does the training given to policy-makers influence the quality of RIAs? Does the attitude to evaluation and policy appraisal in general have an effect on RIAs? What is the role of the management of a department in fostering a positive attitude towards RIAs?

The report's conclusions were sharper than those of previous years. The report argued that RIAs are often not used in the right way. The purpose of RIAs is not always understood by policy-makers, there is a lack of clarity in the presentation of the analysis and persistent weaknesses in the assessments. As a result, in many cases RIAs have not offered a robust challenge to proposals to regulate. In general, RIAs are still often seen as a paper output rather than being integral to the process of policy-making.

This new work represents the next stage in the incremental evolution of the NAO's work away from substantive evaluations of individual exhibits towards diagnosing systemic strengths and weaknesses in policy-making. It represents a shift in audit in general type away from detailed testing of transactions towards testing whole systems. This mimics the general shift in auditing techniques in the UK in this direction over the last decade described above.[15]

CHALLENGES FACING THE EXTERNAL REVIEWER

Undertaking its RIA reviews has required the NAO to confront a series of challenges: in particular, the meaning of quality, the need to maintain independence, the potential rigidity of the RIA tool and the shifting focus of the better regulation agenda. Each of these is now discussed in turn.

The Meaning of Quality

The biggest challenge revolves around the meaning of quality. The NAO audits focus on the quality of RIAs. But quality has a vague, almost unreachable quality to it. Quality of what and to whom? Claudio Radaelli in a series of articles[16] has brought out how there are different logics in policy-making according to the norms of five different groups. Radaelli argues that each of these groups has a different notion of quality in an RIA:

1. the expert, whose principle criterion of quality is efficiency and who follows the logic of the social sciences;
2. the civil servant, who pursues conformity to rules and whose logic is that of standard operating procedures;
3. the politician, who seeks consensus and whose logic is negotiation;
4. the firm, whose criterion is cost minimization, and whose logic of action is what Radaelli calls 'the logic of influence'; and
5. the citizen, who desires cost-effective protection from risk and whose logic of action is that of participation.

But if quality has little objective meaning, how can the auditor make sense of it? The auditor is looking for judgements and analyses to be explicit. The NAO therefore looks for clear objectives; a clear and coherent decision rule; and coherent explanations of how the regulation will impact on society. The NAO wraps this up in the following phrase, 'RIAs have two main roles: informing policy decisions; and communicating those decisions'.[17]

The RIA is seen by the NAO as both a tool of decision-making (helping the policy-maker reach judgements) and transparency (making judgements explicitly). This seeks to sidestep Radaelli's criteria and puts in place a different logic, that of the auditor: namely, is it clear how the RIA has been used to challenge and inform policy decisions and then communicate those policy decisions?

Maintaining Independence

Auditors are scrupulously independent and aim to be apolitical – hence in the UK, the bar on the NAO questioning the 'merits of policy objectives'.[18] But the involvement of the auditor in assessing regulatory impact assessments may make it harder to achieve this. RIAs frequently involve more than purely technical judgements. They can be the result of the trade-off of complex interests. For example, viewed through a business lens, a good RIA might mean an RIA that leads to less regulation. But to an environmentalist, a quality RIA might be one that places an appropriate weight on environmental impacts.

The NAO has sought to maintain its neutrality through two means: first, the NAO has avoided becoming embroiled in contemporary political controversy via a preservation of retrospectivity. The NAO has declined to review RIAs in real time – that is, as they are being prepared – and will only look at completed RIAs once the relevant department has completed them. By a rigorous focus on retrospectivity the NAO is able to preserve its independence while retaining an ability to comment constructively on RIAs. Second, the NAO has been wary of questioning the objectives of the regulation and has confined itself to an analysis of the options identified to achieve those objectives. This approach regards the RIA as a tool of government that is used to deliver a policy objective, and not the policy objective itself. An RIA on a new component of criminal justice policy for example, can be reviewed on its merits as a tool – on the evidence base it uses, on its consultation techniques, on costing and so on – without actually passing any judgement on the merits of the policy. The NAO has no delusions in this regard; political dispute and political judgement are always relevant to a discussion of RIA. But the NAO has a rigorous approach that minimizes this risk.

Rigidity

In a recent contribution, Baldwin has questioned whether better regulation really is 'smarter' regulation.[19] Smarter regulation is soft: it eschews top-down solutions in favour of voluntary codes of practice, risk-based regulation and reliance on third parties. It is inherently networked. In Baldwin's view the RIA's emphasis on cost–benefit analysis may drive policy-makers towards well defined command-and-control solutions – and away from the 'smarter' approach, since it is difficult to predict ex ante how networks are likely to behave. The demand for rigour in RIAs therefore drives policy-makers away from soft solutions and towards command-and-control regulation. In this context Baldwin notes that it is possible that the 'alternatives to regulation' approach favoured by proponents of better regulation are not necessarily advanced by the regulatory impact assessment.[20]

Similarly, Lyons has questioned the rigidity of one tool within the overall RIA – the competition filter test, which seeks to identify RIAs with a potential impact on competition through a checklist. Lyons convincingly shows that this checklist is insufficiently flexible to identify important competition risks.[21]

The NAO has sought to test these assertions in its work. It has focused not only on cost–benefit analysis but also on compliance analysis and innovative consultation – parts of the RIA where softer approaches might score well. The findings have been disappointing: not only do RIAs in the UK tend to avoid extensive exploration of compliance and non-standard consultation, but the cost–benefit analyses do not always have the expected rigour.

The Changing Better Regulation Agenda

By contrast to this rigidity of tools, the better regulation project as a whole is surprisingly flexible. The flexibility is reflected in shifting government agendas and the creation of important new tools of better regulation. In March 2005 the government accepted the recommendations of two reports: the Hampton Report on inspection and enforcement;[22] and the Better Regulation Task Force (BRTF) report, *Less is More*.[23] The Hampton Report recommended the consolidation of regulatory agencies and the adoption of risk-based regulation as a guiding principle of regulatory behaviour. The BRTF report encouraged radical simplification and consolidation of regulations and the adoption of the standard cost model (SCM) – a comprehensive approach to quantifying and reducing the administrative burden imposed by regulation.

The presence of these new tools – risk-based regulation and the SCM – acts as a complement to the existing RIA tool. They both deal with the stock of existing regulation while RIAs address the flow of new regulation.[24] But the new tools also may threaten a displacement of RIAs as the tool of choice for better regulation. Embedded within the Hampton and the 2005 BRTF reports may lie a critique of and dissatisfaction with the quality of RIAs, a critique that is rather supported by the recent Better Regulation Executive consultation on a radical redesign of the RIA itself.[25] And the adoption of the SCM represents a step change in the UK government's attempts to reduce the administrative burden of existing regulation – distinct from the RIAs' focus on the overall costs and benefits of new regulation.

If the SCM is becoming the UK's weapon of choice in better regulation what does this mean for the auditor? It depends on whether the SCM is seen as a measurement approach or a management incentive. On the one hand, if the SCM is intended as a sui generis accounting standard, then the auditor must consider how well the SCM accounts for the costs of regulation. This is particularly true if the current interest in burdens is the first step towards regulatory budgets – which seek to account for the cost of regulation. Regulatory budgets can complement the classic public finance instruments based on public expenditure and taxation; and would require the same rigour of audit as the standard expenditure and tax instruments.[26]

On the other hand if the SCM is a management incentive, designed to address the culture of policy-making, then the auditor's focus becomes different. The focus will not be on measurement issues per se, and more on the effect of the model on behaviours – both within departments and more importantly, in businesses and others affected by regulation. The auditor will wish to examine whether the approach taken to reducing existing burdens is comprehensive and whether new regulations are challenged using the analytical framework of the model. The auditor will also wish to confirm whether the SCM is making a perceptible difference to the experience of regulation on the ground, in businesses across the country.

The point for the NAO is that the SCM is not ultimately different in nature from the RIA. It is a tool of government to be used poorly or effectively. But before embarking on an audit it is important that the purpose of the tool is clear, whether it be a measurement exercise; a management incentive; or both – because the risks that the NAO will address are driven by the intentions underlying the tool. If it is purely a measurement tool, the risks arising from the SCM are about the relevance and reliability of the data gathering and data analysis; if it is purely a management incentive, the risks are that departments slip into pro-forma approaches as with RIAs; and if it is both, the risk is of muddle and confusion within departments.

CONCLUSION

The discussion of the difficulties of auditing RIAs brings out one overarching point: RIAs are not merely technical exercises. They are also tools of transparency that ought to demonstrate to the outside world the biases, judgement and trade-offs within the political system.

This chapter has sought to show how the National Audit Office has adapted the techniques of auditing to the world of RIAs. It shows how this requires a flexible application of the core values of audit: retrospectivity, independence from the substance of decisions and understanding but not questioning the policy objectives. The chapter also notes the shifting nature of better regulation itself. Not only is there an important new game in town – the SCM – there is also a reconsideration of the role of the RIA itself. What remains to be seen is whether these new and revised tools will be better insulated from the problems highlighted in the NAO's past evaluations of RIAs: inadequate analysis (2004 evaluation), a pro-forma culture (2005 evaluation), and the absence of a system to ensure that government departments as a whole improve the way they regulate (2006 evaluation). The NAO will pursue this issue in future evaluations – since Parliament and the public will continue to require an independent view on whether the new SCM tool, and revised RIAs, are another hollow form of lip service to the need to regulate better or genuinely effective tools to challenge and communicate new and existing policy.

NOTES

1. The views expressed in this article are the author's own, not those of the National Audit Office. The author would like to thank members of the NAO's advisory panel on regulatory reform (Claudio Radaelli, Michael Spackman, Rob Baldwin, John Howell and Fiametta Gordon) for their invaluable insights and assistance; and Dushana Arumugananthan for her research efforts.
2. Mather and Vibert (2005).
3. Ambler, Chittenden and Obodovski (2004): 'It is open to question whether ten admittedly unrepresentative RIAs is an adequate sample for national audit of a topic of immense importance for governance and business.'
4. Letter to the Editor, *Financial Times*, 8 August 2005.
5. 'Supermarkets: The Code of Practice and Other Competition Issues', Office of Fair Trading, March 2005 (http://www.oft.gov.uk/shared_oft/reports/comp_policy/oft783.pdf.). This work is presented unequivocally as an audit. For example, Chapter 1, 1.1: 'This paper covers a report on the findings of the audit of supermarkets' compliance with the Supermarkets Code of Practice ("the Code") carried out by PKF on behalf of the Office of Fair Trading (OFT).'
6. The Healthcare Commission's website provides more information on clinical audit at http://www.healthcarecommission.org.uk/serviceproviderinformation/nationalclinical-audit/aboutclinicalaudit.cfm., which asks 'What is clinical audit?' and provides the following description: 'The overall aim of clinical audit is to improve patient outcomes by improving professional practice and the general quality of services delivered. This is achieved through a continuous process where healthcare professionals review patient care against agreed standards and make changes, where necessary, to meet those standards. The audit is then repeated to see if the changes have been made and the quality of patient care improved.'
7. Under Section 6 of the National Audit Act 1983.
8. NAO (2001), Paragraph 5: 'Regulation is one of the principal instruments available to governments to achieve their objectives.'
9. NAO (2001).
10. For a fuller analysis of these issues, see Part 2 of NAO (2001).
11. NAO (2004).
12. NAO (2005).
13. NAO (2006).
14. NAO (2006), Paragraph 4: 'This report therefore evaluates the extent to which departments are embedding impact assessment into their processes and culture.'
15. Indeed, general auditing principles imply that the auditor needs to understand and identify a system before placing reliance on it. This is broadly the approach adopted by the NAO on RIAs.
16. See for example, Radaelli (2005).
17. National Audit Office (2005), Introduction to Part 2.
18. National Audit Act, Section 6(2).
19. Baldwin (2005).
20. See, for example, BRTF (2005a).
21. Lyons (2005).
22. HM Treasury (2005).

23. The BRTF (2005b).
24. It is interesting to note that the distinction between 'stock' and 'flow' is used increasingly in regulatory reform discussions in the UK.
25. BRE (2006).
26. I am grateful to Claudio Radaelli for his assistance in capturing and developing this thought.

REFERENCES

Ambler, T., F. Chittenden and M. Obodovski (2004), *Are Regulators Raising their Game? UK Regulatory Impact Assessments in 2002/3*, London: British Chambers of Commerce.

Baldwin, R. (2005), 'Is Better Regulation Smarter Regulation?', *Public Law*, 485–511.

BRE (Better Regulation Executive) (2006), 'The Tools to Deliver Better Regulation – Revising the Regulatory Impact Assessment: A Consultation', July.

BRTF (Better Regulation Task Force) (2005a), 'Alternatives to Regulation', Report, http://publications.brc.gov.uk/publication_by_year.asp?PublicationYear=2005.

BRTF (2005b), *Less is More*.

HM Treasury (2005), *Reducing Administrative Burdens: Effective Inspection and Enforcement*, March, London: HM Treasury.

Lyons, S. (2005), 'Testing Which Proposed Regulations Need "Competition Proofing"', Trinity Economic Papers 2005/20, Trinity College Dublin.

Mather, G.C.S. and F. Vibert (2005), 'Rebalancing UK and European Regulation', European Policy Forum, Corporation of London, City Research Series No. 5, April, www.cityoflondon.gov.uk/economicresearch.

NAO (National Audit Office) (2001), *Better Regulation, Making Good Use of Regulatory Impact Assessments*, HC 329 2001–02, London: NAO.

NAO (2004), *Evaluation of Regulatory Impact Assessments Compendium Report, 2003–04*, HC 358 2003–04, London: NAO.

NAO (2005), *Evaluation of Regulatory Impact Assessments Compendium Report, 2004–05*, HC 341 2004–2005, London: NAO.

NAO (2006), *Evaluation of Regulatory Impact Assessments Compendium Report, 2005–06*, HC 1305 2005–06, London: NAO.

Radaelli, C.M. (2005), 'Diffusion Without Convergence: How Political Context Shapes the Adoption of Regulatory Impact Assessment', *Journal of European Public Policy*, **12** (5), October, 1–20.

8. Regulatory impact assessment in Australia: a survey of 20 years of RIA implementation

Rex Deighton-Smith

INTRODUCTION[1]

Australia represents a case study of a 'mature' RIA system, having accumulated over 20 years of experience. As it is a federal country, several distinct RIA processes co-exist, enabling the performance of different system designs to be compared within the context of similar institutional, administrative and political environments.

This chapter argues that while RIA has contributed significantly to improved regulatory quality, its role has essentially been subordinate to other regulatory quality initiatives, notably the National Competition Policy programme of wide-ranging reviews of existing legislation. Moreover, the logic underlying RIA has not yet been fully embedded in the regulatory process, leaving the RIA process vulnerable to attack and implying that its role continues to be dependent on the existence of active political support. Progress in expanding the reach of RIA to cover all major legislative instruments has also been intermittent and significant further effort is still required to reach this goal.

DESCRIPTION OF AUSTRALIAN RIA SYSTEMS

The Federal Government adopted RIA requirements for primary legislation in 1985. At the same time the Victorian State Government adopted RIA requirements for subordinate legislation. Most other state governments subsequently adopted RIA requirements based on the Victorian model, commencing with New South Wales in 1989. A third level of RIA requirements was adopted in 1995. This process, agreed by the Council of Australian Governments (CoAG), that is, federal, state and territory heads of government – was applied to laws adopted under regulatory harmonization arrangements and in areas where federal and state governments share constitutional powers.[2] These harmonization agreements became increasingly common during the 1990s and involved states agreeing model legislation (or in some cases, common essential requirements for legislation) in particular areas. CoAG agreed that all such legislation should be subjected to a specific set of RIA procedures.[3]

Federal RIA Requirements

Federal RIA requirements are established as a matter of government policy. Earlier drafts of the Legislative Instruments Act 2003 proposed to legislate specific RIA requirements but these provisions did not appear in the Act passed.[4] Regulatory impact statements (RISs) must be prepared for 'all significant regulations, including international treaties, that have the potential to affect business or restrict competition'.[5] RISs must include benefit/cost analyses covering all impacts of the proposed regulation as well as risk analysis. Feasible alternative means of achieving the regulatory objective must be identified and assessed in identical terms.

Consultation undertaken in the course of developing the regulatory proposal must be documented in the RIS. RISs are intended 'to ensure that all relevant information is presented to the decision-maker'. In respect of primary legislation the decision-maker is the Cabinet. An RIS is therefore not initially a public document, though it is now tabled in Parliament after the introduction of the Bill in most cases.

RISs are required to be assessed for adequacy by the Office of Regulation Review (ORR) a body with statutory independence, prior to being presented to decision-makers. Published ORR data show that 71 RISs were prepared in 2004–05, of which 17 related to primary legislation and 54 to delegated legislation. Another 15 instances were identified in which an RIS should have been prepared but was not.

Requirements Under the CoAG Process

The CoAG process is established under a written agreement by federal, state and territory heads of government. It applies to all 'instruments of a legislative character'. This includes primary and subordinate legislation[6] as well as instruments such as Codes of Practice where there is an 'expectation of widespread compliance'. Thus, this RIA requirement extends to include 'quasi-regulation' or 'grey letter law' and is therefore the widest-ranging of the Australian RIA systems.

Analytical requirements are equivalent to those applying federally, however, some procedural differences exist. The CoAG RIS requirement is in two parts. A 'draft RIS' is released as a public consultation document. Comments received are then used in refining the regulatory proposal and developing a 'final RIS', which is presented to decision-makers. Decision-makers in this context usually comprise a 'Ministerial Council' of federal, state and territory ministers responsible for the particular policy area. RISs are frequently prepared by administrative bodies created jointly by federal and state governments as part of the national uniformity or regulatory harmonization agreement concluded in relation to the particular policy area.[7] These bodies very frequently employ private consultants to complete an RIS. Both draft and final RISs must be assessed for adequacy by the ORR. Twenty-four RISs were prepared under the CoAG requirements during 2004–05.[8]

RIA Requirements in the State of Victoria

Victoria's RIA requirements in relation to subordinate legislation are established in legislation. The Subordinate Legislation Act 1994, like its predecessor legislation, establishes detailed procedural requirements for regulation-making, including those relating to RIA. RISs must be prepared wherever a proposed statutory rule would 'impose an appreciable economic or social burden on a sector of the public'. RIS requirements are consistent with those applying under the federal and CoAG systems, with a comparative assessment of different alternative means of achieving the identified regulatory objective required to be developed, based on benefit/cost analysis. The RISs are made public via a 'notice and comment' process for a minimum of 28 days. They must be assessed by the Victorian Competition and Efficiency Commission (VCEC) prior to release. A notice of the intention to proceed with the regulations (whether amended or not) or not to proceed must also be published. The RIS and procedural matters are reviewed by the parliamentary Scrutiny of Acts and Regulations Committee (SARC), which may recommend disallowance of the regulations on grounds set out in the Subordinate Legislation Act. The Act also establishes a 'sunsetting' period of no more than ten years for all regulations. Regulations remade following sunsetting are subject to the same RIA scrutiny as new regulations.

Requirements for RIA in relation to Victorian primary legislation have only existed since 2004. They are established in government policy, published in the Cabinet Handbook and in guidance material issued by VCEC. The RIA requirement is triggered when proposed legislation potentially has 'significant' impacts on either business or competition. This is reflected in the resulting documents being termed 'business impact assessments' (BIAs), rather than RISs. However, once the BIA requirement is triggered, the substantive analytical requirements are equivalent to those applicable to subordinate legislation and impacts on all sectors must be assessed. VCEC is also required to assess the adequacy of BIAs. The RIS is submitted to Cabinet as an attachment to the 'Approval in Principle' submission. As a Cabinet document, the BIA is not made public – indeed it is treated as confidential.

RIA Requirements in Other States

RIA requirements exist in six of the eight Australian states and territories.[9] RIA requirements in relation to delegated legislation have in most cases been modelled closely on the Victorian legislation, which was the first state legislation to require RIA to be conducted.[10] RIA requirements at state level initially focused on subordinate legislation, however, the current position is that four states apply RIA requirements to primary legislation while only three apply RIA to delegated legislation. Only Victoria applies RIA requirements to both primary and delegated legislation.[11] All state and territory RIA processes require a comparative benefit/cost analysis to be undertaken while publication of RIA documents for public consultation purposes is required in respect of delegated legislation in all cases.[12] Some substantive differences do exist, for example the frequency of 'sunsetting' varies from ten years in Victoria to five years in New South Wales. Jurisdictions also vary in terms of the presence of a requirement for RIS to be assessed by an independent body prior to completion.

ANALYSING THE PERFORMANCE OF RIA

Published Evaluation of RIA Performance

Official data indicates that compliance with RIA requirements is relatively high under federal, CoAG and state processes. However, other data casts some doubt on the quality standards actually being achieved and highlights the subjective nature of these assessments, even in a context in which the required content of RIA documents is set out in explicit and relatively detailed terms.

The Federal Government publishes annual assessments of RIA compliance. These reports cover the federal and CoAG RIA systems, as the federal ORR has responsibilities for RIA assessment under both systems. The ORR reports on whether RIA documents were prepared when required and on whether those RIA documents meet published adequacy criteria. For federal RIA, the seven criteria relate to the following key elements of an RIA document: problem identification, articulation of the regulatory objective, identification of policy alternatives, adequacy of impact analysis, adequacy of consultation undertaken, identification of decision criteria and discussion of implementation and review arrangements.[13]

In 2004–05 a compliance rate with federal RIA requirements of 80 per cent was reported. In 14 of 85 cases, RISs were not prepared where they were procedurally required. However, 68 of 71 RISs that were prepared were found to be compliant with the necessary quality standards.[14] In respect of RISs prepared under the CoAG requirements, compliance was assessed at 88 per cent (RIAs were prepared in all cases, with 21 of 24 RISs complying).[15] The ORR reports appear to indicate a trend of increasing compliance over the past several years while ORR management state that the required standard for RIS compliance has also been progressively increased. State regulatory reform authorities generally do not publish RIA compliance data.[16] However, data are available via the parliamentary scrutiny committees, which have responsibilities for ex post assessment of the adequacy of RIA documents under most states' legislation and can recommend disallowance of subordinate legislation to their Parliaments if RIA requirements are not met.

Review of the Annual Reports of Victoria's Scrutiny of Acts and Regulations Committee (SARC) indicates that on average, it has found concerns with 20–25 per cent of the RISs it has reviewed in recent years. This has led to queries being made via correspondence with responsible ministers. However, no recommendations that regulations should be disallowed due to non-compliance with RIA requirements have been made at least since 1998, with Committee Annual Reports recording that concerns raised were adequately addressed in each case. By contrast, during the earliest years of the RIA process, several regulations were disallowed as a result of Committee recommendations.

This data from the Committee's published reports must be interpreted as indicating that it has found no substantial evidence of non-compliance with RIA requirements over the past several years. However, this conclusion and the conclusions of the federal ORR noted above are at odds with the conclusions of a research report prepared by the present author for SARC in 2001.[17] The report provides a detailed analysis of RIA quality, based on a sample of 62 RISs completed under both the Victorian and the CoAG requirements over several years. The RISs were assessed against ten criteria relating to both their ability to contribute to the public consultation process and more broadly, their ability to contribute to improved policy outcomes.

Many RISs fell short in relation to fundamental quality elements. Only slightly more than half contained an adequate discussion of the nature and extent of the problem and the need for regulatory action. Only around 13 per cent adequately identified and analysed alternatives to the proposed regulation. The costs of the regulatory proposals were quantified adequately in 29 per cent of cases, while the benefits of the proposal were adequately quantified in 26 per cent of cases.[18] Fewer than half of the RISs had made adequate attempts to cite relevant research and integrate the findings into the analysis conducted, indicating that policy-makers are not drawing adequately on existing scientific, social or other research as part of their policy development processes.

Slightly over half of the RISs were found, on a subjective assessment, to have little or no ability to improve the policy outcome. In many cases this was due to the poor quality of the RIS analysis while in others it was due to the lack of real policy choice.[19] Around one-third of the RISs were judged as having moderate ability to improve policy outcomes, while only about 10 per cent were judged as having major ability to effect improvements. Finally, the RISs were assessed in terms of their performance in demonstrating that the best policy option was being pursued. Performance on this criterion was particularly poor with only around 13 per cent of the RISs rating as good and exactly half rated as poor.

These conclusions stand in stark contrast with the published data cited above. Nonetheless they were based on judgements as to what standards of analysis were feasible, as informed by the author's substantial experience in drafting and reviewing RIAs. On one view, these differing conclusions regarding RIA adequacy simply highlight the fact that any generally applicable RIA quality standards necessarily require a significant element of subjective interpretation. Alternatively, the difference can be seen as evidence of strong pressure within the governmental process to ensure that proposed regulations proceed and that the RIA process does not constitute a major impediment.

A third possible view is that the report largely assessed RISs from the late 1990s, while a number of regulatory reform authorities have argued that quality standards have, in general, improved since that time. However, there are reasons to doubt that this constitutes a significant part of the explanation. Available data tend to suggest significant variability in this aspect of RIA quality over time but do not indicate the presence of any clear trends. For example, the report's findings that 29 per cent and 26 per cent of RISs managed to quantify costs and benefits respectively, can be compared with recent data from Victoria suggesting that, in the first year of operation of the VCEC (2004–05), only about 17 per cent of RIAs were regarded as having comprehensively quantified expected costs, while in its second year of operation this level of quantification had improved to 50 per cent of RIAs.[20] Similarly, in a recent speech, the head of the Productivity

Commission stated that only 20 per cent of RISs prepared under federal arrangements included quantification of costs and benefits.[21]

Long-term Trends?

Despite this apparent lack of evidence of improvement in the extent of quantitative analysis, most regulatory reform officials argue that a long-term trend of improving RIA quality is evident and well established. Such a view may be overly optimistic however. The OECD has identified the general tendency for the level of political commitment to regulatory policy to 'wax and wane over time'[22] and the quality of RIA – a major element of regulatory policy and one that is significantly dependent on the resourcing of regulatory reform authorities – can clearly be expected to be affected by this trend. The experience of a number of Australian jurisdictions over 20 years of RIA implementation appears to bear out this observation and raises the obvious possibility of its continuation in the future.

Victorian RIA in the first five years of implementation (to 1990) achieved very limited results, despite a formal requirement for full benefit/cost analysis to be undertaken. In part this reflected a lack of relevant expertise in regulatory agencies, a problem common to virtually all newly implemented RIA systems. An additional issue was that the quality control function for RIA documents was the responsibility of the finance department. The department apparently accorded little priority to RIA assessment and conducted little or no training.

The assessment function subsequently moved to the Regulation Review Unit (RRU), which was also the key government advisory body on regulatory reform issues. The quality assurance function was given high priority throughout the early to mid-1990s and substantial improvements in analytical quality resulted. However, the vigorous execution of this function by RRU[23] became controversial within the administration, particularly because the RIA process led, on several occasions, to politically sensitive regulations being substantially delayed.[24]

The result of the strong approach to RIA quality assurance taken by ORR was that the ORR's survival – and with it presumably, that of the regulatory reform policy itself – came into question, being considered at Cabinet level. This experience clearly highlighted the precarious status of regulatory reform policy and the administration and the need for its advocates to act to broaden constituencies in favour of reform and more generally to cement the role of regulatory policy within government. In the event ORR survived and retained the RIA assessment role. However, organizational and management changes led to a refocusing of priorities on other functions and a downgrading of its regulatory reform role and its RIA assessment role in particular. As discussed in the preceding section a subsequent review of Victorian RIA prepared in the period 1996 to 1999 suggests that quality standards then being achieved were lower on average than had been achieved in earlier years. This situation persisted until recently when a substantial shift in government policy led to the ORR being replaced by the VCEC, which has statutory independence and has, at least initially, been successful in significantly improving RIA quality control.

Both at Victorian and federal level, the importance of the location and status within government of the regulatory oversight body have been highlighted as key determinants of its ability to conduct effective RIA oversight. Thus, for Victorian regulatory reform officials, the recent establishment of the VCEC as a body with statutory independence constitutes an important underlying reason for their expectation of further improvement in RIA standards. In the federal context, the role of exercising quality control over RIA documents was given to a body with statutory independence as long ago as 1993. This move continues to be seen as a watershed in terms of RIS quality by federal regulatory reform officials.

Some of the underlying reasons for the currently observed strong political support for regulatory reform at the political level are also potentially subject to reversal. For example, the current strength of business lobbying for further regulatory reform probably partly reflects the fact that many other issues have lesser prominence in the context of a strongly growing economy and this may not be maintained. In addition, the Victorian experience cited above demonstrates the potential for vigorously pursued regulatory reform policy initiatives to become politically unpopular.

Impact of RIA in Leading to Change in Regulatory Proposals

The preceding sections have discussed some input-based indicators of RIA performance. However, the true measure of RIA effectiveness is clearly its propensity to improve regulatory outcomes. As in most countries, limited data is available in Australia on this question. That which does exist provides some evidence of effectiveness. For example, data published by the federal ORR in 2005 shows that ten of the 71 regulatory proposals subjected to RIA requirements in the preceding year had been changed substantively during the course of the RIA process.[25]

This can be seen as one, albeit rough, 'outcome' measure of RIA effectiveness. However, not all changes to initial regulatory proposals made during the RIA process can be attributed to RIA itself. Clearly in some cases changes have been driven by other imperatives. Moreover, measurement of the number of policy changes tells us little about the size of the improvements in welfare that may have resulted. While regulatory reformers generally assume that changes made as a result of the application of RIA are welfare-enhancing, little evidence exists as to the actual size of such gains, either in Australia or elsewhere.

Regulatory reformers report that while improvements to the detailed design of regulatory proposals as a result of RIA occur quite frequently, more fundamental policy shifts are relatively rare. However, these officials believe that RIA requirements have yielded important benefits as a result of the changes they have prompted. Certainly there is a clear view that RIA itself passes a notional benefit/cost test: that of the gains in social welfare that it brings forth significantly exceed the cost of the resources devoted to the RIA process.

The author's own experience as a regulatory consultant suggests that significant changes to initial policy proposals do in many cases result from the application of RIA. Such changes are however, often difficult to identify when evaluating RIA performance. One reason is that they often occur at a very early stage of the process and so may not come to the attention of regulatory reform authorities.

Arguably the better integrated with the policy process the RIA system is, the less visible will be its impact on policy outcomes when viewed from outside the regulatory agency in question. Similarly, one of the most important impacts of RIA may lie in its ability to prevent low-quality regulatory proposals from being put forward in the first instance.

Scope of RIA Requirements and Extent of Avoidance Activity

As noted above, the RIA processes adopted in the Australian states have until very recently, been exclusively focused on subordinate legislation. Moreover, the scope of the RIA requirements has been too narrow in most cases to include most forms of quasi-regulation and has often been ineffective in ensuring that the impacts of incorporated instruments[26] are captured.

One result of these weaknesses has been the growth of avoidance activity. This takes the form of regulators deliberately choosing to adopt regulatory measures via instruments other than those that are subject to RIA. One result has been significant growth of the use of legislative instruments of uncertain character and limited accountability. Examples include an increasing tendency to draft laws giving ministers wide-ranging powers to make directives in relation to various matters and an increasing tendency to adopt codes of practice and guideline documents that often have or attain over time, a quasi-compulsory nature.[27] Few of these quasi-regulatory instruments contain meaningful procedural safeguards or accountability mechanisms. Thus, RIA in attempting to enhance regulatory quality standards and safeguards can at times have the opposite effect. That said, to the extent that growth in these ill-defined legislative instruments has been driven by attempts to avoid procedural safeguards, it is not only RIA but other forms of scrutiny such as enhanced parliamentary processes that have led to the avoidance activity. This issue was identified in the Australian context as long ago as 1992[28] but has not been addressed effectively through subsequent policy action.

Recognition of these trends can be seen in the RIA requirements adopted by CoAG in the mid-1990s.[29] These explicitly define regulation in the broadest terms and require that RIA be applied to all forms of regulation. '"Regulation", for the purposes of these guidelines, refers to the broad range of legally enforceable instruments which impose mandatory requirements upon business and the community as well as to those voluntary codes and advisory instruments, noted above, for which there is a reasonable expectation of widespread compliance.'

This approach has been relatively successful in ensuring a wide range of regulatory activity is subject to RIA and minimizing avoidance activity. Other recent moves to broaden the coverage of RIA requirements include the extension of state RIA requirements to primary legislation in Victoria and the Northern Territory. Victorian regulatory reform officials believe the application of RIA scrutiny to primary legislation enables them to exercise much more effective scrutiny over proposals to create powers to adopt quasi-regulatory instruments. Notwithstanding these improvements there continue to be serious problems in bringing quasi-regulatory instruments within the ambit of RIA requirements particularly where these are adopted 'by reference'. While the scope of RIA has often been criticized as being too narrow, there has also been continuing concern that relatively trivial regulatory proposals can be subjected to RIA. For example, Victorian data indicate that only 12 of the 33 RIAs for regulations it assessed in 2004–05 had quantified net present costs of more than $10 million over ten years.[30] Both regulators and regulatory reform authorities have expressed these views. For both groups a key concern is that conducting RIA in respect of minor regulatory proposals is wasteful of resources. For regulatory reform authorities there is also concern that requiring RIA to be completed in contexts in which there is little potential for regulatory outcomes to be influenced undermines support for the process from regulators.

Australian RIA processes generally do not specify clear thresholds past which RISs must be prepared, instead relying on concepts that are open to wide interpretation, such as whether an 'appreciable burden' is likely to be imposed by the proposed regulation. Often these thresholds have been 'read down', so that all but the most trivial regulations have been caught within the RIA net. For example, a recent review of a large sample of RISs found that one-quarter related to regulations judged as being 'minor' in scope.[31]

Reviews of the RIA requirements have considered other forms of 'threshold tests', such as the estimated dollar cost associated with regulatory proposals (as used in the United States) or expert examination of regulatory proposals as used in the Netherlands.[32] However, none has been adopted to date.

Embedding RIA in the Policy-making 'Culture'

Despite the accumulation of over two decades of experience, the embedding of RIA perspectives within the policy-making culture remains a work in progress in Australia. After 20 years the question of whether the policy-making culture can be changed in the way sought by RIA theorists must be asked. Consideration of the reasons for observed differences in regulators' attitudes to RIA may be useful in seeking to answer this question.

As in many endeavours, the role of an influential individual can be crucial in promoting change in the early stages. Such individuals within regulatory agencies, if convinced of the ability of RIA disciplines to add value to policy-making, can ensure that RIAs are applied early in the policy process, when opportunities to change outcomes away from initial proposals remain more substantial. However, little longer-term progress will be made if these individuals move to different roles or different organizations in the early stages. Time and experience are required to disseminate these views more broadly so that they may potentially come to constitute the dominant view.

Regulatory reform officials report that views about RIA among senior management in regulatory agencies show a similar range of opinion to those represented among the mid-level policy officers who are actually responsible for conducting RIA. This suggests that the expected movement of officials with RIA training and experience into management positions over time has not had substantial success in promoting cultural change. It is also worrying that senior management, who can be expected to have a broader and more strategic review of policy-making issues are not on the whole, any more favourably disposed to RIA than are their subordinates.

Another factor determining perceptions of RIA's usefulness relates to the dynamics of policy decision-making in particular regulatory environments. There is some evidence to suggest that where it is more difficult to obtain agreement at the political level in favour of a regulatory proposal, RIA may come to be seen as an important tool in support of the policy proposal. The Australian context of regulatory harmonization agreements, necessitating the achievement of consensus among eight state and territory ministers, gives rise to numerous circumstances in which the presentation of sophisticated RIA documents can greatly facilitate the process.

Moreover, a more serious commitment to the use of RIA may sometimes result from experiences in which difficulties in satisfying RIA requirements have led to substantial delays in delivering regulatory outcomes. The need to avoid repeating the political problems arising from these delays has often led to agencies adopting a more serious approach to assessment including providing significant resources (often through consultancies) to produce higher-quality RIA. Arguably however, this is not real cultural change so much as pragmatic acceptance of the need to generate high-quality RIA to achieve regulatory progress.

A notable example in the Australian context is provided by occupational health and safety regulators. Many currently produce highly sophisticated RIA documents, notwithstanding that ideological perspectives within some such agencies continue to regard attempts to bring the costs of achieving safety improvements into consideration as being illegitimate. This reflects the fact that key elements of their regulatory programmes have been delayed or derailed by RIA requirements in the past. For example, in Victoria in the early 1990s, new regulations relating to the use of asbestos were delayed by almost two years due to RIA problems, with the result that an ongoing consultancy was given by the regulator to an academic economist to conduct all future RIA in this area.

Use of External Consultants

The use of external consultants to develop RIS has generally increased over time in Australia. This outcome is not generally predicted in the literature, which tends to assume that policy officials will increasingly develop their own RIA as experience and expertise accumulate.[33]

Two possible explanations for the increased use of consultants can be identified. First, there is some evidence of increasingly rigorous analytical standards being required over time by oversight authorities. This may have reduced the willingness of generalist policy officials to attempt the required analysis and may also have enhanced the case for employing external consultants by highlighting the nature and extent of the specific expertise required. The current situation in Victoria, where the newly established VCEC has substantially increased the required analytical standards for RIA, fits this hypothesis: around three-quarters of RIAs in that state are currently being prepared by consultants.

The generally limited provision of RIA training by regulatory oversight bodies[34] also highlights the difficulties faced by policy officials in developing the skills needed to complete RIA without external assistance.

Moreover, the need to prepare RIAs is likely to be relatively infrequent. For example, 109 RISs were prepared at the federal level in Australia in 2003–04, with 24 different regulatory agencies preparing one or more RIS. This clearly limits the ability of policy officials to develop and maintain RIA expertise, particularly given significant rates of staff turnover: recent surveys of participants in RIA training provided by VCEC in Victoria show that only around 40 per cent of respondents had previously prepared an RIS.

Australia has no experience with the United Kingdom's concept of small RIA units being embedded within each regulatory agency to provide a source of internal 'consultancy' services. However, there is some indication that a small number of Victorian agencies are considering adopting this approach on their own initiative. Another plausible explanation for the increasing use of consultants is a cultural one: it is arguably simply a small part of a broader trend, evident in all Australian governments, toward greater outsourcing of service provision. This trend means that it is easier for policy officials to employ experts to complete RIS than would previously have been the case. There are clear incentives to take this path; particularly, greater certainty that the RIS will be assessed as adequate and that the process will be completed more quickly.

As noted above, the RIA literature generally assumes that as RIA expertise and experience develops among policy officials, the dynamics of decision-making will also shift, increasingly favouring 'rational' models over alternatives and increasingly favouring internal preparation of RIA. Indeed, achieving cultural shifts within agencies, such that comparative policy analysis based on benefit/cost perspectives are normalized as decision-making methods, is seen as the long-term goal of RIA and an essential condition for achieving its maximum potential. The question arises then as to whether the observation of substantial and increasing use of external consultants in Australia, in the context of 20 years of RIA experience, constitutes evidence that this expected dynamic of long-term RIA evolution does not exist.

Evidence suggests that the specific use made of consultants within the RIA context differs substantially between regulatory agencies and that these differences have considerable bearing on the above issues. Where external expertise in benefit/cost and policy analysis is contracted early in the policy process it is likely to have a real opportunity to influence regulatory outcomes. In this model the relationship with external consultants constitutes a dialogue and is clearly consistent with effective RIA. Arguably, the willingness of policy officials to engage external consultants early in the policy process is itself an indicator of the degree of 'cultural change' already achieved by RIA. It may reflect agencies' prior experiences of RIA analysis solving policy implementation problems – perhaps by contributing to policy re-design that has enabled RIA procedural requirements to be negotiated successfully.

However, for many regulators, RIA consultants are still viewed as conducting a 'closed' process: their task is simply to complete the next procedural step in the regulatory process by providing an RIA document that is approved by the regulatory oversight body, with RIA remaining entirely distinct from the 'real' business of policy formulation. In this context RIA consultants are likely to be contracted much later in the policy process and the results of their analysis will have far less opportunity to affect outcomes.

In sum, the propensity to use external RIA consultants is not itself an indicator of the broader attitude of regulators to the RIA process. Rather, it is the way in which such consultants are used that is its determinant. For some regulators the formal RIA requirements appear to act as a sufficient pretext for employing additional, external policy expertise as part of policy development. The RIA consultancy in some such cases acts as the springboard for transfers of knowledge on a broader range of regulatory quality issues, including matters such as different regulatory approaches, risk analysis, design of alternative policy tools and the like. In such cases it is not tenable to argue that continuing and even increasing use of external RIA consultancy is indicative of the failure of RIA to embed itself in the policy process.

Resource Costs of Conducting RIA

A frequent criticism of RIA is that it is resource-intensive and that such resources are inevitably diverted from core policy-making functions. This criticism suggests that there is a conceptual distinction between 'policy-making' and 'RIA assessment'. However, such a distinction becomes untenable when it is recalled that the core business of RIA is to assess the impact of policy proposals and to weigh these against the implications of alternatives.

Nonetheless, the issue of the cost of RIA has frequently been the subject of debate within government. Recent data on the cost of preparing RIS are available from both the federal and Victorian governments. According to the federal ORR, the average cost to regulatory agencies of completing an RIS is around 13.6 person days, valued at around A$4500,[35] while the VCEC reports that of the average cost in the Victorian context is A$15 000.

The difference between these estimates is partly explained by the greater use of consultants by Victorian regulators. This is arguably a result of the substantial government-wide moves toward privatization and contracting out that were taken in Victoria by a reform-oriented conservative administration during the 1990s. A second partial explanation is that the analytical standards currently being required in Victorian RIS have increased substantially since the establishment of the VCEC, while the federal ORR has adopted a more gradualist approach to increasing quality standards. The higher gross cost of using external consultants to prepare RIS must be balanced against the likelihood that the process will be completed more quickly, due to the specific expertise brought to bear. There may also be a valuable knowledge transfer to policy officials as part of the process.

However, in practice, both of the average figures cited above will be underestimates. Regulators typically fail to account for management and corporate overheads in undertaking such costing exercises, while the inputs by regulatory oversight bodies responsible for assessing RIA are also probably excluded. Nonetheless, it is clear that the cost of RIA activities is not disproportionately large. Moreover, as the ORR points out, these are gross cost estimates, 'Where regulators carefully define policy objectives, consider feasible options and their impacts etc., the additional net cost of preparing an RIS would be smaller, because the RIA simply documents the existing policy development process.'[36]

Given these factors, agencies are arguably devoting too few resources to RIA, suggesting that regulatory oversight agencies need to consider means by which they can encourage greater efforts. However, convincing regulatory agencies of the value to them of investing more heavily in RIA remains problematic. For many, RIA remains a diversion from the policy process, rather than being a part of it.

DETERMINANTS OF RIA PERFORMANCE

The following sections highlight key determinants of the performance of RIA in Australia, distinguishing between different RIA systems and different periods of time. Many of these issues have been identified by the OECD[37] as important determinants of the performance of RIA systems generally, however, these factors are discussed with particular reference to their role in the Australian context. Some emerging issues for RIA are also identified.

Adopting RIA Requirements in Law

The OECD argues that there should either be legislative authority for RIA or that it should be supported by a clear government policy statement. Regulatory reform officials in both federal and Victorian governments believe that having RIA requirements established in law substantially assists quality control efforts. Victorian officials note that their dealings in respect of RIA are often with regulators' legal departments rather than with policy officials per se. For such officials accustomed to administering legislation, the ability of the regulatory reform authority to cite specific statutory requirements, backed by guidelines with a clear status, creates a much greater degree of willingness to accede to the reform authority's views on the required analytical standards. Federal officials by contrast have argued that their inability to cite a clear legislative authority for the RIA requirement or specific performance standards has historically diminished their ability to insist on the achievement of better standards of analysis. However, they believe that legislative backing for RIA is ultimately less important than having strong support for the RIA process at senior political levels and among senior civil servants.

While some states have had legislatively-based RIA requirements in place since the 1980s, attempts to establish similar provisions at the federal level have consistently failed. While the Federal Legislative Instruments Act 2003 established a range of procedures designed to assure regulatory quality, it did not incorporate RIA requirements. Previous versions of this Act had included RIA requirements but these were removed due to significant opposition at the parliamentary level.

Regulatory Oversight Bodies: Roles and Performance

Most jurisdictions' RIA systems give regulatory reform bodies responsibility for assessing the adequacy of RIS in terms of explicit quality criteria. In practice it is difficult, though not impossible, for regulatory proposals to proceed without receiving a positive assessment from these bodies. This scrutiny function has contributed substantially to RIA quality over time in line with the OECD view that independent review of RIA is essential to achieving high-quality analysis. The experience of New South Wales, which does not require independent assessment of RIA by a regulatory oversight body within the administration, provides a contrasting study. An OECD review of RIA in New South Wales found that the absence of independent assessment had substantially compromised the standard of the analysis achieved and recommended that a requirement for assessment by a regulatory reform authority should be adopted.[38] The review found that ex post oversight by a parliamentary committee was not effective as a substitute for scrutiny by a reform body within the administration.

Having responsibility for assessing RIS against set quality standards has inevitably led the regulatory reform bodies to adopt other strategies to improve RIA quality. Most provide RIA training to regulators albeit that their efforts in this area have often been insufficient to achieve substantial skills development. In most cases, training is made available infrequently and there is little evidence of attempts to build knowledge over time by progressing systematically from the provision of more basic material to offering more advanced techniques.

Limited RIA training efforts have been exacerbated by frequently high rates of staff turnover within regulatory agencies. High turnover rates mean that there is constant demand for training in the fundamentals of impact analysis. This in turn implies that advanced training can rarely be undertaken, as the focus tends to be on training new entrants to the RIA field for the first time.[39]

Regulatory reform bodies have also sought to enhance RIA quality by offering internal consultancy services to regulatory agencies, to provide relevant expertise and guide them in carrying out RIA tasks. However, they have generally had limited success in carrying out this function, arguably because of perceived conflict between this role and their RIS assessment function. For many regulators, interactions with regulatory reform bodies in the course of reviewing RIS inevitably becomes adversarial in nature. In consequence, developing the cooperative relationships needed to underpin a successful consultancy role becomes difficult if not impossible.

Similar experiences have been reported by occupational health and safety authorities in Australia. These authorities, who have the responsibility for enforcement of occupational health and safety legislation, have also sought to develop cooperative relationships with business and provide guidance to them in complying with their regulatory responsibilities. Most report a degree of reluctance on the part of businesses to engage with them in this role, apparently as a result of fears that openness regarding problems will leave them more vulnerable to prosecution.

A satisfactory answer to this problem has not been found. One possible approach might be the development of small regulatory impact units within regulatory agencies as has occurred in the United Kingdom. However, this approach remains almost untried in Australia.

In common with the trend observed across most other OECD countries, Australian regulatory oversight bodies have increasingly gravitated toward the centre of government. However, while the OECD promotes this 'centre of government' location as a best practice, the developing view in Australia is that such bodies should have statutory independence as do the Federal Productivity Commission and the VCEC. The National Competition Council recently argued that the regulatory reform function in New South Wales should be removed from the Cabinet Office and given a greater degree of independence from the policy-making process.[40] Such independence is seen as essential for these bodies to be able to carry out RIA quality control effectively as well as enhancing their effectiveness in reviewing existing regulation. The substantial contribution to regulatory reform of the Productivity Commission constitutes strong evidence for the effectiveness of the model of statutorily independent regulatory reform bodies.[41]

An area in which Australian RIA arrangements are at odds with published OECD 'best practices' is that few jurisdictions have a minister who has specific responsibilities for regulatory reform policy and for whom this is the central part of the minister's portfolio. Some regulatory reform officials contest the OECD 'best practice' in this area, arguing that any minister who was primarily responsible for regulatory reform policy would inevitably be a junior minister within the government. While such a minister might have clear incentives to promote regulatory reform and be free of conflicting incentives arising from a substantial role as a regulator, his/her lack of authority within the government is likely to severely limit his/her effectiveness.

An example of this problem is given by the experience of the recently disbanded Victorian ORR. This was located within the small business portfolio and hence reported to a junior minister, whose title was 'Minister for Small Business and Regulatory Reform'. This location was widely believed to have substantially impeded the body's effectiveness and was a factor in its replacement with the independent VCEC.

The Use of 'Sunsetting' Requirements

Australia appears to be highly unusual in making extensive use of 'sunsetting' arrangements particularly for delegated legislation. However, it is perhaps more surprising that other countries have been so little inclined to take up sunsetting given its potential to extend the effective scope of RIA.[42]

Sunsetting has been adopted as part of the legislation establishing RIA procedures in most states and territories.[43] Formal analysis of the role of sunsetting is difficult, however experience suggests that the requirements have had a significant effect in bringing forward review activity. At a minimum, sunsetting provides a mechanism allowing stakeholders to challenge regulatory requirements in the context of a structured review process.

Most sunsetting requirements specify a ten-year period of operation for subordinate legislation, with this period being widely regarded as appropriate. The five-year sunsetting period used in New South Wales has been criticized by the OECD in a review of the RIA process in that state as being substantially too short and widely subverted in practice: 'special circumstances' provisions and allowing an extension of regulations for 12 months prior to sunsetting were found to be applied on three, four or more occasions in respect of many or most substantive regulations.[44]

The approach in New South Wales has also led to complaints from regulators regarding the need to divert resources unnecessarily or unprofitably, toward dealing with sunsetting requirements, while the repeated use of the short-term exemption mechanism has also reduced the predictability of the regulatory process.

Sunsetting requirements are supplemented by provisions of the National Competition Policy (NCP) agreements, that the required reviews of all legislation that contains restrictions on competition be repeated at ten-yearly intervals. Thus, automatic review processes apply to a very large proportion of the Australian legislative structure. To date, the NCP reviews have constituted a powerful regulatory reform mechanism, while current moves to launch a 'second wave' of NCP reforms suggest that this will continue to be an important means of applying RIA disciplines to existing legislation.

Broader Regulatory Trends and Their Impact on RIA

A number of trends in regulation-making styles pose significant challenges for RIA. The OECD has noted that the use of performance-based regulation significantly increases uncertainty as to likely compliance costs and performance-based regulation is widely used in Australia. RISs frequently estimate compliance costs for performance-based regulation by reference to various prescriptive guidance documents, where available (i.e. 'safe harbours'[45]), presenting these as 'upper bound' estimates of actual compliance costs. This is based on the logic that anyone who chooses not to use the 'safe harbours' will only adopt alternative means of compliance if they believe that they can do so at lower cost. Nonetheless, such safe harbours are not always available to RIA practitioners so that substantial issues remain in relation to the impact assessment of performance-based regulation.

More challenging still for RIA is the increasing use of process regulation, which generally requires regulated parties to undertake a process of hazard identification, risk assessment and design of appropriate risk controls. In circumstances in which a wide range of productive activities may be regulated, it can be almost impossible to estimate a priori the likely compliance costs. These regulatory approaches are being increasingly applied in many areas in which the likely regulatory costs are greatest.[46] It is arguable that this constitutes one explanation for the frequent complaint of business that RIA disciplines are failing to exercise adequate control over regulatory inflation. The increasing volume and complexity of regulation inevitably poses another substantial challenge in achieving adequate standards of RIA. In particular, the increasing tendency of regulators to adopt a large number of complex technical standards 'by reference' in regulation[47] substantially reduces the effectiveness of RIA, since meaningful assessment of large quantities of such detailed, technical provisions is often all but impossible.

Some attempts were made to address this issue during the 1990s by encouraging change in the means by which the standards-setting body (the Standards Association of Australia) develops and adopts standards. In particular, the Kean Report[48] recommended that the standards development process should recognize that a majority of technical standards were now likely to be adopted in a regulation in one or more jurisdictions and should seek to ensure that the resulting standards were as far as possible appropriate to this regulatory purpose. In effect, this amounted to an attempt to integrate a form of RIA into the development of the standards themselves. However, little appears to have been achieved in this regard and the use of technical standards in regulation remains a significant issue for RIA.

A further change in regulatory approaches in Australia with negative implications for RIA is the trend away from traditional Westminster-based models of regulatory development, involving the publication for consultative purposes of 'Green Papers', canvassing policy issues and options and 'White Papers' setting out proposed government responses. This degree of formal consultation and in particular the focus on problem identification and advancing a range of possible policy responses in the Green Paper context is becoming increasingly rare. Instead, current approaches frequently see specific proposals advanced in the first instance, typically following selective and non-transparent consultation with particular stakeholder groups.

An important result of this change is that governments tend to demonstrate a much greater degree of commitment to the proposal initially advanced, making it increasingly difficult for the results of RIA to lead to fundamental change to these proposals. The problem is exacerbated by the fact that the changing regulatory style appears to have much to do with a desire to shorten the regulatory process. Again, this focus on speed probably reduces ability of RIA to affect regulatory outcomes.

Importance of Political Support for RIA

Political support for RIA has historically been and remains largely bipartisan in Australia. This bipartisanship may be considered somewhat surprising given the frequently more expansive regulatory ambitions of social democratic parties, although the programme of country reviews of regulatory reform undertaken by the OECD suggests that regulatory reform has been embraced by political parties of both left and right wing orientations in many countries. Clearly bipartisan political support is likely to be extremely important to the success of a policy that requires sustained implementation over the long term in order to achieve its potential benefits.

Notwithstanding broad political support for RIA, conflict can clearly arise between broad Cabinet support for the policy and the ambitions of individual ministers to implement favoured regulations, even where these have difficulty withstanding objective scrutiny. Moreover, it can be speculated that the development of an increasingly risk-averse public culture will tend to erode political support for RIA over time. In this view increasing risk aversion among populations both promotes regulatory inflation and increases pressure to adopt more stringent regulations that are increasingly difficult to justify on benefit/cost grounds. Politicians can be expected to respond to these public pressures at the expense of support for RIA. Regulators themselves can frequently be observed to be sensitive to this increasing risk aversion and indeed at times appear to be moving in advance of public opinion in this regard.

CONCLUDING REMARKS

Australia represents a mature example of the implementation of regulatory impact assessment. Despite this, evidence on the influence of RIA on regulatory quality remains limited. There is little evidence of RIA having a substantial effect in limiting or reversing regulatory inflation. In addition, there are new challenges in ensuring that the quality and relevance of RIA are maintained in the face of changes to regulatory styles, including the increasing use of performance-based and process regulation, the adoption of substantial numbers of technical standards 'by reference' and the increasing use of various kinds of quasi-regulatory tools.

If direct evidence of the impact of RIA on regulatory quality is scarce, even data on the quality of RIA documents being produced is partial in nature. In general it appears that the standards of analysis being achieved are improving and that this improving trend has been maintained in the past several years. That said it is not yet possible to state with certainty that this constitutes a secular trend and that regression in the quality of RIA, as has occurred at different times and in different jurisdictions in the past, will not recur.

The Australian experience provides strong support for most though not all of the OECD's RIA best practices. That said, RIA cannot be said to be fully integrated into the policy-making process in Australia, even after 20 years of experience. This inevitably poses the question of whether the hoped-for integration of RIA and policy processes is in fact achievable. The

Australian experience arguably lends itself to analysis in the terms proposed by Raedelli,[49] who states that, 'in order to make an impact on elites and public opinion (and, ultimately, to make an impact on the reform of the regulatory system), RIA needs a broader vehicle, a "big" national problem which attracts political attention'.

In the Australian context, the National Competition Policy (NCP) process has arguably performed this function. The policy requires all legislation containing restrictions on competition to be assessed in public benefit/cost terms and all new proposals containing such restrictions to be assessed similarly. Since 1996 it has led to the application of RIA-type analysis to a huge proportion of the stock of regulation in Australia – at both federal and state/territory levels – and requires that these reviews be repeated on a ten-yearly cycle. However, there remains a clear view of RIA and NCP as separate vehicles, which suggests that RIA may not necessarily profit from the NCP process in the long run.

It was noted above that in particular circumstances, RIA serves the interests of policy-makers by facilitating agreement on policy outcomes, notably at the political level.[50] As well, policy-makers have sometimes found that RIA assists them in achieving policy outcomes that receive a greater degree of consent from stakeholders. These benefits provide plausible explanations for the embrace of RIA by policy-makers in particular circumstances.

On the other hand, the strong tendency for robust RIA to favour empirically-based decision-making at the expense of other models (such as expert, consensus or political)[51] can be inimical to the values and/or objectives of policy-makers at the political level. Ministers ultimately responsible for regulatory decision-making can frequently assign a zero or even negative value to the insights and conclusions provided by RIA because RIAs may constrain their ability to make particular decisions that, while rational within the political frame of reference, may well be inconsistent with the underlying RIA objective of maximizing social welfare.

The lengthy experience with implementing RIA in Australia suggests that this political dynamic is an enduring one and that the logically compelling claims of RIA in terms of objective welfare maximization are able to make little headway against it. Arguably this conclusion is unduly pessimistic. The current context is one in which the degree of rigour with which RIA is conducted and its real influence on regulatory outcomes is at a historical high point. However, Australia's long experience with RIA underlines the need for sustained commitment both at the political level and by regulatory reformers, realism as to the likely effectiveness of RIA in improving regulatory quality and a clear understanding that RIA is only one among a range of regulatory quality assurance tools.

NOTES

1. The author acknowledges the valuable inputs of Simon Corden, Assistant Director, Victorian Competition and Efficiency Commission, and of Professor Peter Carroll, University of Tasmania. Australian Federal Government regulatory reform officials also assisted in the preparation of this chapter. The views expressed are solely those of the author.
2. This includes both areas in which states/territories agree to adopt nationally harmonized or uniform regulation and those in which regulatory powers are shared between federal and state/territory government, where harmonization focuses on ensuring that federal and state regulation is well integrated.
3. Council of Australian Governments (1995, 2004).
4. The Act was first introduced to Parliament in the early 1990s and was redrafted several times. In its final form it sets out a range of procedural requirements designed to contribute to enhanced quality of 'legislative instruments', broadly defined. Issues addressed include drafting standards, consultation processes, inclusion on a register of legislative instruments, parliamentary scrutiny and sunsetting requirements.
5. Office of Regulation Review (2004, p. 5).
6. Primary legislation is that made by the Parliament itself – that is, Acts of Parliament. Delegated legislation is that which is made under a legislative authority delegated by Parliament. Thus, most Acts confer authority on the minister responsible for its administration to make Statutory Rules (or 'regulations'). Other forms of delegated legislation include Ministerial Orders, management plans, policies, and so on.
7. These bodies include the National Transport Commission and Food Safety Australia and New Zealand (FSANZ). They resemble federal regulatory agencies in many respects but typically include board-like structures and involve a measure of state decision-making.
8. Office of Regulation Review (2005).
9. The exceptions are Western Australia and the Northern Territory.
10. Victorian RIA requirements were initially based on 1984 legislation and this has served as the model for most states. New legislation was passed in Victoria in 1994, but varied the substantive requirements little.
11. See Office of Regulation Review (2005, pp. 85–90).
12. By contrast, RIAs on primary legislation are generally considered to be part of the Cabinet process and, as such, are not published.
13. See Office of Regulation Review (2005, p. 14).
14. The latter figure is unsurprising given that ORR is formally required to provide advice on the adequacy of the RIA document at the time that it is forwarded to decision-makers.
15. See Office of Regulation Review (2005).
16. An exception is Victoria where in recent times the VCEC has published summary RIA data, as well as publishing all RIA documents on its website www.vcec.vic.gov.au.
17. Deighton-Smith (2001).
18. In some cases the degree of quantification was regarded as adequate even though no substantial attempted quantification was made. This occurred where the impact of the proposed regulation was small or where the identified effects were largely intangible in nature.
19. In the latter case this was due either to the primary legislation specifying the required form of delegated legislation to a high level of precision or else the adoption of Australian Standards or other 'off the shelf' options meant that there was little likelihood that regulators could be persuaded to adopt different approaches.
20. VCEC (2006, p. 66). For example the report's findings that 29 per cent and 26 per cent of RIS managed to quantify costs and benefits respectively can be compared with recent data from Victoria suggesting that, in the first year of operation of the VCEC (2004–5), only about 27 per cent of RIA were regarded as having comprehensively quantified direct costs, while in its second year of operation this had improved to half of RIA quantifying direct costs.

21. New RIA guidance recently published by the Federal Government explicitly requires quantification of impacts for the first time, while a 'costing tool' has also been published. Officials expect that performance will significantly improve as a result. The Productivity Commission is the independent statutory authority that has the central regulatory reform/regulatory oversight function at Federal Government level. The Office of Regulation Review, with responsibility for quality control over RIA, is a subsidiary of the Commission. See 'Regulation-making in Australia: Is it Broke? How Do We Fix It?', July 2005. See www.pc.gov.au.
22. See OECD (2002, p. 40).
23. Later the Office of Regulation Reform (ORR).
24. For example, new regulations on the use of asbestos were delayed by 18 months due to the inability or unwillingness of the regulatory agency to meet the analytical standards demanded by ORR. In some cases these long-run failures to meet RIA quality standards may have arisen from a failure to understand the nature of the skills required and to take the RIA process sufficiently seriously as to ensure that those with the relevant skills were recruited. In other cases delays appeared to be more closely related to concerns that transparent analysis of the regulatory proposals would cast unwelcome light on their shortcomings.
25. See Office of Regulation Review (2005).
26. These are technical standards and other material incorporated in regulation 'by reference'.
27. Similarly, matters of regulatory detail normally found in delegated legislation are sometimes adopted in primary laws in jurisdictions where these are not subject to RIA.
28. See Administrative Review Council (1992).
29. See Council of Australian Governments (1995, 2004).
30. VCEC Annual Report 2004–05.
31. Deighton-Smith (2001).
32. See for example, Scrutiny of Acts and Regulations Committee (2002, p. 47). See also Law Reform Committee (1997).
33. For example, the OECD lists 'train the regulators' as one of ten RIA best practices and argues that RIA quality standards should be progressively increased over time as experience and expertise in RIA disciplines accumulate among regulators. (See OECD, 2002, p. 127.)
34. In fact, the federal ORR has in recent years focused increasingly on training. In 2004–05 209 officials were trained, while more than 350 officials were trained in each of 2002–03 and 2003–04. However, this represents something of an exception to the longer-term observation of limited training provision by regulatory oversight bodies.
35. See Office of Regulation Review (2005). A$1 = US$0.75 approximately at the time of writing.
36. Ibid., p. 26.
37. See OECD (1997) and OECD (2002).
38. OECD (1999, p. 59).
39. A recent exception is provided by the federal ORR, which has trained some hundreds of officials in RIA disciplines in each of the last several years. A notable development is that much of this training has been tailored toward the requirements of individual regulatory agencies and is provided 'on request' to those agencies.
40. National Competition Council (2004, Vol. 1, p. 4.7).
41. See www.pc.gov.au.
42. Radaelli (2004) notes: 'impact assessment can be inserted in the whole regulatory process, as shown by the sunset clauses used in countries such as Australia.'
43. The Victorian Subordinate Legislation Act 1994 establishes ten-yearly sunsetting of all regulations, as do the South Australian Subordinate Legislation Act 1978 and the Tasmanian Subordinate Legislation Act 1992. The New South Wales Subordinate Legislation Act 1989 establishes five-yearly sunsetting.
44. OECD (1999, pp. 39–40).
45. Small business and other groups frequently argue that the use of performance-based regulation implies significant uncertainty for regulated groups as to what specific actions

must be taken in order to ensure compliance. A common response by regulators is to provide prescriptive guidance material to supplement the performance-based regulations and conferring on this material 'deemed to comply' status. Such material is sometimes referred to as a 'safe harbour'.

46. An example is given by food safety regulation. Amendments to the Victorian Food Act 1984 passed in 2001 require all premises handling food to develop individual Food Safety Programmes. Following substantial concerns raised by small retail food premises (cafes etc.), 'template' plans were developed and disseminated by the relevant regulatory agency to reduce the effective regulatory burden. Note however, that RIA was not applied to the primary legislation in Victoria at the time this requirement was introduced.
47. That is, regulations specify that work undertaken must comply with say, a certain ISO technical standard. This formula effectively makes compliance with the standard mandatory and, in effect, makes it part of the regulatory structure.
48. Government of Australia (1995).
49. Radaelli (2004).
50. The example has been advanced of using RIA to assist in gaining agreement among a council of ministers in the context of a regulatory harmonization agreement. Here RIA's emphasis on an analytical basis for decision-making facilitates achievement of agreement on a 'right' outcome.
51. See OECD (2002, p. 46) for a discussion of five models of decision-making and the influence of RIA in respect of the models used.

REFERENCES

Administrative Review Council (1992), 'Rule Making by Commonwealth Agencies', Report No. 35, Government of Australia.

Council of Australian Governments (1995 – revised 1997, 2004), 'Principles and Guidelines for National Standard Setting and Regulatory Action by Ministerial Councils and Standard-Setting Bodies', www.pc.gov.au/orr/reports/external/coag/.

Deighton-Smith, R. (2001), 'The Quality of the Regulatory Impact Assessment Process in Victoria', Report to the Victorian Parliamentary Scrutiny of Acts and Regulations Committee, prepared as part of the Inquiry into the Subordinate Legislation Act 1994. Inquiry Report available at: www.parliament.vic.gov.au/sarc/SLA_Inquiry/Final/Final%20Report.pdf.

Government of Australia (1995), 'Report of the Committee of Inquiry into Australia's Standards and Conformance Infrastructure' (The Kean Report).

Law Reform Committee (1997), 'Regulatory Efficiency Legislation: Report', Parliament of Victoria.

National Competition Council (2004), *Assessment of Governments' Progress in Implementing the National Competition Policy and Related Reforms*, Canberra: Government of Australia.

OECD (1997), *Regulatory Impact Analysis: Best Practices in OECD Countries*, Paris: OECD.

OECD (1999), 'Report by the Public Management Services of the OECD on Regulatory Impact Assessment in New South Wales', Regulation Review Committee, Parliament of New South Wales, Report No. 18/51, January.

OECD (2002), *Regulatory Policies in OECD Countries: From Interventionism to Regulatory Governance*, Paris: OECD.

Office of Regulation Review (2004), 'Regulation and Its Review 2003–04', Productivity Commission Annual Report Series, Canberra: Government of Australia.

Office of Regulation Review (2005), 'Regulation and Its Review 2004–05', Canberra: Government of Australia Annual Report Series, www.pc.gov.au/research/annrpt/reglnrev0405/index.html.

Radaelli, C.M. (2002), 'The Politics of Regulatory Impact Analysis in the OECD Countries: Best Practice and Lesson-Drawing', Paper delivered to the workshop *Regulatory Impact Analysis In a Comparative Perspective*, London School of Economics, 11 March 2002.

Scrutiny of Acts and Regulations Committee (2002), 'Inquiry into the Subordinate Legislation Act 1994: Final Report', Parliament of Victoria.

VCEC (Victorian Competition and Efficiency Commission) (2005), 'Annual Report 2004–5', Melbourne: Government of Victoria, 29 December 2005, www.vcec.vic.gov.au.

VCEC (Victorian Competition and Efficiency Commission) (2006), 'Annual Report 2005–6', Melbourne: Government of Victoria, 22 December 2006, www.vcec.vic.gov.au.

9. Regulatory impact assessment in developing countries

David Parker and Colin Kirkpatrick

INTRODUCTION

Up until the 1980s, international donor agencies tended to emphasize the positive role of government in economic development. However, from the 1980s, attitudes changed with the arrival of what is sometimes referred to as 'the Washington consensus' with its emphasis on privatization and market liberalization programmes and evidence of state-led development failures (World Bank, 1995). The reduction and some might even say the destruction of the state became the prevailing orthodoxy. This policy thrust was understandable in so far as there was evidence that government economic intervention had undermined private investment and damaged economic growth. Government expenditure was perceived to have 'crowded out' private capital formation and led to corruption and cronyism, while at the same time a number of state-owned enterprises appeared to be very inefficient. Government regulations stymied private enterprise by introducing barriers to the establishment of new firms and the growth of existing ones. However, by the late 1990s, questions were being raised again about the ability of market liberalization on its own to bring about a sustained improvement in economic development. This led to a further shift in development strategy, to one where the state plays a key role in sustaining the regulatory framework for the operation of what are often imperfect or missing markets. The focus is shifting away from 'less government' towards 'better government' in developing economies. In the search for better government, regulatory reform is critical (Kirkpatrick, 2006).

Institutional quality is a core element of the transition from a state-led economy to one rooted in resource allocation through markets and there is a growing body of theoretical and empirical literature that links economic growth to the soundness of a country's institutions (North, 1990; Jalilian, Kirkpatrick and Parker, 2006). Appropriate state regulatory structures are needed to tackle market failures in transition economies, which can take the form of pervasive externalities in market transactions, monopoly abuse, underdeveloped or missing markets and information asymmetries (Parker, 2002). Regulation may also be needed to ensure that market-led development contributes to the objectives of social development and environmental protection. While the regulatory institutional structures needed to support the growth of the market economy will vary across countries and over time, it is possible to identify a number of general principles for 'good' regulation. Jacobs (2003) lists the following five characteristics needed of modern regulatory systems, which can be delivered only by building good regulatory capacity within government:

- security – legal security, consistent respect for market solutions, predictable enforcement;
- transparency – clear and simple rules, openness through the entire policy process, less corruption;
- legitimacy – must protect safety, health, environment, consumers, public interests;
- efficiency – low-cost rules, orderly and timely decisions, move swiftly to meet market needs;
- expertise – good regulatory skills and understanding of complex markets and technologies.

In developing economies, the quality of the political and legal infrastructure is a critical component of the regulatory framework. The evidence of a positive correlation between governance, the rule of law and economic performance means that where the political and legal systems are unsatisfactory the development process is seriously impeded. As the World Bank (2002) has remarked: 'Investors are becoming more selective in choosing their investment destinations. As a result, investment is flowing to countries with better domestic investment climates: good governance, sound institutions and a system of property rights.'

The need for effective regulatory structures to sustain the process of economic growth is now well recognized. As the UK's Department for International Development wrote in 2000: 'Effective governments are needed to build the legal, institutional and regulatory framework without which market reforms go badly wrong, at great cost – particularly to the poor. Whilst excessive or cumbersome regulatory barriers stifle incentives and discourage investment, effective regulation remains essential . . .' (DFID, 2000, pp. 24–5).

Although there is no generally agreed definition of regulation, it can be broadly defined as a government measure that is intended to affect individual or group behaviour. The OECD has defined regulation in broad terms to refer to 'the diverse set of instruments by which governments set requirements on enterprises and citizens' (OECD, 1997). Hence, regulation extends beyond sector-specific regulation (e.g., in financial services, telecommunications, energy, transport and water and sewerage) to all laws, directives and other government instruments that impact on individual or group behaviour.

State regulations can produce both 'goods' and 'bads'. Regulation can both promote economic and social welfare and lead to significant economic and social costs. Hence, if social welfare is to be promoted by state regulation, rather than reduced, then regulation needs to be both effective and efficient. Effective in the sense of achieving its planned goals and efficient in the sense of achieving these goals at least cost, in terms of government administration costs and the costs imposed on wider society in terms of complying with the regulations.

This chapter is concerned with the potential of regulatory impact assessment (RIA) to improve regulatory governance at central, regional and local levels within developing economies and within regulatory agencies such as utility regulators. In the chapter we look particularly at the how best RIA might be introduced in the context of a developing country. And then, in the search for further policy lessons, we consider the findings of a survey of actual RIA practices in those developing countries that currently claim to use some form of RIA, drawing on a recent questionnaire study.

APPLYING RIA IN DEVELOPING COUNTRIES

RIA is a method for improving the quality of regulation in any country whether developed or developing. On the face of it therefore, RIA is applicable to developing countries and has the potential to improve regulatory governance. International bodies are active in pursuing regulatory reform programmes aimed at improving the operating environment for private investment and, more generally, enhancing the quality of public governance processes (European Commission, 2005; World Bank, 2005). It is in this context that the interest in RIA is spreading internationally.

Regulatory impact assessment (RIA) has been described as:

> an information-based analytical approach to assess probable costs, consequences, and side-effects of planned policy instruments (laws, regulations etc.). It can also be used to evaluate the real costs and consequences of policy instruments after they have been implemented. In either case, the results are used to improve the quality of policy decisions and policy instruments, such as laws, regulations, investment programmes and public investments. Basically, it is a means to inform government choices: choices about policy instruments, about the

design of a specific instrument, or about the need to change or discontinue an existing instrument. (SIGMA, 2001, p. 10)

RIA contributes to the broader process of better governance through more consultative and accountable procedures. The consultation with consumers, business and civil society that is inherent in RIA helps to build legitimacy in law-making and can help promote equity and fairness. The various ways in which RIA can support better regulation policy-making in, and strengthen the process of, regulatory governance are summarized in Box 9.1.

However, often developing countries have weaknesses in their regulatory rule-making, leading to a lack of accountability, transparency and consistency in policy formulation and implementation, which means that regulatory governance falls well short of the 'good governance goals' set out in Box 9.1. Investors, both foreign and domestic, are discouraged from investing when they believe that regulatory governance in a country is not transparent and is inconsistent and arbitrary and this is the case in too many of the low-income areas of the world. In this respect, RIA has the potential to improve regulatory governance in terms of both regulatory outcomes (ensuring that regulation has net benefits for economic and social welfare) and regulatory processes within government (including proper consultation and evaluation before a new regulation is introduced and periodic reassessment of existing regulations to ensure that they are still appropriate).

BOX 9.1 GOOD GOVERNANCE GOALS OF REGULATORY IMPACT ANALYSIS

Analysis: calculating the costs and benefits of government action	⇒	Faster learning, increasing benefits of government action, finding lowest cost solutions, reducing policy failures
Consultation and responsiveness to a wider range of interests	⇒	Transparency, building trust, and reducing regulatory risks for private sector, reduce 'information monopolies'
Integrating multiple policy goals (social and economic policies)	⇒	Policy coherence in a complex world; break down vertical silos and promote horizontal thinking
Accountability for actions and results (within ministries, to the public)	⇒	Client-oriented, credible and responsive government

Source: Jacobs (2003).

RIA also has the potential to form an integrating framework within government to improve regulatory design and implementation. By spreading best practice in regulation evaluation and monitoring from one department to another, and from central government to local government and governmental agencies, improved administration should result. By adopting standard approaches to evaluation and monitoring of cases across departments, inconsistencies in government should be reduced. In this sense RIA supports horizontal coordination at the level of the central administration. RIA can also support greater policy coherence and 'joined-up' government by encouraging inter-departmental cooperation when undertaking RIA studies. The establishment of firm RIA guidelines applied across the different levels of government should reduce the likelihood of significant and damaging inconsistencies in regulatory policy.

At the same time however, RIA cannot on its own be a solution for government failure in developing countries. The way in which the outcome and process dimensions of RIA are put into practice can be expected to vary considerably between countries, reflecting different priorities and objectives for the regulatory reform process and different institutional endowments, including existing capacity and probity in public administration. Countries with a tradition already of 'good government' are most likely to introduce effective RIA methods. That is to say, RIA is not a substitute for good government, it is a complement. Therefore, the introduction of RIA will often have to be accompanied by more fundamental and wider reforms in public administration.

The fundamental goal of development policy is poverty reduction and the aim of regulation policy in developing countries should be to change private sector behaviour in ways that are consistent with the goal of raising the income levels of the poor. Whilst the impact of economic growth on poverty reduction is the focus for continued empirical investigation, it is generally agreed that the benefits of growth will not necessarily 'trickle down' to improve the income levels of the poorest. Regulation therefore, has a potentially important role to play in ensuring that the benefits of more efficient market processes are distributed in accordance with society's social preferences. This implies a wider range of objectives for regulation policy beyond those that lie at the core of the OECD RIA guidelines (OECD, 1995), namely, promoting market efficiency (Kirkpatrick, 2001). If the positive and negative impacts of regulation in terms of, for example, prices and job opportunities and access to credit are to be properly recognized, an RIA must specifically address the social effects of regulatory changes. It may be appropriate therefore, for RIAs in developing countries to be 'pro-poor' by placing an explicitly heavy weighting on poverty reduction and skewing the assessment in favour of regulatory changes that assist the poor.

Also, the application of RIA in developing countries is far from simply a matter of adopting international RIA guidelines, such as those published by the OECD, for other reasons. The role of the 'institutional endowment' or the pre-existing legislative, administrative and judicial arrangements of a country in the design of effective regulatory arrangements is now well recognized (Levy and Spiller, 1995). The institutional endowment will impact on the extent to which RIA can be successfully adopted. RIA is more than a method of analysis; it requires an open and transparent process of decision-making within government. The result is that RIA is likely to be context-specific, reflecting the realities of a country's political and business behaviour. For example, the consequences of institutional weaknesses may be a lack of long-term commitment to RIA within government, especially if it is seen as imposed by external donor agencies.

RIA needs rule of law, open and transparent government and an active civil society that will respond positively to consultation. This is evidenced by the fact that RIA has been established most successfully in the OECD countries where in general there is rule of law and democratic governments. Also, the application of RIA needs to reflect the level of expertise, resources and information available in a country. It should not demand expertise, resources and information that go well beyond the capability of government departments to furnish. For example, national and local government departments may lack the capacity to collect the necessary data to undertake a meaningful RIA. Moreover, if RIA is to promote sustainable development and poverty reduction by improving regulatory practice, it is essential that its introduction does not impose unacceptable delays in government decision-taking (Deighton-Smith, 1997, p. 213).

Also, RIAs can be 'captured' by elite interests, leading to highly normative evaluations of the data gathered. For example, ex ante RIA will involve risk assessment in which probabilities must be applied to possible outcomes including, for example, risks to safety or health. The valuation of probabilities in a highly politicized decision-making environment can be manipulated to bring about the result initially desired by the policy-makers. In developing countries with underdeveloped conventions and rules on probity within government, RIA will need protecting from such rent-seeking behaviour. Difficulties and dangers will be compounded when benefits and costs are problematic to quantify with any accuracy.

The problems arising from a failure to match the regulatory instrument to a country's existing institutional endowment is clearly evident in the area of banking and financial regulation in developing countries in the 1990s. The financial regulatory system in most low-income developing countries was severely constrained by weaknesses in obtaining accurate financial information, lack of skilled regulatory staff, weak accounting and legal frameworks and pervasive political interference in the regulatory authorities (Brownbridge and Kirkpatrick, 2000, 2002). The adoption of the financial market liberalization model in the context of these regulatory capacity constraints contributed directly to the financial crises that affected many developing countries, subsequent to the implementation of financial market liberalization.

Regulatory capacity constraints are likely to occur in most low-income economies and the RIA framework that is proposed needs to be adapted in a way that recognizes these constraints. Nevertheless, it is our view that RIA still has the potential to improve regulatory governance and therefore economic growth in developing countries. However, there will be a need to adopt an approach to the introduction of RIA that is appropriate to the needs and adaptable to the resource and capacity constraints of each individual developing country. Although the OECD guidelines (OECD, 1995) are a useful comparator for developing an RIA in any country, they need translating to reflect the particular issues that arise when regulating in developing countries, including issues to do with regulatory capacity, poverty reduction and development goals. At present it does not appear that there exists a clear framework of principles for applying RIA in developing countries.

The discussion below draws from Kirkpatrick and Parker (2004) to begin the process of creating such a framework and is concerned with:

- building an effective regulatory management system in the country;
- improving the quality of new regulations in the country; and
- upgrading the quality of existing regulations.

Building an Effective Regulatory Management System

The first step in providing a framework for RIA in a developing country involves building an effective regulatory management system. Reform principles and the use of RIA need to be endorsed at the highest levels of government if RIA is to be taken seriously. A precondition for success is to improve understanding of RIA and the need for improved regulatory governance. Opposition can be expected on two fronts. First officials may be suspicious of RIA as a reform, especially when it is seen as being imposed by outsiders such as donor agencies. As a consequence it will be important to find local champions of RIA within the government who have influence over policy-making. To this end a Regulatory Impact Assessment Unit (RIAU) within government can be useful to act as that champion, especially when it has the status of being located in the prime minister's or president's office. Its budget and staffing will certainly need to be protected from attack by any ministers, parliamentarians or outsiders, such as business interests, disgruntled by the RIA process. The mandate of the RIAU should be to establish explicit standards for regulatory quality and principles of regulatory decision-making within the government. The body should aim to ensure consistency, credibility and quality of RIA at the departmental level and will need adequate authority and skills to perform its function successfully.

The use of RIA may need to be mandated by a law or decree so that it carries weight. Hence, there may be a case for primary legislation so that RIA is established as an important and mandatory reform. Short of that, a starting point would be to recommend an RIA in the form of an explanatory memorandum to be attached to important pieces of legislation. The RIAU should immediately develop national RIA guidelines and training programmes, drawing on OECD guidance and other international experience, probably assisted by outside consultants. Training is an essential part of the implementation of RIA and will need to be provided not only to the officials responsible for implementing RIA but to the staff in each of the departments responsible for regulatory policy. It will be important to provide effective training schemes in regulation theory and practice, to give regulators and relevant civil servants the skills required to undertake high-quality RIAs.

In addition, each government department should be encouraged to have its own RIA official or small unit to champion the method at the departmental level. While the RIAU champions the development of RIA across government, it is important to locate responsibility for undertaking RIAs within regulatory departments and agencies. This improves 'ownership' and integration into decision-making. Departments will also need to develop processes and systems for effective and comprehensive data collection. Data quality is essential for successful RIAs and the framework should clarify data needs, quality standards for acceptable data and suggest strategies for collecting data at minimum cost and within the required time limits. Also, while methods for estimating the costs and benefits of a regulation are now relatively well developed in a number of the OECD countries, this cannot be expected to be so in many developing economies. The RIAU will need to investigate and disseminate information on the types of data needed to undertake meaningful RIAs. The unit should also ensure that departments are fully aware of the need to consult interested parties before regulatory changes are made. Systematic public consultation procedures with affected interests should be introduced to ensure the widest possible input into regulatory decision-making. Interest groups should be consulted widely and in a timely fashion and treated even-handedly. This will require data on relevant interest groups to create a directory of relevant interests that is made available within ministries.

Improving the Quality of New Regulations

The second step will be to improve the quality of new regulations. Procedures should become embedded within departments to ensure that RIA is built into the process of regulatory appraisal and at the earliest possible stage in the design of important new regulations and proposed regulatory changes. RIA should be gradually applied to all significant policy proposals, whether implemented by law, lower level rules or ministerial actions. Methods for assessing regulatory options, including not regulating, will need to be developed and disseminated, as will an understanding of when and when not to use RIAs. Resources should be concentrated on those regulations where the impacts are likely to be the most significant and where the prospects are best for altering regulatory outcomes.

Systems will need to be introduced to ensure improved regulatory coordination within government. The method adopted should include facilities for peer review within government, perhaps by the RIAU or an audit body (in the UK the National Audit Office has taken on this role enthusiastically). Peer review unearths poor practice and publicizes the benefits of good practice. The objective should be to identify RIA 'successes' that can be used as examples to win over doubters within government of the value of RIA. Once RIA takes hold within at least some government departments, it can then be rolled out across other departments and into regional and local government and government agencies.

Upgrading the Quality of Existing Regulations

The third step should be to upgrade the quality of existing regulations. This will be achieved by systematically reviewing and updating existing regulations, building on the lessons learned from the application of RIA to new regulations and utilizing the central and departmental RIA bodies.

In summary, the following principles for the successful implementation of RIA in the context of a developing country are:

- Championing across government, so that RIA becomes a normal feature of regulatory policy-making. This requires powerful political support within government if bureaucratic and political inertia is to be overcome, especially as RIA may be seen as another 'Western' gimmick. Probably essential will be the creation of an RIAU, preferably at the highest political level, to champion the implementation of RIA and disseminate best practice.
- Development of the necessary local knowledge of what RIA is and the skills and resources needed to implement RIAs effectively through

awareness of international experiences and guidelines and through training and skills development. This will usually require resort to outside help from RIA consultants.

- Development of processes of data-gathering so that meaningful RIAs take place within a reasonable time and without excessive cost.
- Spreading understanding of the need to consult and evaluate before regulatory changes are made, even though this can be time-consuming and resource-heavy within hard-stretched government. Minimum time periods for consultation should be established so that interested parties have time to formulate their responses in detail. The use of a common format when reporting results will be helpful. This should be developed by the RIAU.
- RIAs may involve multiple stages with each new regulation facing an initial RIA, another RIA after consultation and redrafting and a final RIA on the legislation as passed by the legislature. This places a large burden on departments. A sensible approach to minimize these costs is to develop a method to prioritize where detailed RIAs should be undertaken by using a screening procedure to identify when a regulation is likely to have major effects on the economy, society or the environment. It is important however, that the decision on when to use an RIA is not made simply on political grounds.
- Ex post auditing of RIAs and publication of the results can form a useful barrier to capture of the RIA process. Governments should consider implementing a method for ex post auditing of RIAs undertaken so as to police quality, ensure public confidence in the process and improve conformance with best practice. These reports should be available for debate in the legislature to reinforce proper accountability.

We now turn to consider the limited evidence on the existing use of RIA in lower- and middle-income economies in the light of the above principles.

EVIDENCE ON THE USE OF RIA IN DEVELOPING COUNTRIES

While RIA is now used in most OECD countries albeit to varying degrees, there is little recorded evidence of its use in developing countries. Where its use is recorded it seems that serious implementation problems have occurred. For example, RIA is used in the middle-income economies of South Korea and Mexico (OECD, 1999, 2000). In Mexico almost 1500 regulations were reviewed between 2000 and early 2002 (OECD, 1999). In

South Korea a regulatory review committee reviewed nearly 3000 regulations between 1998 and 2002, declining 387 draft regulations and returning 1157 to sponsoring agencies for revision (OECD, 2000; World Bank, 2004, p. 74). However, in spite of what on the face of it appears to be an impressive record in both countries, serious 'implementation gaps' have been identified. Inadequate skills within government have been particularly highlighted as a significant cause of implementation failure.

The experiences of Mexico and South Korea illustrate some of the challenges that arise when attempting to adopt RIA where institutional capacity is underdeveloped at the government level. For example, on Mexico an OECD report (1999, p. 159) comments: 'The biggest problem for the Costs and Benefits Section of the RIA is that the quality of data is generally poor and thus a quantitative analysis of proposals is virtually impossible. Regulatory authorities are not asked to produce net benefit estimates for fear of creating additional incentives to distort already inadequate data'. The report on South Korea notes that 'the bulk of the RIA is still being conducted at a low level of sophistication' (OECD, 2000, p. 153).

To assess the extent to which RIA is used in other low- and middle-income economies and their experiences, in 2003 the Centre on Regulation and Competition at the University of Manchester sent a questionnaire on RIA to 311 government departments and agencies with regulatory responsibilities in 99 developing and transition countries. In most cases the questionnaire was sent to more than one informant in each country as a potential cross-check on the accuracy of the information received. The questionnaires completed and returned came from 40 countries in Latin America and the Caribbean, Asia and Africa. Replies were also received from some of the ex-communist transition economies, namely Albania, Estonia, Georgia, Lithuania and Moldova. In total, 68 useable questionnaires were returned giving an overall response rate from government officials of 17 per cent. The regulatory activities covered included economic, social and environmental regulation but with a bias towards economic regulation. The majority of the responses were from regulators of utilities. Box 9.2 lists the countries from which completed questionnaires were returned.

The questionnaire had three main parts, namely, RIA as an assessment method, RIA as a process and RIA as part of a more general strategy for regulatory reform. The main questions were concerned with:

- existing familiarity with RIA as a concept and the OECD guidelines;
- the existing use of RIA within the country;
- legal requirements to adopt RIAs and the existence of published RIA guidance within government;

BOX 9.2 COUNTRIES FROM WHICH COMPLETED QUESTIONNAIRES WERE RETURNED

Asia (9 countries)
India, Jordan, Korea, Malaysia, Oman, Pakistan, the Philippines, Sri Lanka, Thailand

Africa (16 countries)
Algeria, Botswana, Cameroon, Gabon, Ghana, Guinea Bissau, Kenya, Malawi, Mauritius, Morocco, Nigeria, South Africa, Tanzania, Uganda, Zambia, Zimbabwe

Latin America and Caribbean (9 countries)
Barbados, Brazil, Colombia, Jamaica, Mexico, Nicaragua, Peru, Uruguay, Venezuela

Transition economies (6 countries)
Albania Estonia, Georgia, Lithuania, Moldova, Romania

- the forms RIAs take when used;
- the processes used within government when undertaking RIAs;
- RIA transparency, in terms of published documentation;
- public consultation and participation in RIA exercises;
- RIA as part of wider governmental reforms.

The questionnaire answers confirmed that there is some understanding of RIA and its principles amongst regulators in a number of developing economies. At the same time this understanding did not seem deep or widespread. There was evidence of much variation in knowledge between different agencies and government departments within the same country (a fuller summary of the study results can be found in Kirkpatrick et al., 2004).

Taking Asia first, the questionnaire results confirmed that RIA was applied in eight of the nine countries in Asia from which replies were received. In Africa RIA seemed to be used to some degree in 11 of the 16 countries; however, in only one of these countries was there a claim that RIA was being systematically applied to all new state regulations. By contrast, in Latin America and the Caribbean the results suggested that RIA was being used to assess some or all new regulation proposals in six of the nine countries from which questionnaires were returned. This finding is perhaps surprisingly low given this region's longer and more developed operation of regulatory systems, especially in the utilities sectors (Pargal, 2003). Finally, for five of the six transitional economies that took part in our survey, respondents claimed that RIA was being applied in some measure to assess the potential impact of new regulation proposals.

While it appears that some form of regulatory assessment was being applied at least to some degree, in the majority of countries from which completed questionnaires were received, there were marked regional differences in familiarity with RIA principles. Three-fifths of the replies from Africa reported little or no awareness, whereas the majority of respondents from Asia said that they were fully aware of the concept. Only six of the respondents however, were familiar with the OECD's RIA guidelines. In four countries respondents reported that guidance on how RIA should be undertaken had been prepared within their government; but these countries included Mexico and South Korea, which are OECD members. None of the respondents from Africa claimed that their country had developed guidelines for the conduct of RIA.

RIA is a method for assessing the actual impact of existing regulations as well as the potential impact of proposed new regulatory measures. The questionnaire therefore, sought to elicit information on the extent to which ex post assessment methods were being applied. Returns from 19 countries reported using RIA to evaluate existing regulations. It seems that where RIA is being applied in developing economies, it is mostly being used for ex ante appraisal rather than for monitoring or ex post evaluation purposes. This may reflect a lack of resources within governments to undertake such appraisal or alternatively, reluctance on the part of governments to dwell on whether previously introduced regulatory measures were having their desired effects. In OECD countries too there has been a similar lack of interest in publishing ex post assessments.

The questionnaire also attempted to gather information on the extent to which RIA is applied to economic, social and environmental proposals. The results identified the application of RIA across the three main areas of regulation but with a heavy concentration in terms of monitoring economic issues (see Table 9.1). Twenty-eight of the 30 countries in which respondents reported the use of RIA recorded its application to this area of government activity. The questionnaire also attempted to obtain more detailed information on the application of RIA to economic, social and environmental regulation, by asking what proportion of regulations in each area had been subject to RIA during the past five years. Overall, the results confirmed that no country is applying RIA consistently to all major economic, social and environmental regulations.

The concentration of RIA activity on economic regulation probably reflects the traditional focus of government regulatory activity in areas of market failure, particularly in utilities services where 'natural monopoly' can be pervasive. It in addition reflects that fact that the majority of the

Table 9.1 Application of RIA to economic, social and environmental regulation in lower-income economies

Region	Economic Regulation	Social Regulation	Environmental Regulation
Asia (no. of countries)	8	8	5
Africa (no. of countries)	10	5	7
Latin America (no. of countries)	5	3	5
Transitional economies (no. of countries)	5	5	4

Source: Kirkpatrick et al. (2004).

completed questionnaires came from regulators of utilities. The responses to the questionnaire also indicated that in the majority of those developing and transition countries where RIA had been adopted, the assessments included both potential costs and benefits of the regulatory proposal. Of the 30 countries that reported using RIA, 18 countries claimed that both benefits and costs were estimated. Another two countries indicated that only benefits were assessed and replies from ten suggested uncertainty about the coverage. In five cases respondents replied 'don't know' and in another five countries inconsistent answers were received from different respondents, suggesting that practice varies across different regulated activities within the same country. None of the last five countries had adopted uniform guidelines for undertaking RIAs.

The replies to the questionnaire also revealed that a variety of practices exist for the quantification of costs and benefits. Of the countries that assessed both costs and benefits, only a minority quantified the estimated impacts in both physical and value terms; although in the four countries where guidelines were in place, quantification of benefits and costs was carried out using both measures. This finding is perhaps not surprising given the difficulties associated with the economic and social valuation of benefits and costs in the practice of impact assessment. The problems associated with valuation are reflected in the responses received from the countries where RIA is being applied. When asked if in their judgement, the application of RIA in their country had provided a 'high level of detailed analysis of costs and benefits', respondents in only eight of the countries replied in the affirmative.

The questionnaire was also concerned with the process aspects of RIA in contributing to the principles of 'good governance'. The responses received indicated that in the majority of countries where RIA was applied to new regulations, public consultation did occur with a main emphasis on the use of public notices and invitations to comment on proposals. Consultation involved outside experts, government bodies and the private business sector; but consumer groups and other bodies representing civil society were less commonly included. In most cases (34 countries) consultation occurred before or after the government prepared detailed regulations. However, fewer countries (15) made the views of participants in the consultation exercise public, suggesting scope for improved regulatory transparency.

The final section of the questionnaire was designed to gather information on the role of RIA as part of a government-wide strategy for regulatory reform. The impact of regulatory impact assessment is likely to be enhanced where RIA is adopted as part of an overall strategy for regulatory governance reform and institutional capacity-building (Stern and Holder, 1999; Kirkpatrick et al., 2004). Of the 40 countries for which replies were received, 22 were reported to have a strategy in place for promoting government-wide regulatory reform. The countries having a government-wide strategy in place were cross-checked with the 30 countries applying RIA. This confirmed that in ten of the countries RIA was being applied as part of a broader programme of regulatory governance reform. An interesting area for further research investigation would be to assess the results of RIA where a wider programme of regulatory reform is underway, against the results in countries where such reform is yet to occur.

Overall, the findings from the questionnaire study suggested that the level of awareness and application of RIA in developing countries was perhaps higher than what might have been expected, based on the limited information previously available. This conclusion should be qualified however, by acknowledging the possibility of sample bias. The questionnaire returns may have been mainly from countries where regulatory practices were well established. The heavy concentration of responses from the utilities sector may be indirect confirmation of this potential bias. The relatively high number of countries (59) from which no return was received may reflect the absence of any form of RIA in these countries. Also, although respondents were provided with a definition of RIA at the start of the questionnaire, the possibility that they used different definitions when completing the questionnaire cannot be ruled out.

Finally, just over a half of the countries from which completed questionnaires were received appear to have engaged in a programme of regulatory governance reform and RIA had been part of this process in a number of cases. In the remaining countries RIA appeared to have been adopted on a 'stand-alone' basis, which may have limited its impact in terms of improving regulatory governance. If RIA is to contribute to economic development and poverty reduction, it is important that it is operated appropriately, including clarity about regulating goals, the use of full consultation and without 'capture' of the process by special interest groups, as set out in the principles laid down earlier in this chapter. RIAs that simply exist to impress outsiders, such as donor agencies, and rubber stamp all decisions made by the executive are not worth the cost and effort. The questionnaire study reported mixed results in this respect. In particular, it found that where RIA was being used, in most cases consultation had been incorporated as part of the process. At the same time consultation tended to be limited to government and the business sector, with consumer interests and other civil society interest groups being under-represented in the consultation process.

CONCLUSIONS

This chapter has been concerned with the potential and actual application of RIA in developing countries, countries with pressing poverty reduction and economic development objectives. We have argued that RIA has the potential to improve regulatory governance significantly in these countries and thereby promote private investment and economic growth. International experience demonstrates that RIA has the potential to form an integrating framework within government to improve regulatory design and implementation. However, we should not be blind to the difficulties of introducing RIA given the institutional weaknesses evident in many developing countries. In this context, while the OECD 'best practice' guidelines provide some pointers to how a RIA framework might be developed, they are unlikely to be a complete template or model for transfer and adoption in countries with very different institutions and objectives. The OECD guidelines need translating to reflect the particular issues that arise when regulating in different countries, including issues to do with regulatory capacity, social and environmental goals and development aims.

The chapter has also reported findings from a questionnaire study sent to regulators in a large number of lower- and middle-income economies on the actual use of RIAs at the present time. The results confirm that a number of difficulties exist. The evidence points to the following requirements if RIA is to be successfully planted in a country.

First, RIA needs the development of appropriate cost and benefits analysis skills within the government machinery, including skills in enumeration and valuation. Generally, qualitative effects will involve much judgemental or subjective evaluation and physical units introduce serious problems of aggregation. There may be a temptation therefore, to diminish the RIA to include only an evaluation of measurable financial costs and benefits. Or the assessment could be reduced to looking solely at the cheapest way of achieving the regulatory outcome (in effect providing a cost-effectiveness study only) in which the benefits are taken as given. This lesser form of RIA risks ignoring important differential benefits from differing forms of regulation.

Second, RIA requires the extension of consultation procedures to ensure that appropriate information is collected and analysed in reaching a view on the regulatory impact. There may be little tradition of consulting widely before undertaking regulation or those chosen for consultation in the past may not have been representative of the relevant stakeholders. The international evidence provides a very mixed picture on the scope and depth of consultation with interested parties.

Third, the need to consult and evaluate can be time-consuming and resource-heavy within hard-stretched governments. RIAs may involve multiple stages with each new regulation facing an initial RIA, another RIA after consultation and redrafting and a final RIA on the legislation as passed by the legislature. A sensible approach to minimize these costs is to prioritize where detailed RIA should be undertaken by using a screening procedure to identify when a regulation is likely to have major effects on the economy, society or the environment. It is important however, that the decision on when to use an RIA is not made simply on the grounds of political expediency or administrative convenience. Evidence of the patchy application of RIA within governments where regulators claim that RIAs occur suggests that decisions on when to undertake RIAs could be motivated by political expediency.

Fourth, RIA needs to be championed across government if it is to be used consistently and become a normal feature of regulatory policy-making. It therefore needs clear and powerful support within government if it is to overcome bureaucratic and political inertia, such as a Regulatory Impact Assessment Unit located at high level within government. The functions of the unit should include coordinating legal changes to provide a sound basis for impact assessment, ensuring that departments are consulting interests and carrying out impact assessments at the beginning of the policy-making progress and not simply as a rubber stamping exercise when the legislation is already at final draft stage; to provide a resource centre on RIA techniques and publish and disseminate guidance; to advise and report on the quality of RIAs submitted by departments; and to undertake reviews of the RIA process so as to further cultivate best practice. Unfortunately such units do not exist even in a number of countries that claim to apply RIA.

Fifth, RIA must also confront the possibility of 'regulatory capture'. In practice, the nature and content of regulation can be 'captured' by special interest groups, who have the time, resources and incentives to invest in influencing the regulatory process. In market economies resources flow to where the perceived returns are highest and this is no less true in the shaping of regulation policy. There will be constant pressure from external groups and their spokespersons within the legislature and government to advance regulations that promote their members' economic rents. For this reason regulatory policy-making may not be the objective and rational process that RIA presumes, with its emphasis on fact-finding and a disinterested analysis of the evidence. At the same time however, RIA can help to control rent-seeking activity within government by promoting wider consultation and by requiring the explicit identification and evaluation of costs and benefits.

Finally, RIA requires a cultural change within government involving more open policy-making as part of a broader process of governance reform. This can be a particularly difficult hurdle to overcome where government has traditionally been secretive and exclusive rather than inclusive.

In summary, RIA has the potential to improve regulatory governance in lower- and middle-income economies but no one should underestimate the difficulty of introducing and operating effective RIA processes.

REFERENCES

Brownbridge, M. and C. Kirkpatrick (2000), 'Financial Regulation in Developing Countries', *Journal of Development Studies*, **37** (1), 1–24.

Brownbridge, M. and C. Kirkpatrick (2002), 'Policy Symposium on Financial Regulation and Supervision', *Development Policy Review*, **20** (3), 243–316.

Deighton-Smith, R. (1997), 'Regulatory Impact Assessment: Best Practice in OECD Countries', in *OECD Report on Regulatory Reform: Synthesis*, Paris: OECD.

DFID (Department for International Development) (2000), *Making Markets Work Better for the Poor: A Framework Paper*, London: DFID.

European Commission (EC) (2005), *Impact Assessment Guidelines*, SEC (2005) 791, Brussels: EC.

Jacobs, S. (2003), 'Assisting Economic Transition: An RIA Strategy for Developing Countries', Paper to *Conference on Regulatory Impact Assessment: Strengthening Regulation Policy and Practice*, Centre on Regulation and Competition, University of Manchester.

Jalilian, H., C. Kirkpatrick and D. Parker (2006), 'The Impact of Regulation on Economic Growth in Developing Countries – A Cross-country Analysis', *World Development*, November.

Kirkpatrick, C. (2001), 'Regulatory Impact Assessment in Developing Countries: Research Issues', *Working Paper No. 5*, Centre on Regulation and Competition, IDPM, University of Manchester.

Kirkpatrick, C. (2006), 'Regulatory Impact Assessment', in M. Crew and D. Parker (eds), *International Handbook on Economic Regulation*, Cheltenham, UK and Northampton, MA, USA: Edward Elgar.

Kirkpatrick, C. and D. Parker (2004), 'Regulatory Impact Assessment and Regulatory Governance in Developing Countries', *Public Administration and Development*, **24**, 333–44.

Kirkpatrick, C., D. Parker and Y. Zhang (2004), 'Regulatory Impact Assessment in Developing and Transition Economies: A Survey of Current Practice', *Public Money and Management*, **24** (5), 291–6.

Levy, B. and P. Spiller (1995), 'A Framework for Resolving the Regulatory Problem', in B. Levy and P. Spiller (eds), *Regulations, Institutions and Commitment: Comparative Studies in Regulation*, Cambridge: Cambridge University Press.

North, D.C. (1990), *Institutions, Institutional Change and Economic Performance*, Cambridge: Cambridge University Press.

OECD (1995), *Recommendation on Improving the Quality of Government Regulation*, Paris: OECD.

OECD (1997), *The OECD Report on Regulatory Reform: Synthesis*, Paris: OECD.

OECD (1999), *Regulatory Reform in Mexico*, Paris: OECD.

OECD (2000), *Regulatory Reform in Korea*, Paris: OECD.

Pargal, S. (2003), *Regulation and Private Sector Investment in Infrastructure: Evidence from Latin America*, Policy Research Working Paper No. 3037, Washington DC: World Bank.

Parker, D. (2002), 'Economic Regulation: A Review of Issues', *Annals of Public and Cooperative Economics*, **73** (4), 493–519.

SIGMA (2001), *Improving Policy Instruments through Impact Assessment*, SIGMA Paper No. 31, Paris: OECD.

Stern, J. and S. Holder (1999), 'Regulatory Governance: Criteria for Assessing the Performance of Regulatory Systems. An Application to Infrastructure Industries in the Developing Countries of Asia', *Utilities Policy*, **8**, 33–50.

World Bank (1995), *Bureaucrats in Business: The Economics and Politics of Government Ownership*, Oxford: Oxford University Press for the World Bank.

World Bank (2002), *Global Economic Prospects and the Developing Countries*, Washington DC: World Bank.

World Bank (2004), *Doing Business in 2004: Understanding Regulation*, Washington DC: World Bank.

10. Regulatory impact assessment: a tool for improved regulatory governance in Sri Lanka

Malathy Knight-John

INTRODUCTION

Empirical evidence from around the world, as set out in analyses such as Nicoletti and Scarpetta (2003), Estache (2004) and Loayza, Oviedo and Serven (2004), for example, suggests that good governance in general and regulatory governance in particular, are critical to a sustainable development process. A similar line of thinking is reflected in country-specific research, which argues that regulatory reform would have a significant impact on productivity growth (Beardsley and Farrell, 2005). At a sector-specific level, studies by Samarajiva and Dokeniya (2004) and by De Silva and Khan (2004), for example, find a strong association between the telecommunications regulatory environment and investment in telecommunications in Sri Lanka and Bangladesh.

Several studies also find positive links between strong governance and institutional frameworks on the one hand and growth in per capita incomes and increased investment on the other, using quantitative indicators constructed for this purpose (see for example, Kaufmann, Kraay and Zoido-Lobaton, 1999, 2000, 2002; Hellman, Jones and Kaufmann, 2000). As pointed out in Minogue (2005), however, the aggregate nature of the indicators that support these studies detract from the usefulness of the findings. Moreover, the indicators cannot determine an association between a particular type of reform and specific performance improvement and are also too generalized to be of any value in identifying the underlying causes of particular governance problems and coming up with practical reform targets (Manning, Mukherjee and Gokcekus, 2000).

The specific research and policy questions being explored in this chapter deal with the extent to which regulatory impact assessment (RIA) can usefully be employed in the development of practical regulatory reform strategies and in the pursuit of improved regulatory governance practices in Sri Lanka. RIA is broadly defined as:

> an information-based analytical approach to assess probable costs, consequences, and side effects of planned policy instruments (laws, regulations, etc.) . . . [and] to evaluate the real costs and consequences of policy instruments after they have been implemented . . . a means to inform government choices: choices about policy instruments, about the design of a specific instrument, or about the need to change or discontinue an existing instrument. (Lee, 2002, p. 12 citing SIGMA, 2001, p. 10)

The rationale for choosing a broader definition of RIA for this analysis is two-fold. First, given that the regulatory process is a complex, 'messy' process involving several interconnected policy variables, rather than a logical sequence of events, any analysis of regulation is complete only if it can be extended into the broader policy bowl. Second, in view of the strong parallels between regulatory governance and governance in general, lessons that can be drawn from the RIA process could provide valuable insights on broader governance issues.

Regulation in Sri Lanka has for the most part been incompatible with the needs of an economy and a society undergoing extensive reforms (Knight-John, 2004a and 2004b). In the case of privatization for instance – a process that was carried out extensively in Sri Lanka since the late 1980s – privatization often preceded the establishment of regulation, reflecting the prominence accorded to fiscal imperatives and leading to unfavourable distributional consequences (Knight-John, 2005). In addition, weak regulation coupled with privatization produced a huge source of continued rent-extraction for politicians and their cronies (Jayasuriya and Knight-John, 2002). Studies that document the general governance climate in the country also indicate an unfavourable situation, with Sri Lanka scoring 3.5 out of 10 on the international corruption perception index compiled in 2004 by Transparency International for 146 countries, the police being perceived as the most corrupt public institution in the country and nearly all Sri Lankan households surveyed admitting to bribing the judiciary (Lanka Business Online, 'Informed Choice', 2 June, 2005 http://www.lbo.lk).

The chapter focuses on the opportunities and challenges associated with the introduction of RIA as a strategy for improved regulatory governance in Sri Lanka. It draws on the results of a consultative process that was designed to elicit the view of a wide range of stakeholders in Sri Lanka, including experts from regulatory agencies, operators, the media and the non-governmental sector. This consultation process informed the development of a Concept Paper on RIA for submission to the government. The next section sets out some crucial conceptual concerns pertaining to the use of RIA in a developing country, drawing also from the feedback received from the Expert Consultation on the RIA Concept Paper for Sri Lanka. The third section details salient issues in the Concept Paper and the fourth section concludes.

SOME KEY CONCEPTUAL ISSUES

The interest in regulation as a mode of governance has spawned a huge literature – largely relating to developed countries – on the regulatory state, regulatory space, regulatory capture and independent regulation (see for instance, Hansher and Moran, 1989; Wilks, 1996; Majone, 1997, 1999; Stern, 1997; Scott, 2000; Moran, 2002). The focus on RIA as a means of regulatory reform also has its roots in advanced economies, with the USA and Member Countries of the OECD spearheading the process, whereas research on the subject as it relates to a developing country context is still at an embryonic stage. Analyses by Kirkpatrick, Parker and Zhang (2004) based on a questionnaire administered to a sample of developing and transition economies, and by Jacobs (2005b) on the role of RIA in the democratization process in selected transition states in Central and Eastern Europe, indicate that whilst there is a growing awareness of the concept, its application is patchy and inconsistent.

Why has the spread of RIA been so limited in less developed countries? Is it an issue of policy transfer, where the 'international best practices' promulgated by the OECD do not sit well in economies that strive not only towards greater efficiency in resource allocation but also towards reducing poverty? Or is it a 'chicken and egg' dilemma where RIA requires a pre-existing level and genre of 'good governance' that is not present in developing countries. Conversely, can RIA facilitate the creation of islands of good governance amidst oceans of bad governance? Or, given the messy nature of policy-making, where interest groups, politics and patron–client relations drive and shape the decision-making process, does the rational-synoptic and technocratic perception of the policy process, implicit in the OECD's RIA template, 'lead to impact assessment systems which crash against the walls of administrative feasibility, lack of legitimacy and proliferation of instruments badly assimilated by civil servants and politicians' (Radaelli, 2002)?

Majone (1997, p. 301) has cautioned against inappropriate policy transfer: 'The notion that regulatory models established in developed economies can be transferred into a contextless environment is clearly a dangerously naive conception, and there may well be a need to adapt idealised models of regulation to particular variations between national, political and administrative cultures, so that an adaptive process must be specific to each national regime'. What is significant in this regard is that a persistent concern expressed by the various stakeholders commenting on the Concept Paper, was the applicability of this methodology in developing countries in general and in Sri Lanka in particular.[1]

A related concern aired at the Expert Consultation was the feasibility of adopting the quantitative requirements – or the cost–benefit component – of the RIA method as set out in the processes followed in the advanced economies, given the significant data and technical inadequacies in Sri Lanka. It was pointed out that basing an RIA on erroneous data would distort the decision-making process and have counterproductive consequences for regulatory reform.[2]

Whatever the merits or otherwise of the case for cost–benefit analysis may be, the redeeming feature for RIA is its inclusion of the *process* element – where for instance, consultation procedures can be used not only to enhance transparency and accountability and incorporate principles of good governance, but also as an assessment technique. As such, RIA could be employed usefully through mechanisms such as perceptions surveys and focus groups, in countries such as Sri Lanka where quantitative methods have a weaker base.

THE RIA CONCEPT PAPER

The RIA Concept Paper developed to be handed over to the government was the result of a consultative process involving a number of stakeholders from the regulatory and policy space. This section sets out some key elements of the Concept Paper, before proceeding to its details. It should be noted that whilst Sri Lanka does not have a formal RIA process in place, there have been two significant attempts at incorporating the policy in a partial manner – one embedded in the Regulatory Manual of the Public Utilities Commission of Sri Lanka and the other in the Deregulation Process undertaken by the Public Interest Program Unit set up by the previous government to spearhead the reform process. However, a change of regime and the associated reversals of policies, which have now become a regular feature of governance in Sri Lanka, prevented further progress in this area.

The definition of RIA adopted for the purpose of the Concept Paper is 'a process used to assess the likely consequences of proposed regulation, and the actual consequences of existing regulations, to assist those engaged in planning, approving and implementing improvements to regulatory systems' (Lee, 2002). Whilst recognizing the value of using a broader definition of RIA, those who compiled the Concept Paper were of the view that emphasizing RIA as a tool for regulatory reform – as against its potential as a tool for broader policy reform – at least at the initial stage, would bring about less resistance from vested groups and be a better 'marketing strategy' as far as the government was concerned.

In setting out the objectives of RIA in the Sri Lankan context, the Concept Paper emphasizes the role of RIA as a tool for pro-poor growth (equity) and enhanced regulatory governance, and argues that the well-being of the citizen has to be at the heart of the process. This citizen-centric approach is reflected in the examples set out in the paper, ranging from the obstacles faced by farmers as well as investors due to inefficient land legislation, the hardships faced by businesses because of a badly conceptualized Economic Service Charge, the loss of revenue to the country with the illegal by-passing of international traffic given inadequacies in the International Traffic By-Pass Control Rules, and the threats to consumers and small businesses from the 'politically-motivated' stripping of monopolies and mergers provisions from the Competition Law.

In the short to medium term, RIA should be targeted and developed in central government, given the need for endorsement at the highest political level. As previous experience with reforms in Sri Lanka indicate, it is easier to introduce new processes at the provincial and local government levels, if first legitimacy has been established at the centre. As such, the paper proposes an incremental approach, starting with the centre and gradually moving into the other levels of government using strategies such as pilot studies that have local relevance.

Given the need for political endorsement at the highest levels, the Concept Paper suggests three options for the location of a central RIA unit: the President's Office, the Cabinet Office or the Ministry of Finance. Whilst the last was chosen because of the central, coordinating role it plays in the development process and the links it has with the other ministries, one pertinent concern that remains is the possibility of fiscal imperatives taking precedence over other objectives of RIA if the Ministry of Finance overlooks the unit.

An issue for decision-makers is the duration of the unit's life – specifically, if it ought to function as a sunset body that fades out as RIA practices get progressively embedded in the regulatory culture of the country. Alternatively, if there is justification for a continuing entity to provide for regulatory oversight and guidance, a recommendation for the medium to long term is to convert the unit into a separate legal entity, under an Act of Parliament and with the involvement of the Constitutional Council in the appointments procedure.

The mandate for the RIA unit should be to establish standards for regulatory quality and principles of regulatory decision-making, and to provide the necessary support to the line ministries and regulatory agencies that will in turn carry out RIAs. This requires the formulation of an RIA template to guide the decision-making process. The RIA template should address the following three issues: the role of RIA in achieving sustainability and poverty reduction goals; the timing and extent of public consultation in an RIA and processes for coordination within government; and coordination of RIA with more narrowly focused impact assessment processes, such as environmental impact assessment (EIA) and social impact assessment (SIA). In order to rationalize time and resource costs associated with the implementation of this process, the RIAs should be confined to those regulations that have the most significant positive and negative distributional or efficiency impacts. This can be achieved by the use of screening criteria. The following screening criteria can be used for this purpose: 1) identify the key stakeholders affected by the proposed regulation (for example, consumers, businesses, investors, regulators, law enforcement authorities), together with a rough quantification (e.g., *x* number of businesses); 2) identify the potential impacts, positive and negative, on each of the key stakeholders (e.g., for business the additional costs to be incurred to comply with the regulation, for consumers the better safety standards, for regulators the increased costs of monitoring compliance); 3) considering the above two points together, give an impact rating of high, medium or low to each positive/negative impact; and 4) where one or more impacts are rated as 'high', or two or more impacts are rated as 'medium', the screening process would suggest that it is advisable to undertake an RIA.

A practical issue of concern requiring the urgent input of key decision-makers is the need to coordinate the RIA process with the already well-established EIA process in Sri Lanka. Whilst analyses of RIA in the UK (see for example, Jacobs, 2005a) indicate that the departments responsible for EIA in the UK were willing to place these under the RIA umbrella, given the broad and flexible nature of the RIA process, it is likely that there will be significant resistance to such an approach in Sri Lanka. This anticipated problem with coordination, coupled with the fact that the EIA process in Sri Lanka is in itself a rather fragmented and haphazard one, could create significant obstacles to the effective implementation of RIA if it is not tackled at the very outset. As expressed at the Expert Consultation, for instance, it is vital that the powers in charge of regulatory reform establish some ordering or sequencing for the application of these different methods, to prevent a situation of regulatory overkill.

Technical capacity would be a priority for the RIA unit and it would need to be able to attract high-quality professionals in order to fulfil its mandate effectively. In this regard and in order to have the flexibility to pay market-based salaries, the Concept Paper recommends that the RIA unit be exempt from the standard Administrative and Financial Regulations that govern public sector entities, whilst adopting a transparent operations manual that should be open to public inspection to ensure adherence to principles of accountability. The paper calls for the setting up of a multi-skill professional base in the unit, drawing from the fields of economics, engineering, law, and ideally also sociology and environment, with staff being recruited on a full-time basis. Moreover, it is recommended that the organizational structure should be skills-based, with teamwork being accorded priority, minimal hierarchy, and outsourcing and contracting-out given precedence over staff expansion to preserve a lean entity.

The paper suggests that there should be a Cabinet decision requiring that all secretaries to ministries, heads of departments and chairpersons of authorities that exercise regulatory powers undertake an RIA, before placing any new regulation that meets the predetermined screening criteria for ministerial signature. To underpin this, it should be further required that the draft regulations and their accompanying RIAs should be submitted to the unit for review, and the non-binding opinion of the unit obtained within a specified number of days, before the regulation can be passed. Moreover, it is recommended that the unit publicizes its opinion in order to enhance transparency and accountability and improve regulatory governance.

Finally, the Concept Paper sets out cases that have a direct impact on the population as possible pilot studies, as a practical strategy to solicit political and broader stakeholder buy-in for the RIA process, as well as to identify through applied research the opportunities and challenges associated with the use of RIA in Sri Lanka. Examples of cases selected as potential pilot studies include the price control formula on pharmaceutical products, the calling party pays tariff in mobile telephony and amendments to the value-added tax (VAT).

CONCLUSIONS

The importance of building 'well-governed' institutions based on 'international best practice' to promote growth and to reduce poverty has become a much chanted mantra in the donor community with this ideology being transferred to developing countries through donor-funded programmes and policy advice. Whilst recognizing that good governance is indeed critical to the sustainable development of a society and an economy, the pertinent questions remain: what is good governance and what is 'best practice'? Can what is defined as good governance in developed societies or a version of it be assimilated into a developing country context? And if not, what are the specific factors that need to be taken into consideration in attempts to improve governance practices in developing countries?

In spite of recent attempts through donor-funded projects to improve governance and regulatory governance in particular, the focus on governance is more rhetorical than real in Sri Lanka, largely due to the configuration of interest groups and rent-seekers that benefit from maintaining the status quo. This raises significant doubts as to the robustness of the concept of 'independent' regulation as defined in the context of well-governed societies in countries that have weak governance structures. As argued in Samarajiva (2002), 'workable independence' maybe a better way to conceptualize the issue in developing countries. Moreover, such public policy – including regulation – is inherently a political process. As such, regulatory strategies have to be attuned to political nuances if they are to be effective and not result in implementation deficits (Minogue, 2005).

Politicians and civil servants are seldom interested in reforms that produce results in several years' time (Downs, 1957). Hence, it is the political electoral cycle that matters, even in developed societies such as the USA. This phenomenon is more pronounced in countries like Sri Lanka, where dissolving of parliament, fresh elections, and ad hoc changes in ministerial portfolios and civil servant positions, even without regime changes, are frequent occurrences. This brings a new dimension to the reform process and to getting deep 'buy-in' for reforms, such as RIA, which could take several years to demonstrate results. More often than not, such reforms are taken on board merely to satisfy international donors with little commitment from those that implement them, resulting in a patchy and distorted application of the processes.

The issue then is to develop strategies that blend with the vote-maximization objectives pursued by politicians and that do not pose a threat to the position of civil servants. One solution – which is the one adopted in the RIA Concept Paper developed for Sri Lanka discussed in this chapter – is to aim for 'buy-in' from a broad spectrum of stakeholders, putting the citizen at the centre of the process by undertaking pilots on cases that affect the average citizen. This strategy has the twin benefits of being able to evaluate the opportunities and challenges associated with RIA in Sri Lanka, as well as being palatable to politicians and decision-makers that cater to the general masses. In the final instance the key questions are: what is the counterfactual; what is the situation in the absence of RIA; can regulatory governance be improved if RIA becomes established in Sri Lanka's regulatory culture?

NOTES

1. To cite one of the participants at the Expert Consultation: 'An approach of looking at "best practice" elsewhere and applying it here won't work or sell. We need to do it the other

way around – look at the "holes" in our regulatory governance and then identify practices that can be tailored to stitch these up. The mechanism maybe RIA – or it maybe some other regulatory reform approach. But we must not rush into adopting blueprints.'

2. As reflected in an article titled 'The Regulator's Best Friend?' in *The Economist*, 31 March 2005, which claims that Europeans embrace the logic of cost–benefit analysis just as Americans grow suspicious of it, players in Sri Lanka's regulatory space are perhaps not alone in their wariness.

REFERENCES

Beardsley, Scott and Diana Farrell (2005), 'Regulation That's Good for Competition', in *The McKinsey Quarterly*, No. 2. McKinsey Global Institute.

De Silva, Harsha and Abu Saeed Khan (2004), 'Regulation and Investment: Case Study of Bangladesh', World Dialogue on Regulation, Discussion Paper, http://www.regulateonline.org/content/view/224/65/.

Downs, Anthony (1957), *An Economic Theory of Democracy*, Addison-Wesley Publishing Company.

Estache, Antonio (2004), 'Emerging Infrastructure Policy Issues in Developing Countries: AQ Survey of the Recent Economic Literature', Background Paper for the October 2004 Berlin meeting of the POVNET Infrastructure Working Group.

Hansher, L. and M. Moran (1989), *Capitalism, Culture and Regulation*, Oxford: Oxford University Press.

Hellman, J.S., G. Jones and D. Kaufmann (2000), 'Seize the State, Seize the Day: State Capture, Corruption and Influence in Transition', Paper presented at World Bank Annual Bank Conference on Development Economics, April, Washington DC.

Jacobs, Colin (2005a), 'Improving the Quality of Regulatory Impact Assessments in the UK', Centre on Regulation and Competition Working Paper No. 102, Manchester: Centre on Regulation and Competition, University of Manchester.

Jacobs, Colin (2005b), 'The Role of Regulatory Impact Assessment in Democratisation: Selected Cases from the Transition States of Central and Eastern Europe', Centre on Regulation and Competition Working Paper No. 101, Manchester: Centre on Regulation and Competition, University of Manchester.

Jayasuriya, Sisira and Malathy Knight-John (2002), 'Sri Lanka's Telecommunications Industry: From Privatization to Anti-Competition?', Centre on Regulation and Competition Working Paper Series, Paper No. 14. Manchester: Centre on Regulation and Competition, University of Manchester.

Kaufmann, Daniel, Aart Kraay and Pablo Zoido-Lobaton (1999), 'Aggregating Governance Indicators', Policy Research Working Paper No. 2195, Washington DC: World Bank.

Kaufmann, Daniel, Aart Kraay and Pablo Zoido-Lobaton (2000), 'Governance Matters: From Measurement to Action', *Finance and Development*, **37** (2), 101–13.

Kaufmann, Daniel, Aart Kraay and Pablo Zoido-Lobaton (2002), 'Governance Matters II: Updated Indicators for 2000/01', World Bank Working Paper No. 2772, Washington DC: World Bank.

Kirkpatrick, Colin, David Parker and Yin-Fang Zhang (2004), 'Regulatory Impact Assessment in Developing and Transition Economies: A Survey of Current Practice', Centre on Regulation and Competition Working Paper

No. 83, Manchester: Centre on Regulation and Competition, University of Manchester.

Knight-John, Malathy (2004a), 'Privatization and Regulation', in Saman Kelegama (ed.), *Economic Policy in Sri Lanka: Issues and Debates – A Festschrift in Honour of Gamani Corea*, Sage Publications.

Knight-John, Malathy (2004b), 'Regulation and Regulatory Governance in Sri Lanka', in P. Cook, C. Kirkpatrick, M. Minogue and D. Parker (eds), *Leading Issues in Competition, Regulation and Development*, Cheltenham, UK and Northampton, MA, USA: Edward Elgar.

Knight-John, Malathy (2004c), 'Adopting Regulatory Impact Assessment in Sri Lanka: A Tool For Better Regulatory Policy?', in *Law and Governance*, **3**, 2003/2004, 44, British Council.

Knight-John, Malathy (2005), 'Distributional Impacts of Privatization: The Sri Lankan Experience', in John Nellis and Nancy Birdsall (eds), *Reality Check: The Distributional Impact of Privatization*, Washington DC: Center for Global Development.

Knight-John, Malathy, Shantha Jayasinghe and Andrew Perumal (2004), 'Regulatory Impact Assessment in Sri Lanka: The Bridges that have to be Crossed', Centre on Regulation and Competition Working Paper No. 74, Manchester: Centre on Regulation and Competition, University of Manchester.

Lee, Norman (2002), 'Developing and Applying Regulatory Impact Assessment Methodologies in Low and Middle Income Countries', Centre on Regulation and Competition Working Paper Series, Paper No. 30, Manchester: Centre on Regulation and Competition, University of Manchester.

Loayza, Norman, Ana Maria Oviedo and Luis Serven (2004), 'Regulation and Macroeconomic Performance', Mimeo.

Majone, G. (1997), 'From the Positive to the Regulatory State: Causes and Consequences of the Changes in Modes of Governance', *Journal of Public Policy*, **17** (2), 139–67.

Majone, G. (1999), 'The Regulatory State and its Legitimacy Problems', *West European Politics*, **22** (1), 1–24.

Manning, Nick, Ranjana Mukherjee and Omer Gokcekus (2000), 'Public Officials and their Institutional Environment: An Analytical Model for Assessing the Impact of Institutional Change', World Bank Working Paper No. 2427, Washington DC: World Bank.

Minogue, Martin (2005), 'Apples and Oranges: Problems in the Analysis of Comparative Regulatory Governance', Centre on Regulation and Competition Working Paper Series, Paper No. 94. Manchester: Centre on Regulation and Competition, University of Manchester.

Moran, M. (2002), 'Understanding the Regulatory State', *British Journal of Political Science*, **32**, 391–413.

Nicoletti, Giuseppe and Stefano Scarpetta (2003), 'Regulation, Productivity, and Growth: OECD Evidence', Policy Research Working Paper No. 2944, Washington DC: World Bank.

Radaelli, C.M. (2002), 'The Politics of Regulatory Impact Analysis in the OECD Countries: Best Practice and Lesson-drawing', Mimeo.

Samarajiva, Rohan (2002), 'Utility Regulation and Competition Policy in Sri Lanka: Prospects for Change', in Malathy Knight-John (ed.), *Competition Policy and Utility Regulation: The Sri Lankan Experience*, Colombo: Law & Society Trust.

Samarajiva, Rohan and Anupama Dokeniya (2004), 'Regulation and Investment: Sri Lanka Case Study', World Dialogue on Regulation, Discussion Paper, http://www.regulateonline.org/content/view/207/65/.
Scott, Colin (2000), 'Accountability in the Regulatory State', *Journal of Law and Society*, **27** (1), 38–60.
SIGMA, (2001), 'Improving Policy Instruments through Impact Assessment', SIGMA Paper No. 31, Paris: OECD.
Stern, Jon (1997), 'What Makes an Independent Regulator Independent?', *Business Strategy Review*, Summer, 67–75.
Wilks, S. (1996), 'Regulatory Compliance and Capitalist Diversity in Europe', *Journal of European Public Policy*, **3**, 536–59.

11. Regulatory impact assessment in East Africa

Darren Welch

INTRODUCTION

This chapter discusses the growing interest in regulatory impact assessment (RIA) that is being witnessed in East Africa and describes the first attempts at adoption of RIA systems in the three countries that comprise the East African Community: Uganda, Kenya and Tanzania. The chapter will focus mainly on Uganda as a case study, as that is where most progress has been made at the time of writing (spring 2006).[1]

There are six sections to the chapter. The next section discusses the growing interest in RIA in East Africa. This is followed by a summary of the benefits of RIA that East African and other developing countries are aiming to realize. The next section looks at the contribution of RIA to the policy process. After that, we describe how RIA methodologies and systems have been modified in the case of Uganda, and the final concluding section discusses the need for a phased and change management approach to establishing RIA in developing country contexts.

GROWING INTEREST IN RIA IN EAST AFRICA

Over the last five years there has been a growing interest in RIA in East Africa with Uganda, Kenya and Tanzania all taking steps towards adoption of RIA as part of their efforts to improve the business environment, in order to stimulate growth and investment.[2] These efforts are supported by donors, generally under private sector development initiatives, although there are close links with public sector reform programmes, given that RIA is about creating an improved policy-making function. In Uganda the introduction of RIA is taking place under the broad auspices of that country's Medium-term Competitiveness Strategy. In Tanzania a group of donors are funding RIA work under the government's Business Environment Strengthening for Tanzania (BEST) programme; and in

Kenya RIA forms part of the donor-supported Economic Recovery Strategy for Wealth and Employment Creation.

Some of the interest in RIA is inevitably driven by donor countries, many of which have themselves adopted and embedded RIA systems over the past 20 years as a means of improving their regulatory environments, for example, the US, UK, Canada and the Netherlands. As these countries, and indeed the European Commission too, have seen the benefits of RIA, they are increasingly making it a feature of their development assistance. Multilaterals too are pressing the advantages of RIA; the 2005 *World Development Report* (World Bank, 2004) contains strong exhortations and advice to reduce the burden of regulation, noting that most countries have huge scope for improving regulation, including through the use of RIA, without compromising broader social interests. The World Bank's Foreign Investment Advisory Service is supporting RIA initiatives in countries as diverse as Slovakia and Bangladesh.

Each East African Community country is finding that RIA has the ability to address the specific issues and challenges that have resulted from the country's own historical context and from the trajectory of its economic development. These factors are described briefly below, along with a description of progress with adopting RIA in each country.

Tanzania

Tanzania is emerging from a history of heavy-handed socialist regulation influenced by the communist-Chinese model and embodied in the 1967 Arusha Declaration and the economic and social policies of Julius Nyerere. As such the country is hampered by the legacy of a highly regulated economy and a command and control approach to administration and enforcement. Regulatory systems are not well developed to support a flourishing market economy that will create growth and jobs. It is anticipated that RIA will assist the government to strike a better balance in regulatory matters, reducing burdens on business and adopting a facilitative approach to a liberalized, market-based economy.

As noted, RIA is a key component of the Government of Tanzania's Business Environment Strengthening for Tanzania (BEST) programme. BEST was approved in 2002 as a five-year programme to reduce the burden of regulation and improve the services provided by government. The programme was provided with US$25 million of funding by four donors – the UK's Department for International Development (DFID), Danish International Development Agency (DANIDA), Swedish International Development Cooperation Agency (SIDA) and the Royal Netherlands Embassy. The BEST Programme document has RIA in its first and fourth components, 'Achieving better regulation' and 'Changing the culture of government', respectively.

RIA is already being used to a limited extent for new policy reforms in Tanzania; members of the BEST programme's technical working groups are preparing basic RIAs to accompany their proposals for new legislation. The Government's Better Regulation Unit (BRU) in the Office of the President is spearheading efforts to improve RIA practice, building capacity levels and strengthening the robustness of systems. At present the RIA system is not backed up by an institution with a mandate to assure quality, although this is under consideration.

So far the government has carried out significant awareness-raising and capacity-building for RIA. In 2004 a number of seminars were organized for senior public and private sector representatives with the aim of raising awareness of the need for better quality regulation and for a reduction in regulatory burden. This exercise aimed to begin a process of changing mindsets amongst public officials, orienting them towards a different role for government. The private sector representatives were informed of the important role they could play in bringing pressure to bear on government for reform, and in using evidence-based analysis of regulatory burden when advocating reform.

One instructive finding from Tanzania is that participants in RIA training wanted joint training for public and private sectors rather than separate events. The history of consensual policy-making in Tanzania meant that participants felt that separate training hinted at a more confrontational future relationship between public and private sectors, something that was perceived as an unwelcome development. This points to the need to take account of contextual factors when approaching the institutionalization of regulatory best practice (RBP) and RIA.

Following this initial awareness-raising exercise, the government commissioned more in-depth training for senior Tanzanian officials on the specific tool of RIA. A one-week, full-time training course was provided for about 50 members of the government's business environment reform working groups. The aim was to equip participants with the skills necessary to carry out more substantial RIAs as part of their work proposing reforms to business regulation. Towards the end of the course participants developed a plan for introducing a more formal system of RIA into government processes and presented this to the BRU, suggesting roles and responsibilities for institutions to ensure that RIA becomes an integral part of policy-making.

A further phase taking place in 2006 will include building local capacity for RIA training, training of trainers, rolling out of training in both central and local government, as well as taking forward plans for the institutionalization of RIA.

Kenya

Kenya's economic development since independence has been characterized by political and economic patronage, regional instability, drought, the autocratic leadership of Daniel Arap Moi and pervasive corruption. In 1990 donors withdrew support from Kenya following the assassination of the Foreign Minister, Robert Ouko, who had threatened to reveal the names of corrupt ministers. Poor quality policy-making has held back economic development with negative growth during the 1990s in the majority of sectors. In 2003 the new government adopted its Economic Recovery Strategy for Wealth and Employment Creation (ERS). This strategy included a section on regulatory reform with activities aimed at reducing costs on small businesses and at reducing the informal sector. This has included simplifying rules and regulations and removing unjustified regulatory requirements.

RIA has not yet become a central element of enabling environment activity in Kenya under the ERS or other development initiatives, and Kenya is perhaps the least advanced country in East Africa in terms of adopting RIA. There are however, activities underway to adopt an RBP approach to regulation more generally, including through the abolition of some of the most costly business licences.

In keeping with trends elsewhere in enabling policy environment reform, initial better regulation activity in Kenya focused on pure deregulation, that is, removal of regulatory and administrative barriers to market entry and to enterprise growth. There were, for example, two phases of DFID activity targeted at deregulation between 1996 and 2003. Some notable successes were achieved including in the area of business licensing where a single business permit was introduced in 1998.

Only later after the Moi administration did there begin to be a growing awareness of the need to have techniques for improving the quality of regulatory proposals on a systematic basis. Recent enabling environment work has included an enabling environment project to promote and facilitate a more conducive business climate for growth. DFID continued to sponsor enabling environment work in Kenya and provided funding to the Kenya Institute for Public Policy Research and Analysis (KIPPRA) in order to advance work on RIA and on the better regulation agenda more generally. KIPPRA did produce a Better Regulation Guide in 2002 that encouraged the use of RIA but this failed to find support within the administration and RIA is not widely used.

As of mid-2006 there are signs that more headway is being made. For example, the government announced it its budget speech that there were plans to establish an RIA unit within government and that a regulatory reform strategy would be developed and embedded in the Ministry of Finance.

Uganda

The case of Uganda is dealt with as a case study in detail below. The country's Poverty Eradication Action Plan makes clear that constraints on private sector competitiveness need to be removed in order to promote economic transformation, growth and job creation. Better regulation and RIA within it are seen as key tools that the government will use to achieve its economic growth targets. The government has been supported in its reform efforts by a number of donors, notably DFID, which has supported a Deregulation Programme (2000–03) and a second phase known as the Regulatory Best Practice Programme (2003–06). The RBP programme has moved beyond the reduction of individual regulatory burdens to a phase of embedding the process of regulatory reform within institutions in Uganda, including through the introduction of RIA. With specific regard to RIA, the programme has:

- developed guidance on RBP and secured endorsement by the President of Uganda for RBP principles to be adopted by government. Cabinet too, in 2006, endorsed RBP principles as the basis for regulation;
- developed a methodology for RIA that meets the needs of the Ugandan context;
- trained officials in the use of the methodology and created local training capacity in RIA;
- helped establish an RIA unit within the government that will monitor and police the quality of RIAs;
- provided advice on institutional arrangements to support RIA;
- provided ongoing mentoring, training and assistance to officials as RIA takes hold within the system, including training in microeconomic methods for calculating the impact of proposed regulations.

Table 11.1 shows how far each East African country has attained levels of good practice along certain dimensions of RIA adoption.

THE BENEFITS OF RIA

The benefits of RIA and of a RBP approach to government are well known and have been documented by the World Bank, OECD, EU, national

Table 11.1 Good practice activities to support RIA in Kenya, Tanzania and Uganda

Good Practice Activities to Support RIA	Kenya	Tanzania	Uganda
Senior political commitment to RBP/RIA expressed	✓ – RBP only, in Kibaki govt's economic recovery strategy	✓ – through adoption of BEST	✓ – presidential level
Awareness-raising activity for public sector		✓ – initial workshops	✓ – sustained activity
Awareness-raising activity for private sector/NGOs		✓ – initial workshops	✓ – sustained activity
Efforts to make public aware of need for RBP/RIA			✓ – sustained media activity and training of business journalists
Formal guidance on components of good regulation			✓ – guide to good regulation
Formal RIA methodology			✓ – under consideration by govt. Draft guidance produced
Formal requirement for RIA			✓ – proposed Cabinet memo will introduce formal requirement. Ministry of Finance already interpreting its role as requiring impact of costs of regulation to be considered
Training available locally in RIA methodology		✓ – under development	✓ – Uganda Management Institute offering RIA training
Training offered to government officials who will use methodology			✓ – govt policy analysts trained
RBP unit established in government		✓ – under BEST, BRU performs	✓ – from 2006, RBP unit being established in Ministry of Tourism, Trade & Industry.

Table 11.1 (continued)

Good Practice Activities to Support RIA	Kenya	Tanzania	Uganda
		part of the role	Until 2005, activity focused on donor project housed in Ministry of Finance
RIA unit established in government		✓ – under consideration	✓ – embryonic RIA unit functioning in Cabinet Office (Office of the President)
Designated officials in ministries given RIA responsibility		✓ – members of BEST programme working groups, drawn from ministries, responsible for RIAs	✓ – policy analysts in ministries
Parliament encouraged to demand RIAs to improve quality of debate			✓ – seminars run for Parliamentarians
Independent review (audit) of sample RIAs undertaken			

governments and other organizations. They are discussed in other chapters of this book.

The benefits that RIA brings to governments are largely the same whether the country is developed or developing, that is, evidence-based policy aimed at delivering economic growth through more efficient regulation and fewer burdens for business. However, the problems that RIAs seek to address are perhaps more acute amongst developing countries and therefore the advantages correspondingly greater.

In particular, RIA has the potential to make a strong contribution towards poverty reduction. Figure 11.1 suggests that at the aggregate level, broad economic growth could be closely associated with a reduction in poverty – the 'rising tide lifts all boats' theory. Whilst many see a clear link between better regulation, economic growth and poverty reduction, RIA

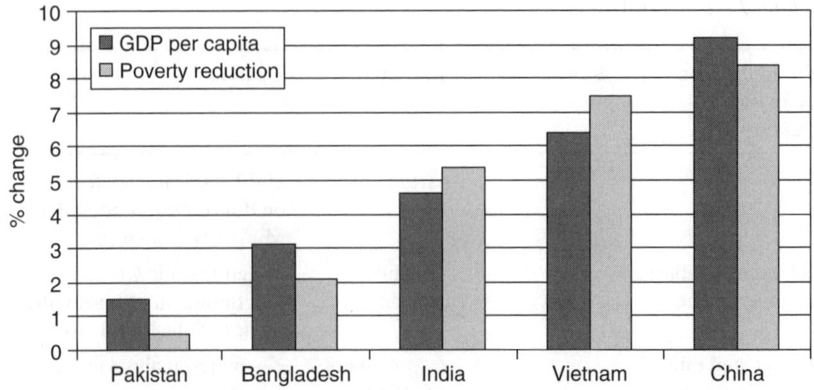

Source: World Bank (2004, p. 3).

Figure 11.1 Growth and poverty reduction (percentage change per year, 1992–98)

can help ensure that economic growth is pro-poor. It can do this by encouraging policy-makers to focus on the needs of micro and small enterprises and to assess the impact of proposed new regulations specifically on the poor.

Micro and small and medium-sized enterprises (MSMEs), constitute the majority of businesses in many countries but especially so in the developing world. These MSMEs are more vulnerable to regulatory burdens than larger firms as they are not able to take advantage of economies of scale. It is in this sector that most of the poor make their livelihoods. MSMEs account for a substantial share of total employment and gross domestic product and they contribute significantly to poverty reduction. Many of them operate in the informal sector and allow individuals to support a significant number of family members. On average the informal economy in Africa is estimated to have been 42 per cent of GDP in 1999/2000 (Schneider, 2002). Uganda and Tanzania were at the high end with 43 per cent and 58 per cent respectively (Figure 11.2).

Micro and small enterprises are particularly important to growth and development of the Ugandan economy and to the government's efforts to lift people out of poverty. It is estimated that 70 per cent of Ugandan enterprises employ fewer than five people. Establishing a micro-business, perhaps simply as a sole trader, offers an escape route from poverty for some people and the government understands the importance of putting as few barriers as possible in the way of that process. Therefore, as part of the RIA methodology being introduced in Uganda, policy-makers are

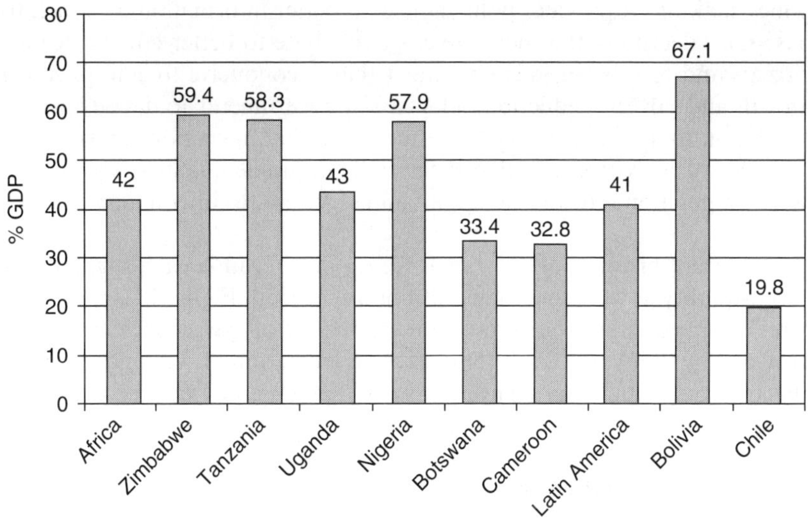

Source: Schneider (2002).

Figure 11.2 Informal economy as a share of national income (percentage of GDP in 1999/2000)

encouraged to specify whether their proposal will entail additional costs to small businesses, what any such costs are and how much the typical small business in the sector is likely to have to pay.

It would be a mistake to think that informal economy enterprises operate beyond the reach of the effects of regulation. For example, non-compliance with regulation leaves enterprises vulnerable to demands for bribes from enforcement officers. Perhaps more importantly the high level of burden that an enterprise needs to overcome in order to embrace a greater degree of formality can cause many enterprises to remain in the informal economy, something that can deny them, and indeed society, the benefits of more formality, including a broader tax base and greater access to finance for the business.

Beyond the overarching goal of economic development and poverty reduction, the intermediate-level benefits of RIA as they relate to East Africa will briefly be discussed below.

Improving the Quality and Efficiency of Government Interventions

RIA is designed to increase the information brought to bear on the policy-making process and is an important contributor to rational, evidence-based policy-making. It provides politicians with better information on which to base their decisions and therefore can contribute to better governance for citizens and to a business environment that is conducive to enterprise-led growth and poverty reduction. RIAs assist governments to devise efficient regulation that addresses market failures and that in economic terms, sets the price of activities such that the socially desirable quantity is provided. Where regulation is inefficient, goods and services are either under- or over-provided.

The recent histories of Tanzania, Kenya and Uganda each suggest that better-quality government interventions are needed. Figure 11.3 shows the three countries' low relative position on one set of governance indicators provided by the World Bank. This gives an indication of weak government effectiveness, notably for Kenya but with Uganda and Tanzania also lying some way down the country rankings.

Enhancing Competitiveness

Unnecessary regulatory burdens reduce the competitiveness of individual businesses directly and indirectly reduce national competitiveness in the global economy. They reduce the resources available for investment in equipment and human capital and reduce economic efficiency. The World Bank's Doing Business Indicators show that East Africa has relatively high levels of regulatory burden. Although the region does better than many other parts of Africa, the highest-scoring country, Kenya, lies at position 68 with Tanzania at position 140 (Table 11.2).

Developing a strong competitive position becomes increasingly important as regional and global economic integration picks up pace. In East Africa regional integration is taking place through the development of the East African Community. This regional integration is allowing goods and services to flow freely between the member states, although there are time-limited protections in place to shield selected Ugandan and Tanzanian industries from Kenyan imports, given that country's head start in industrialization.

Theory and experience suggest that production will shift to those countries with a comparative advantage in the production of certain goods and services. This comparative advantage includes a conducive regulatory environment, as well as other endowments, such as a skilled labour force and natural resources. Similarly, businesses will move to those states that have the most favourable overall environment for wealth creation.

Whilst much attention is traditionally placed on tax competition between states in attracting investment and especially foreign direct investment, the regulatory environment is also a key factor in the decisions

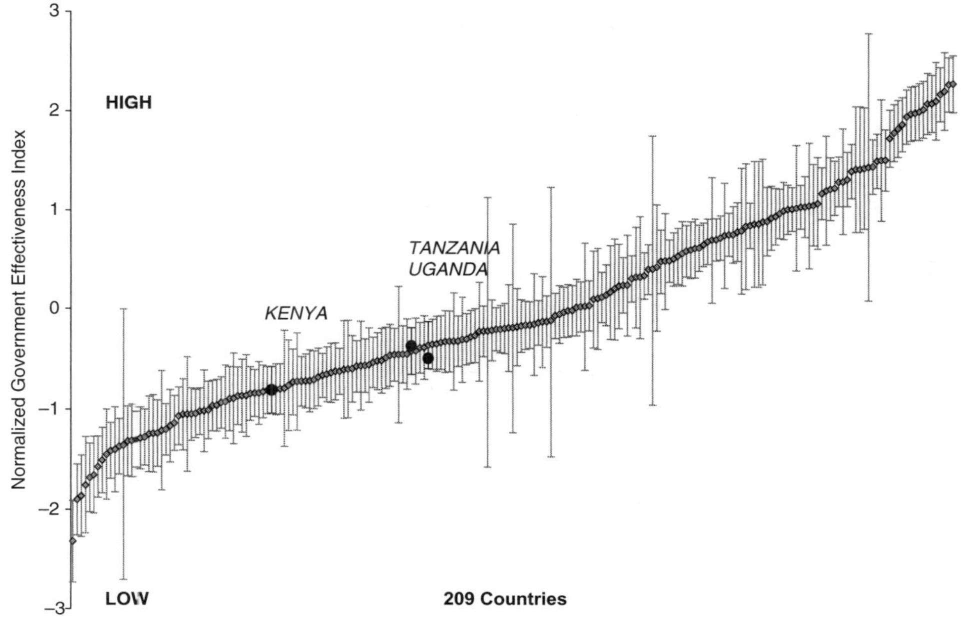

Note: Dots represent estimates for the 2004 governance indicators. The thin vertical lines represent standard errors around these estimates for each country in world-wide sample.

Sources: 'Governance Matters IV: Governance Indicators for 1996–2004', by Daniel Kaufmann, Aart Kraay and Massimo Mastruzzi (2005), Paper for the World Bank.

Figure 11.3 Government effectiveness – 2004, Kenya, Uganda and Tanzania

Table 11.2 Ease of doing business in Africa

Economy	Ease of Doing Business	Starting a Business	Dealing with Licences	Hiring and Firing	Registering Property	Getting Credit
Botswana	40	74	113	16	80	4
Zambia	67	44	85	38	111	107
Kenya	68	93	15	42	113	13
Uganda	72	100	92	10	97	127
Ghana	82	131	71	48	120	116
Nigeria	94	105	117	27	152	38
Malawi	96	70	110	41	83	85
Lesotho	97	111	56	51	117	118
Ethiopia	101	94	57	47	140	114
Mozambique	110	139	54	113	94	70
Zimbabwe	126	140	147	19	71	90
Mauritania	127	146	89	126	56	67
Benin	129	107	135	121	72	108
Cameroon	130	133	121	106	122	91
Madagascar	131	124	128	118	146	94
Senegal	132	125	68	128	137	136
Angola	135	155	122	117	145	77
Sierra Leone	136	64	134	151	139	122
Eritrea	137	150	109	40	115	143
Rwanda	139	58	106	104	124	149
Tanzania	140	113	150	136	143	125
Burundi	143	88	138	107	123	110
Guinea	144	145	144	97	133	144
Cote d'Ivoire	145	130	133	99	147	141
Mali	146	143	123	147	91	135
Congo, Rep.	148	128	81	146	136	130
Niger	150	142	129	153	90	119
Sudan	151	68	–	77	–	123
Chad	152	154	102	134	108	112
Central African Republic	153	112	116	143	87	111
Burkina Faso	154	138	149	154	148	109
Congo, Dem. Rep.	155	153	132	139	142	140

Source: World Bank (2005).

businesses make about where to locate. The World Bank's 2005 *World Development Report* states that the way in which states regulate and tax the private sector has a strong influence on the investment climate and therefore the decisions of investors and businessmen and businesswomen (World Bank, 2005, Chapter 5). This is not to say that the minimum of regulation makes for the best business environment. Business flourishes where there are the regulations necessary to provide protections and assurances to businesses and citizens to give them stability, predictability and confidence to invest without being unnecessarily burdensome. RIA helps governments to strike the right balance – a message that is important where there are fears that RIA is about stripping away social, labour and environmental protections in a laissez-faire approach to regulation.

Increasing Transparency and Accountability

RIA also contributes to transparency in government by encouraging policy-makers to set out ex ante the reasons for their policy decision, how it addresses an identified and quantified problem and the anticipated costs and benefits. Best practice in RIA stipulates that such assessments should also contain an analysis of whether any particular groups either gain or lose disproportionately from the regulatory proposal. This helps identify whether any groups are being given favourable treatment. In many jurisdictions where RIA is used, the assessments are made available publicly and are also submitted to Parliament along with draft Bills. This can improve the quality of Parliamentary debate as more information is available and thus assist the legislature to hold the executive to account on behalf of the people.

In multi-ethnic societies, the focus that RIA brings to the distribution of impacts can be particularly enlightening and encourages policy-makers to identify whether one ethnic or religious group benefits at the expense of another. In Africa generally societies are less homogeneous than in other parts of the world. Hameso (1997) provides evidence that many African countries have suffered decades of misrule and conflict due to a misunderstanding of ethnicity and the management of ethnic relations. The continent's ethnic diversity places a special responsibility on African governments to assess the distributional impacts of their proposed regulations. National unity is not served well when one group is seen unjustifiably to benefit at the cost of other groups.

East African countries are developing more accountable and transparent regulatory processes although significant impediments remain. One important factor is the level of capacity within business representative associations and civil society groups to respond in a meaningful way to opportunities to have greater input into the policy process. In both Uganda and Tanzania, the introduction of RIA in government is being accompanied by measures to sensitize external stakeholders to the need for them to engage in policy dialogue with government, using evidence-based arguments to press the case for reform. Both countries are also offering capacity-building support to stakeholders so that they can use analytical techniques to calculate compliance costs in a way that can be persuasive and useful.

Greater transparency should help contain levels of rent-seeking behaviour and contribute to economic efficiency.

Reducing Opportunities for Corruption

The more complex and open to interpretation a regulatory obligation is, the greater are the opportunities for corruption. Enforcers can use their discretion to extract bribes and the regulated businesses are incentivized to pay bribes as a way of circumventing more costly bureaucratic requirements. By encouraging minimum burdens on business and simple, clear regulations, RIAs can contribute towards an environment that is hostile to corruption. Out of 145 countries ranked on Transparency International's Corruption Perceptions Index, Kenya, Uganda and Tanzania rank at positions 129, 102 and 90 respectively (Transparency International, 2004), so there is much room for RIA to help bring about improvement. Corruption is more pervasive in many developing countries than in the OECD countries and can impede growth at the enterprise level. Small businesses in Uganda can be unwilling to invest in new equipment or in taking on employees because this would signal to the local authorities that the business was creating wealth, something that would risk inviting requests for bribes. In a 2006 survey of businesses in Uganda[3] 35 per cent of respondents said that they thought businesses like theirs had been asked to make informal or unofficial payments or facilitation fees.

Transparency International notes that corruption hits the poor harder than the rich. Its 2003 Corruption Barometer Survey revealed that 40 per cent of poor people surveyed said that corruption had a very significant effect on their family and personal life, whereas 25 per cent of comparatively wealthy people said this was the case (Transparency International, 2003). By reducing opportunities for corruption, RIA can have an especially significant impact on the quality of life of the poor.

A Tool for Policy Monitoring and Evaluation

After a regulation has been passed, the RIA carried out on that measure can provide data for ex post monitoring and evaluation and help governments review the effectiveness of their interventions. It also assists businesses to press successfully for improvements if the regulation turns out to be more burdensome than anticipated, and enables citizens to hold their governments to account for delivery of the benefits promised.

Tools also exist that enable governments to monitor the quality of their policy proposals, and more specifically the degree to which these adhere to RIA and RBP principles.[4] By evaluating a sample of proposals at the beginning of the introduction of RIA, a numerical score, or benchmark, can be established against which improvements in regulatory proposals can be measured over time.

THE QUALITY OF THE WIDER POLICY PROCESS

Putting an RIA system in place contributes to improving the quality of the policy-making process generally and to supporting a regulatory best practice approach to governance. For example, it can be a useful way of preventing policy-makers from rushing straight to drafting legislation before policy options have been considered. However, RIA alone can only contribute so far to a better policy-making process. It is important also to consider the wider policy process into which RIA fits. The policy process can be divided into the following stages, although the process is more dynamic than this implies:

1. strategic planning and prioritization;
2. initiation;
3. policy development;
4. funding provision;
5. policy approval;
6. ensuring policy implementation;
7. policy monitoring and evaluation;
8. with coordination and consultation being ongoing activities.

The inter-relationships in this process are illustrated in Figure 11.4.

RIA directly improves stages:

- Stage 3 by facilitating consultative, rational, evidence-based policy development.
- Stage 7 by providing a benchmark against which policies can be monitored and evaluated, that is, are they delivering the benefits outlined in the RIA, are the costs no more than were anticipated?
- Stage 8 by encouraging policy-makers to involve all those likely to be affected.

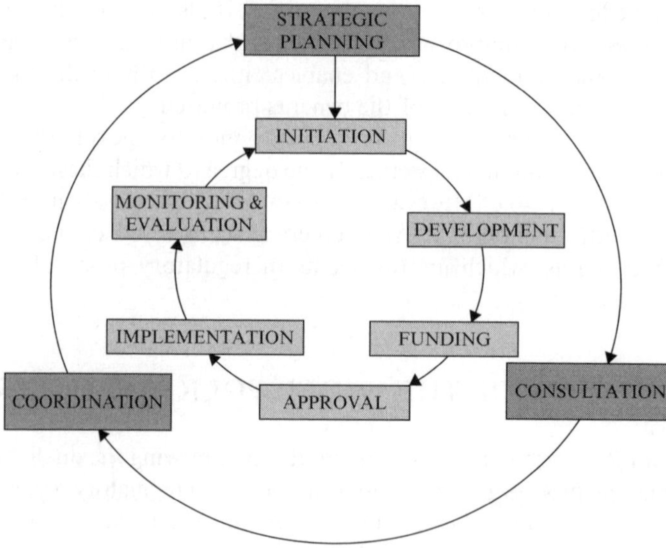

Figure 11.4 The policy process

This however, leaves a large part of the policy process untouched. For example, there is little point enabling business associations and NGOs to carry out RIA if they are unaware of the government's legislative agenda and unable to prepare analyses in time to influence the policy debate and the process of strategic planning. Nor will the best-designed policy have any impact unless the necessary resources are allocated in the budget process for its implementation. Similarly, RIA needs to find traction in the political policy approval process if it is to have real impact. RIA must therefore be part of a wider programme of policy reform and capacity-building if its full benefits are to be captured.

THE UGANDA EXPERIENCE

Although there is diversity between different countries' RIA methodologies, the role that RIAs play in the policy process and institutional responsibilities for RIA, it is possible to discern a high degree of commonality, notably in the methodologies used. Box 11.1 sets out the typical structure of an RIA methodology.

The OECD has issued best practice guidance on RIA systems as part of its regulatory reform practice area (OECD, 1997). This guidance highlights good practice and identifies common elements in OECD countries'

> **BOX 11.1 TYPICAL STRUCTURE OF AN RIA METHODOLOGY**
>
> 1. Title of proposal.
> 2. Establish the *purpose* and intended effect of the proposal.
> 3. Analyse and quantify the *policy problem*.
> 4. Determine *options* for intervention.
> 5. Assess *impacts* of options.
> 6. Analyse the *distribution of impacts*.
> 7. Consult and report the results of *consultation*.
> 8. Determine appropriate mechanisms for *enforcement and sanctions*.
> 9. Establish mechanisms for *monitoring and evaluation*.

approaches to RIA. The UK system is fairly typical in that it contains the core elements recommended in best practice guidance. It has: political support, a central unit to monitor RIAs and provide guidance to officials, an agreed methodology, published RIAs and training to support RIA use (see Chapter 3). The RIA system being implemented in Uganda is based upon this UK system, not least because of a shared Westminster-style administrative system. It comprises: 1) an RIA methodology; 2) a set of institutional arrangements that govern the use of RIA; and 3) training and guidance for officials.

Kirkpatrick and Parker (2003 and see also Chapter 6) have noted that OECD RIA systems may not transfer readily to the developing country context; and very few developing countries have adopted RIA. In designing an RIA system for Uganda, it was found that the basic components of the RIA system set out above did not need a significant amount of amendment to be applicable to the developing country context. However, it was necessary to propose changes in the way that the RIA process and notably the methodology is used.

RIA Methodology

There are common elements to many countries' RIA methodologies – regulations are usually evaluated in terms of costs and benefits, options for regulation are considered, consultation is shown to have been undertaken and often the impact on small businesses or other vulnerable groups is assessed. The core methodology used can be made content neutral and allows policy-makers in different countries to focus the methodology on addressing their own values and concerns. For example, one of the main differences in countries' RIA frameworks are the groups that are selected for special consideration as to the distribution of impacts.

Whilst the UK and Ugandan systems share an interest in ensuring that the burden of regulation does not fall disproportionately on small businesses, Uganda has a range of other groups that it wishes to consider in the policy process in order to take account of any disproportionate impact. In the guidance on RIA being piloted in Uganda, officials are encouraged to look at distributional impact on different tribes, religious groups and the various regions of the country. For example, a proposed Bill to regulate domestic relations was contested by some of Uganda's Muslim population, which has special concerns to be considered in the policy process. This is not to say that regulations with a disproportionate impact are unjustified, only that the impacts need to be carefully considered for the purposes of equity.

There are also vulnerable groups in Uganda whose needs are especially relevant in the context of the fight against poverty. The RIA methodology is providing a structure for ensuring that these groups' special needs are taken into account. Policy-makers have undertaken consultation to identify such groups whose needs require particular consideration. As a result of this consultation, the RIA will require policy-makers to consider the needs of the very poor, of people living with HIV/AIDS and gender issues. For example, in assessing the impact of new regulations on the poor, officials are encouraged to take into account the following facts:

- Adjustment is expensive for the poor who lack savings. Support measures, transition periods and exemptions might be appropriate.
- The poor are more vulnerable to changes in prices which can significantly diminish or increase real incomes.
- Social ties are very important, as they constitute a line of defence against risk. Regulations should not damage the social capital of the poor.
- The poor often lack access to services – regulation should improve access not make it harder.
- The poor often rely on informal mechanisms and may suffer if these become subject to regulation.

Another difference is in the local political objectives that are introduced into the consideration of impacts. For example in the UK, policy-makers are required to consider whether their proposals will have any impact on the country's ambition to be a leading jurisdiction for electronic commerce. Such a requirement would clearly be inappropriate for Uganda, which is at a different phase in its economic development and is focusing on sectors where it has comparative advantage, such as agriculture and fishing. It may be more appropriate for the Ugandan RIA system to require officials to state that their proposals will not unnecessarily harm those sectors that the government has selected for development as part of its export-led growth strategy. Such requirements are easily added to the impacts section of the framework as part of tailoring the way the methodology is used.

The RIA methodology tailored to the Ugandan context had to take account of the lack of reliable data available to inform policy assessment. OECD countries can generally call upon a host of business surveys to assist with the calculation of compliance costs. They also enjoy access to networks of well resourced business associations and civil society groups. A well developed insurance market can provide insights into shadow prices where impacts of proposed measures do not have a market value. None of these factors is readily available in the Ugandan context. To take account of this, policy-makers have to be trained to be creative in the way they ascribe values to the impacts of regulations. In the absence of existing data, the importance of consultation is being emphasized as a way of gaining information on impacts and their distribution and introducing user-friendly techniques for arriving at shadow prices, working with ministry economists where available.

Institutional Arrangements and Political Support

To provide institutional support for the introduction of RIA in Uganda, a new RIA unit has been established in the Cabinet Office in the Office of the President. The creation of this unit is seen as an important mechanism to ensure sustainability. Ongoing mentoring is being provided to two Ugandan officials in this new unit who are responsible for 'policing' the RIA system, providing support to ministries and checking the quality of RIAs that accompany Cabinet papers. This new unit will in the early phase of RIA introduction not be overzealous in its critique of RIAs submitted for comment. It is important that this new RIAU acts collaboratively with ministries rather than confrontationally, so that officials come to view RIA as a useful tool rather than a test that they are being set up to fail. Nonetheless, as gatekeeper for the Cabinet, this unit has significant influence to ensure that RIA is used.

The Ugandan RIAU will also compile a resource library of studies, reports and other reference materials that ministries can draw upon in their analyses to make the most of the information that is available. There are many very useful reports by donors, consultants, NGOs and the international financial institutions that currently go unused despite the fact that they contain a wealth of valuable information about Uganda's economy and society. By building links to research units in other countries in the region, the unit will be looking for ways to borrow judiciously from analysis that has been undertaken in similar environments in order to draw out lessons and maximize the use of available comparative data. The RIAU will also act as a reference point for data so that data gathered by one ministry is available to others. It will work with training providers to ensure suitable local training is available, and by working with the Ministry of Public Service it will also build a requirement for RIA competences into civil servants' career development plans. This will create an incentive for civil servants to take up RIA training.

In addition to the RIAU in the Cabinet Office, two further units have important roles in the RIA system – the Prime Minister's Office oversees the implementation of policy and has monitoring and evaluation responsibilities. The Ministry of Tourism, Trade and Industry also has a Regulatory Best Practice Unit that represents the interests of business in the RIA process, making sure that the voice of the private sector is heard and that RIAs address business concerns. The Prime Minister's Office and the Cabinet Office jointly chair regular meetings of policy analysts embedded within ministries. These policy analysts are the individuals primarily responsible for carrying out RIAs within line ministries and have been given extensive training and mentoring. There is also a Parliamentary task force that is receiving support in order to help members of Parliament demand good-quality RIAs from government as part of Parliament's scrutiny process.

The Ugandan government has given visible political support to RIA and to RBP. The President has confirmed his support for the initiative by issuing instructions to ministries to carry out RIAs and Cabinet has formally endorsed RBP principles as the basis for government policy-making, the first African country to do so.

One factor that has affected the implementation of institutional support mechanisms for RIA has been the challenge in Uganda of attracting and retaining high-quality staff at the pay levels available. This has meant that plans to increase the staffing in the RIAU have been slow to progress.

Training and Guidance

RBP, and RIA as a tool within it, embodies a new way of making policy and of governing. This concept of a more rational approach to policy-making is new to many developing countries and challenges established ways of doing things. It is important therefore, first to work to build awareness of what RIA is and how it can contribute to national development goals, in order to overcome any misunderstandings and resistance to change. It should be emphasized that RBP and RIA are not the same as deregulation, which has, rightly or wrongly, become associated amongst some with an unreconstructed 'Washington consensus' approach to unfettered markets, imposed by the developed world on developing countries.

This phased approach, starting with awareness-raising, is the approach that was taken in Uganda, which began with a series of sensitization workshops to familiarize officials, Parliamentarians and business representative organizations with the concept of RBP and its benefits. These workshops briefly introduced RIA as a tool. Similar awareness-raising workshops have also been provided in Tanzania, both for officials and business associations.

Once this awareness-raising phase was complete, the formal introduction of RIA was supported with more in-depth training in the RIA methodology. This training was offered by international experts, whilst simultaneously building the capacity of a local training organization, the Uganda Management Institute (UMI), to deliver ongoing training in RIA to Ugandan officials. UMI has been assisted to produce a one-week training course in RIA that will equip officials with the skills and knowledge necessary to carry out basic RIAs and to know where to get help with more complex cases. This training course includes local case studies and has been offered to government policy analysts in advance of the introduction of the formal RIA requirement. Indeed, in both Uganda and Tanzania, local consultants have been engaged throughout the introduction of RIA, in order to build local capacity and expertise in the subject. In Tanzania the Tanzanian Public Service College is involved in developing and delivering RIA training courses.

Civil society organizations and business associations also need training. These organizations often have limited capacity to contribute to consultation undertaken by government as part of the RIA process. In Uganda the capacity of a number of business organizations and NGOs is being strengthened so that they are ready to contribute to consultation exercises and have a good understanding of the types of information on compliance costs that government will be looking for them to solicit from their members. RIA skills will strengthen the capacity of business associations to articulate a convincing argument for pro-business regulatory reform. Ministry policy analysts will be trained to ensure they listen to all points of view, in an effort to prevent regulatory capture, or undue influence by those best placed to argue their case.

Similarly, as noted above, a group of supportive Parliamentarians (and their research staff) are being given training and mentoring in order to strengthen their capacity to analyse the government's RIAs and to challenge them in Parliamentary debate. This capacity-building will contribute to a healthy democratic debate on the merits of proposed regulations.

The Need for a Phased Approach and Change Management

RIA has evolved into a something of a science in the countries where it has been practised for some years. The UK's Better Regulation Task Force and now the Better Regulation Executive, for example, have issued guidance for officials on RIA that has been revised several times over the past decade and covers 90 pages with a large volume of supporting material from the Treasury on calculating costs and benefits. Whilst OECD countries generally strive for guidance that can be used by most policy officials, the level of analysis that is undertaken would stretch the resources of most developing countries and often draws heavily on inputs from economists from within and outside government. Expectations as to the resources available for RIA in developing countries need to be realistic, although this should not be used as a reason for delaying the adoption of RIA.

The RIA system in Uganda has been carefully designed to ensure that it takes account of local circumstances and especially the level of resources available to carry out RIA within ministries. Any system that was too complicated to be of practical use to policy-makers in ministries would soon fall into disuse. Officials were also aware that any system that was in itself burdensome and that clogged up the machinery of government business would soon fall foul of ministers who have an ambitious change agenda. There was clearly a balance to be struck between making the RIA as robust as possible and developing a system that did not overload the policy process. There was equally a danger of the best becoming the enemy of the good, by striving to incorporate every last facet of emerging RIA practice. This temptation was avoided. To address the needs for a system that is both simple and useful, RIA requirements have been kept to a minimum and accompanied by simple guidance produced in collaboration with Ugandan officials. This can be enhanced over time.

More broadly, the introduction of RIA is based on a phased and common sense approach to using and enforcing the discipline. Guidance and training for officials are stressing that the amount of effort put into an RIA should be commensurate with the importance of the policy proposal and its likely impact. If the proposal is likely only to have a limited impact, then clearly there is no point in producing a long and sophisticated RIA, such as would be appropriate for a policy with a major impact. Generally it is expected that the use of RIA and the complexity of analysis will develop over time as officials gain confidence in its application and new skills.

The guidance provided also emphasizes that an RIA does not have to be a long, technical, complex document to have value. At almost any level of complexity, the structured approach to policy analysis that is encompassed in an RIA will improve policy-making by requiring the policy official to answer a number of questions that will steer the policy decisions towards an efficient solution. There is no 'right' standard for the analysis that is performed under RIAs. The important thing is for levels of analysis to be proportionate to the likely impact and for the quality of analysis generally to improve over time. As capacity for RIA increases, so the standards expected can be raised – a pattern that was also followed in OECD countries.

To start with, RIA is being piloted in a number of ministries in Uganda. These ministries have volunteered and selected some current policy issues that they are willing to subject to RIA. A cross-government peer support group of policy analysts has been established. The individuals in this group will work on their RIAs in their own ministries, but meet together under the auspices of the Cabinet Office RIAU to share lessons learnt and provide support to one another. International RIA experts are supporting this process with mentoring and advice.

In addition to resource and capacity/skills issues that suggest a phased approach there are institutional change considerations that arise when implementing RIA systems. The introduction of a formal RIA system in any country usually involves a shift in the balances of power along three dimensions, that is, between institutions at the centre of government, the centre of government and line ministries, and ministers and officials.

Since RIA has horizontal implications, its use needs to be coordinated across the central ministries of government. RIA systems can strengthen the hand of those institutions given the task of policing the system. It may be that these institutions effectively acquire a new power of veto over proposals. It may also be that central ministries that previously enjoyed a free remit to make proposals suddenly find themselves constrained by the requirement for an RIA, enforced by another central institution. In any country this can result in tensions between Ministries of Finance, Cabinet Offices, Prime Minister's Offices, President's Offices and others located at the centre of government. In Uganda the Cabinet Office in the Office of the President coordinates policy proposals on their way to Cabinet and the Prime Minister's Office coordinates and ensures the delivery of agreed policies. A project is underway working with both these organizations to ensure there is adequate coordination of RIA activities. For example, it has been suggested that RIA is placed regularly on the agenda of the monthly meetings of policy analysts hosted by the Prime Minister's Office and attended by the Cabinet Office. A proposed Cabinet Memorandum will set out clearly the institutional roles and responsibilities in the RIA process.

Similarly, RIA can act as a brake on the regulatory activities of line ministries, which find that they are required to overcome an additional hurdle in the policy process and satisfy the requirements of the centre of government. If not carefully managed this can breed resentment and incentivize ministries not to take the RIA system seriously. To bring line ministries along with the development of the RIA system as mentioned already, training in RIA is being offered to ministry policy analysts in order to equip them for the new task, and also to improve their status within ministries. The policy function has generally been relegated to less prominent locations within ministries and policy analysts have accordingly not been central to policy development. Working with line ministries can help them appreciate the value of evidence-based policy analysis as part of the policy-making process.

Ministers do not always welcome the introduction of an additional bureaucratic hurdle that can be perceived as a challenge to their right to govern. Whilst understanding and espousing the need for better regulation and policy advice, ministers are not in practice always keen to see the requirement to carry out an RIA get in the way of their own policy proposals. RBP with its emphasis on rational policy-making and justification of costs gets in the way of the normal way of doing business, which may involve satisfying vested interests. Officials who are used to adopting a passive stance are not always ready for the creative thinking that goes into RIAs, especially the section that requires them to think about all available policy options. These possible concerns are being taken into account in the implementation of RIA in Uganda and elsewhere. The new Ugandan RIA system has been developed in close collaboration with the government to ensure ownership. It will be endorsed by the Ugandan Cabinet so that ministers have an opportunity to comment on its use and to commit themselves to the new system. The President of Uganda has endorsed his government's new approach to regulation, including the use of RIA, sending a clear signal to his ministers of his expectation that the system will be adhered to. It is important to emphasize that RIA is a tool that assists with decision-making by politicians and does not seek to mechanize the policy process in a way that reduces their discretion.

CONCLUSIONS

RIA can help all governments improve the way they regulate to ensure regulatory efficiency, minimize barriers to business growth, provide effective protections for citizens and reduced opportunities for corruption. East Africa is a leading region in Africa in the adoption of RIA with relatively strong progress being made in Uganda and Tanzania. The experience of Kenya demonstrates that advances made in RIA can be readily lost, unless efforts are planned strategically as part of a reform package, given significant dedicated resources and owned by the government.

The benefits of RIA are particularly valuable to developing countries where the poor suffer most from a business environment hostile to growth and job creation, and from corruption. Experience in East Africa (and elsewhere) suggests that core RIA methodologies used in OECD countries need amendment for the developing country context in order to take realistic account of the limited level to which policy analysis can often be undertaken. The methodology can readily be amended to take account of those groups that may be in need of special consideration in the policy process, and these groups need to be identified in each country. Similarly, the methodology can allow for local political priorities to be included as something that officials should take account of, or even 'mainstream', as part of policy development.

Whilst RIA undeniably requires resources to support its introduction, these can be relatively modest in the context of donor development assistance and the use of governments' own resources. Resource constraints need not be a barrier to adoption of RIA and an RIA approach can help improve policy at almost any level of complexity. In order to reap the full benefits there is a need to build capacity through a phased approach, including awareness-raising and skills-building before the methodology is made a formal requirement. Training is required within government but also with government's main interlocutors so that they are well placed to respond to consultation exercises and able to argue for policy reform on the basis of evidence. The methodology needs to be placed within a system that governs how RIA is used within the policy process, setting out roles and responsibilities and providing political support. As with any significant change programme there will be change management factors to consider, otherwise there is a risk that the introduction of RIA will falter. Similarly, RIA must be considered as one part of the policy reform process, an essential part but one that's impact will be limited without wider reform.

NOTES

1. This chapter draws on the experience of DAI Europe Ltd, which has since 2003 been running a two-year project, funded by the UK's Department for International Development (DFID), to improve the regulatory environment for businesses in Uganda. DAI Europe has also worked on regulatory reform issues in Kenya, and is advising the Government of Tanzania on strengthening the business environment through the adoption of RIA.
2. DAI Europe Ltd defines regulatory impact assessment as 'a methodology for designing precise, targeted regulations that achieve legitimate policy aims with the minimum of burden on those affected. It is a tool that provides a framework for a high quality, participative policy development process, guiding users through a series of steps designed to address the main stages in the development of high quality policy.'
3. Carried out by DAI Europe Ltd.
4. DAI Europe Ltd has developed such a tool.

REFERENCES

Hameso, S.Y. (1997), *Ethnicity in Africa: Towards a Positive Approach*, London: TSC Publications.

Kirkpatrick, C. and D. Parker (2003), *Regulatory Impact Assessment: Developing its Potential for use in Developing Countries*, Manchester: University of Manchester.

OECD (1997), *Regulatory Impact Assessment – Best Practices in OECD Countries*, Paris: OECD.

Schneider, F. (2002), *Size and Measurement of the Informal Economy in 110 Countries around the World*, RRU, World Bank.

Transparency International (2003), *A 2002 Pilot Survey of International Attitudes, Expectations and Priorities on Corruption*, London.

Transparency International (2004), *Corruption Perceptions Index*, London.

World Bank (2004), *World Development Report: A Better Investment Climate for Everyone*, Washington DC: World Bank.

World Bank (2005), *World Development Report*, Washington DC: World Bank.

12. Regulatory impact assessment in Mexico

Cesar Cordova Novion*

INTRODUCTION

Since colonial times Mexico has suffered from a burdensome regulatory system. During the 1930s, the regulatory machine accelerated its output of red tape year by year. By the end of the 1980s, Mexico was gripped by full-fledged 'regulatory inflation'.

This growth in the burden of regulation was due to various factors. Nationalism was replaced by a form of interventionist populism without any checks and balances to control it. The President and ministers were uncontested by Congress or opposition groups. Senior officials were often proud to adopt the latest regulations and standards coming out of developed countries and international organizations with little consideration for enforcement and compliance costs. The business sector found regulation to be a useful protection tool against national and foreign competitors (Salas, 2004). When compliance became too burdensome, businesses were given privileges. The rule-making system was a stronghold of lawyers who worked behind the scenes to produce complex and sometimes indecipherable legal documents. The heavy ship of public administration was navigating in a legalistic world often quite unrelated to the realities of the Mexican economy. The absence of systematic and fair enforcement however, led to a largely informal business environment. Furthermore, the regulatory system was often contradictory and corruption was seen as the most viable solution to any government interference.

However, by the end of the 1980s, Mexico progressively began opening up its economy. It joined the GATT in 1986 and then the North American Free Trade Agreement (NAFTA) in 1994. The government launched a fiscal austerity programme to control inflation and reduced its direct participation in the economy though a programme of privatization and market liberalization. An integral part of this new strategy was an aggressive government-led deregulation campaign (Cordova and Haddou-Ruiz, 2006).

The battle to improve the regulatory framework and develop a sound regulatory policy has been described in a series of recent documents. This chapter will, however, concentrate on describing how the Mexican government used one of the key regulatory policy tools – regulatory impact assessment (RIA) – as a top-down and systematic approach to transforming the rule-making process in the economy.

The chapter has four further sections. The next section describes the development of an RIA framework in Mexico. Section 3 provides a detailed account of the current system and procedures for RIA. Section 4 assesses the results of the RIA system and the final section provides a summary and conclusions.

THE DEVELOPMENT OF RIA IN MEXICO

The Mexican government started its regulatory reform efforts with a strong deregulation programme. From 1982 to 1994, 80 per cent of the national legislative framework was extensively modified. The government's main aims were threefold: to support market mechanisms and links to the global economy; to reduce the state's role in market structure and function; and to improve the relationship between the constitutional branches of government, states and municipalities, and business and citizen groups (López Ayllón, 1997).

To support this major effort the government established a new body, the Unidad de Desregulación Económica (Economic Deregulation Unit or UDE), a small but powerful department of the Trade and Industrial Development Ministry (Secretaría de Comercio y Fomento Industrial – SECOFI). Within a few years the UDE played a central role in deregulating a number of key industries, including trucking, ports and the telecommunications industries.

However, by the early 1990s, the government felt the need to add a 're-regulation' component to its new regulatory framework. The UDE moved its focus from a strategy of ad hoc sectoral deregulation to a more horizontal and systematic approach that would benefit the economy across the board. In less than a year the UDE designed groundbreaking laws on consumer protection, technical standards and competition policy (Cordova and Haddou-Ruiz, 2006).

Two initiatives are worth noting during this first phase when the Mexican government started to improve the general structure of the regulatory framework. The first addressed the analytical basis for regulation; the second, the procedural aspects of rule-making.

Based on international best practices the UDE included an open and transparent procedure for preparing technical standards in the 1992

Federal Metrology and Standards Law (Ley Federal sobre Metrología y Normalización). The process required not only public consultation but also, and for the first time in Mexico, a cost–benefit analysis (CBA) for proposed technical rules. Unfortunately the system's efficacy was limited by the over-representation of producer interests within the Standardization Council. As a result, the requirement for a CBA test was only loosely enforced. The consultative committees in charge of preparing the CBA had few incentives to produce rigorous and objective analysis and paid little attention to compliance costs for SMEs. In the end this first attempt at CBA led to little more than a qualitative description of benefits and political considerations set against a description of minor transition costs and became an extra layer of red tape, rather than a useful guide to decision-making.

The second major effort during this period was the enactment, in 1994, of the modern Federal Administrative Procedures Law (Ley Federal de Procedimiento Administrativo – LFPA). This law incorporated a series of requirements with direct impact on rule-making and regulatory adjudication. The law established a 'silence is consent' rule applicable to all administrative procedures, or 'trámites' as they are known in Mexico.[1] The LFPA also completely revamped the inspections system in order to reduce corruption by limiting the authorities' discretion in applying laws and regulations and in adjudicating resolutions (Cordova, 2005). However, the law was subordinate to other laws – that is, it was applicable only when a specific law did not already regulate procedures, thereby limiting its effect on the administrative culture of the bureaucracy. Many sectors and policy areas continued to be administratively regulated as before.

A key aim of these horizontal reforms was to ensure the compatibility with and raise governance standards to those of Mexico's NAFTA partners. This evolution was accelerated by a major macroeconomic crisis in 1994–95. In the aftermath of the so-called 'Tequila Crisis', a new administration launched a more wide-ranging reform under an executive order entitled 'The Agreement for the Deregulation of Business Activity' (ADAE), in November 1995.[2] The ADAE can be considered the first explicit Mexican regulatory policy, as defined by OECD (1997, 2002).

The ADAE organized the reform strategy under three distinct components: simplification of existing regulations, reorganizing the ways in which new regulations were prepared and setting up strong institutional stewardship. First, the ADAE renewed the UDE's mandate to advocate reform and deregulation of the existing regulatory framework. Importantly it added a systematic review of all federal formalities to its remit. This massive undertaking was informally referred to as the regulatory 'guillotine'. The ADAE ordered 12 ministries and Mexico City, which was still a federal entity at the time, to submit all formalities[3] that were required to open and operate a business to the UDE, in a standardized format and under precise timelines. Formalities not submitted would be considered unjustified and automatically repealed at the end of the general review.

For the submission, ministries needed to complete a template for each formality containing a small RIA-type checklist based on the 1995 OECD Recommendations (OECD, 1995). This template included: the legal and economic justification, a description of the positive and negative impacts of the formality (i.e., what would happen if the formality was eliminated), as well as the human and budgetary resources required for enforcement.

Based on this submission the UDE together with an ad hoc Economic Deregulation Council (see below), completed a thorough revision of each formality before including it in the Federal Registry of Business Formalities if deemed sufficiently justified and simplified.

The process took longer than expected; the review of nearly 3000 formalities and in particular the 'legalization' of the reforms, that is, modifying the hundreds of laws and subordinated regulations, took more than five years.[4] However, the initiative was considered a success – in particular the first phase when the massive submission froze the production of new formalities by the federal machinery. In six months the UDE compiled a list of all formalities and posted them on the Internet. During the process of submitting their initial list, many ministries failed to report certain formalities and thus tacitly eliminated a significant number.

The second significant innovation of the ADAE was the requirement that all new proposals be sent to the UDE to ensure that ministries and agencies did not include new unjustified formalities. These ex ante checks applied both to substantive laws and lower-level rules related to the opening and operation of businesses. In order to enforce this 'informal' RIA, the UDE counted on strong support from the newly created Presidential Legal Counsel,[5] which used the UDE to filter out low-quality regulatory proposals.

The third component of the ADAE was the establishment of a new institutional architecture. The UDE was put in charge of formulating and applying horizontal regulatory policy. The UDE reported directly to the Minister of Commerce.[6] Not only was UDE assigned a newer and more powerful mandate but the decree also established the Economic Deregulation Council (CDE), whose responsibilities included actively participating in the review of existing federal government formalities, assisting in the review of proposed requirements in draft laws and regulations and presenting proposals to enhance the regulatory framework for business.

The CDE membership was designed to reinforce the inter-ministerial support for the implementation of its decisions – primarily by involving key public officials but also by opening the body to businesses and members of the civil society (see Box 12.1).

BOX 12.1 MEMBERSHIP OF THE ECONOMIC DEREGULATION COUNCIL – CDE

Government – five seats:

- Ministry of Trade and Commerce, President;
- Ministry of the Comptroller General, Vice-President;
- Ministry of Finance;
- Ministry of Labour and Safety;
- Central Bank.

Labour unions – three seats.
Business sector – five seats.
Agricultural sector – two seats.
Academic sector – four seats.

Because the UDE and the CDE did not have the mandate to issue regulations or sanction violators, the key enforcement role of the ADAE was delegated to the Ministry of the Comptroller General.[7] It was charged with monitoring the discretionary powers of public servants, a potential source of corruption, as well as helping to implement CDE decisions within the bureaucracy. However, the 'informal RIA' soon showed its limits. As the guillotine process started to operate and the UDE and private sector initiated their sequential review of formalities, some ministries and agencies found loopholes or resisted openly.

Many ministries alleged that the UDE lacked the technical knowledge and authority to undertake the review of their proposals. On one hand, UDE, as part of a line ministry (SECOFI), was poorly placed in the hierarchy to control properly the flow of new measures. On the other hand, because the ADAE was only an executive order, it did not stand up well against the legal mandates promoted by ministries. Indeed, there was a serious risk that numerous laws allowed ministers to issue important administrative regulations without UDE oversight. In the end the 'informal RIA' relied mainly on the good working relationship between the Presidential Legal Counsel and the UDE.

Another external reason that pointed to the need for a stronger oversight instrument was the government's recognition of the fact that Mexico was the only NAFTA member that had no procedures requiring that drafts of legal measures issued by executive agencies be made easily and publicly available.[8] After very delicate negotiations with powerful ministries the government decided to amend the Federal Administrative Procedures Law in 1996 and legally establish for the first time RIA and public consultation requirements. This move was an essential strategy to avoid bureaucratic backtracking on the early ADAE results.

With the support of the private sector and Presidential Legal Counsel, the President proposed an amendment to the LFPA in the fall of 1996, establishing full-fledged RIA in Mexico for the first time.[9] This one paragraph amendment simply stated that all federal ministries and agencies needed to submit all draft regulations having a potential impact on business activity to UDE for review along with a 'manifestación de impacto regulatorio' (MIR) or regulatory impact assessment (RIA). Following strict rules and deadlines the UDE could issue a non-binding public opinion on the proposal and its respective RIA. 'In short, the battle for the RIA was won, but full enforcement of public transparency of drafts in addition to RIAs was not there yet: the UDE was not bound to make public received draft proposals' (Salas, 2004).

At that time, a clear goal was to foster a cultural change among regulators, enhancing accountability and transparency. To that end the UDE prepared a detailed RIA manual accessible to and acceptable by ministries. The preparation of this manual took more than eight months, as it had to be negotiated with all ministries. After incorporating their comments the federal government published the manual in September 1997. The UDE also provided technical assistance before and after introducing the manual to assist regulators in improving the quality of their RIAs.

At the same time the government reformed the Federal Standardization Law (May 1997) in order to harmonize the procedures for technical standards with those managed by COFEMER (Comisión Federal de Mejora Regulatia). A new specific RIA replaced the ineffective CBA and its review was entrusted to COFEMER specialists. The reform also included a five-year sunset clause for each technical standard. That is, all technical standards are required to be ratified and reviewed every five years or they are automatically cancelled.

This period was a time of exceptional learning for all regulatory policymakers, from the UDE and the Presidential Legal Counsel to the ministries and agencies. The revised review system began to provide UDE and the CDE with a more detailed picture of the existing regulatory capabilities and feedback on how to help regulators to consider ADAE criteria earlier in the regulatory process. The bureaucracy slowly became accustomed to the new and modern rule-making processes, where transparency and accountability were the norm. During this period the UDE made important investments in developing a better monitoring system and in simplifying and streamlining the submission procedures. It also launched an important outreach campaign to convince the 32 federal states to revitalize their own rule-making practices. In sum the UDE provided all stakeholders with assistance in managing (and struggling with) a new accountable and transparent regulatory system.

With this reform, Mexico joined the limited but growing number of OECD countries using RIA as a tool to improve the quality of regulation and the small group of countries where such a requirement is established by law.

THE CURRENT SYSTEM

Nevertheless, beginning in the late 1990s, some problems started to become evident. An OECD report in 1999 praised the system and declared that the RIA mechanism was in compliance with OECD best practice. However, it also pinpointed the need for further progress and some important improvements (OECD, 1999).

Some ministries and agencies were increasingly opposing the UDE's review of their proposals as they rarely allocated sufficient time to incorporate third-party comments. More dangerously, some ministries, backed by private and public interest groups, were considering using the Congress to initiate laws to bypass the new 'checks and balances' process controlled by the UDE and Presidential Legal Counsel.

Moreover, reformers inside the government realized that there was a real danger that after the general election due in summer 2000 the incoming administration might backtrack and not enforce – or even disband – the RIA procedures and the disciplines enshrined in the Federal Registry of Formalities. This fear was reinforced by what happened in Mexico City when the 'Federal District' became a self-governed entity with powers equivalent to those of the other 31 federal states. The change of party in the administration of Mexico City led to a wholesale reversal of new rule-making procedures.

Consequently the administration prepared a thorough reform of the LFPA as one of its last acts before the election. In May 2000 the Congress passed the reform unanimously. An entirely new section on regulatory improvement was incorporated.[10] The main objective of the LFPA reform was to institutionalize new rule-making procedures based on RIA and public consultation. The LFPA replaced the 1995 ADAE as the main legal document supporting the regulatory policy. A revised Federal Regulatory Improvement Commission succeeded the UDE. The COFEMER became a technically and administratively independent body of the Ministry of Economy in charge of coordinating and monitoring a new National Regulatory Improvement Programme. In addition to more autonomy and extended powers, COFEMER also experienced an increase in budgetary and human resources. Since 2000 COFEMER has had a staff of 60 professionals and a budget exceeding $5 million annually. This was a significant increase with respect to the 15 officials and $1 million per year that the UDE had between 1997 and 2000.

As for the CDE, its name was changed to the 'Federal Council for Regulatory Improvement' emphatically replacing 'deregulation' with 'regulatory improvement' and thereby signalling a philosophical shift in the government's approach. Its membership was also enlarged to include the competition authority and the consumer protection agency as permanent members.

The amendment of the LFPA also widened the scope of regulatory reform policy. The new disciplines extended to all proposed regulations and formalities produced by any ministry and agency, including in areas such as public procurement, public works and social security. Importantly, rules and regulations prepared by sectoral regulatory agencies were also brought under the new mandate.[11] Only a handful of exceptions remained, in areas such as security and defence. Among these exemptions once again was the Ministry of Finance, which fought and obtained an exclusion for tax formalities, though not for regulation of the financial sector.[12]

At the core of the policy the LFPA established a precise administrative procedure – which was later complemented by a detailed presidential decree – clearly defining the rights and obligations of the ministries and agencies and as well as those of COFEMER and the Presidential Legal Counsel. These changes incorporated international best practice and the five years of hands-on experience that the UDE had gained in undertaking substantive reviews of RIAs and formalities. The reforms included the following major characteristics and innovations:

- making the general director of COFEMER a Presidential appointee;
- enshrining the participation of representatives of the private sector, unions and civil society in the rule-making process with the creation of the Federal Council for Regulatory Improvement;
- requiring each ministry and agency to prepare and report on regulatory reform progress in its biennial regulatory improvement programmes;
- assigning an undersecretary (vice-minister) to be responsible for the regulatory improvement in each ministry or agency;
- establishing a transparent process – including a 'notice and comment' process of at least one month – for analysing all regulatory proposals;
- providing greater legal certainty for citizens and businesses on all applicable formalities through their mandatory registration in the Federal Registry of Proceedings and Services; and

- setting the legal framework for cooperation among federal, state and municipal governments on regulatory issues.

Since then COFEMER has continued to perfect its tools and interventions. In 2001, it published a new detailed manual regulating the procedures defined by the LFPA. In early 2004 a new ministerial decree – the Internal Rules of the Cofemer – further clarified COFEMER's competencies.[13] This complemented the already extensive text in the LFPA, which describes in great detail the RIA process and explicitly establishes the rights and obligations of COFEMER to ensure its credibility and fairness.

The law and its decree also mandated that COFEMER develop and publish an RIA format – which has since been adapted as an e-government tool (see Box 12.2). It includes six parts. First, a justification section that describes the proposed regulation, identifying the problem that the proposal seeks to ameliorate. Second, an analytical section that identifies the specific risks that the proposal intends to reduce or eliminate. Third, a legal section that verifies if the ministry or agency has the adequate legal mandate to regulate the issue in question and if the proposal conforms with the national legal framework (including with those of the subnational governments). Fourth, an implementation section that ensures that the ministries will have sufficient resources to inspect, enforce and sanction the proposed regulation.[14] Fifth, an alternatives section that discusses possible alternatives to the regulation that may solve the problem or risk identified at a lower cost. Finally, an impact section that analyses in detail the costs and benefits for the individuals and public enforcers when the proposal is approved.[15]

A key aim of the new process was to reduce compliance costs for ministries and agencies when preparing an RIA, without losing the essential information to appraise proposals properly. As mentioned earlier, ministries had characterized the review process as a bottleneck that impeded important regulations and even regulatory improvement. The earlier RIA review process was undermined by confrontation and lengthy, sometimes sterile, negotiations. To address these issues COFEMER set in place three important mechanisms. First, it enhanced communication with RIA drafters and provided incentives for incorporating quality regulation criteria earlier in the drafting process, thereby avoiding 'unpleasant surprises' for the ministries at a later stage.

Second it established a two-stage approach that permits those regulations (and their RIAs) without significant impacts to be rapidly assessed and cleared (see Figure 12.1). The trigger to require a more thorough assessment is discussed between COFEMER and the relevant ministry officials. As a guideline COFEMER indicates that if a proposal is expected

BOX 12.2 THE RIA ELECTRONIC SUBMISSION SYSTEM

As an integral part of its 2001 reform, COFEMER launched an ambitious programme to modernize its internal processes, to enhance compliance with RIA obligations, to reduce the administrative burdens on RIA drafters, and to increase the quality of individual submissions.

The challenge was to provide COFEMER with a system and software that were efficient and effective as well as transparent and accountable. Key to meeting this goal was the re-engineering of the requirements surrounding the submission of RIAs to COFEMER to create a just-in-time mechanism. This system would also offer a mechanism for monitoring compliance by ministries and agencies. This was translated into the creation of a technological infrastructure that provided swift communication between rule-makers and COFEMER and from COFEMER to the general public.

COFEMER and its technological partner developed a technical and institutional solution based on an Internet application feeding an RIA central repository. More than a simple mechanism to transmit data and information, the new software creates a 'collaborative space' where agents from ministries and COFEMER can interact on an ongoing basis as a regulation matures. It also provides a forum for posting the drafts for public comment at different stages of the development process. The website (http://www.cofemermir.gob.mx), which has been operational since October 2001, includes two parallel areas: a public area where all stakeholders can download draft RIAs and regulations; and an 'intranet' area where ministries and agencies draft the RIAs, consult an online manual and communicate with COFEMER. The intranet permits COFEMER to track the whole rule-making process as well as assess and comment online about individual RIAs. It is also linked to the specific system managing the federal registry of licences and services (Registro Federal de Trámites y Servicios).

Four years after having been established, the electronic RIA system is an unqualified success. Although its use is mandatory for the submission of RIAs, its non-mandatory functions – such as the online help, active consultation – are being increasingly used. More importantly, the use of the public interface and, in particular, the notice and comments features have hugely enhanced public consultation in Mexico. In many ways, these tools have deepened and engrained democratic aspects of Mexican public life.

to have a high impact (that is, if its annual compliance costs are greater than 800 million pesos (around US$70 million) or if it may impose significant costs on one sector or specific branch of the economy, a group of consumers, or a specific geographic area) the proponent ministry should prepare an extended RIA incorporating a quantitative and qualitative

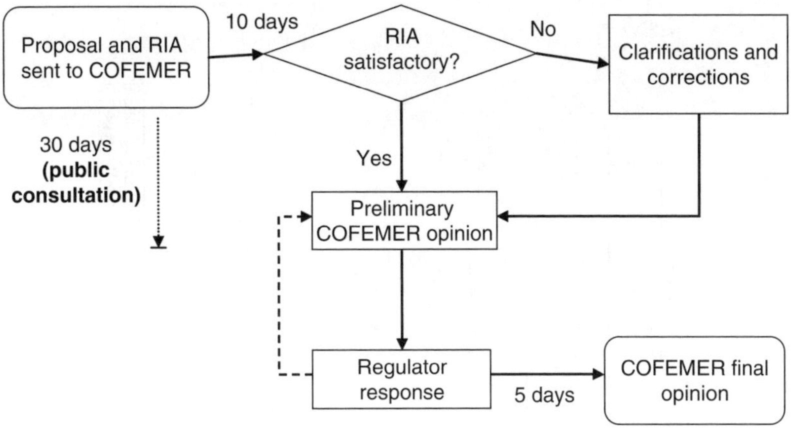

Figure 12.1 Process of the Mexican RIA system since 2000[16]

analysis. This targeted approach also frees scare resources both within the ministries and COFEMER to focus efforts on fewer but more relevant regulations and RIAs.

In order to make the best use of the RIA template, this 'ordinary' procedure was subsequently modified (see Figure 12.2 for the diagram of the complete flow):[17] three important elements need to be highlighted about this modified process. First, COFEMER cannot veto regulations. If the ministry or agency does not agree with COFEMER on the need to conduct a complete cost–benefit analysis, an independent expert approved by COFEMER is assigned to provide a third and final opinion.

Second, COFEMER has invested heavily in training and guidance (in addition to the e-government tool). More than 40 seminars have been organized and nearly 2000 officials have been trained since the new system was established. Generally the courses concentrate on how to conduct an RIA and, in particular, on how to make the best use of the online system. Courses also address how to improve communication and the relationship between COFEMER and ministries; how to develop evidence-based skills to assess regulations impacts; and the importance of the search for non-regulatory alternatives.

Third, in May 2004 the President issued a one-year moratorium (extended for another year in May 2005) on the production of all regulations with an RIA indicating that they will impose costs for businesses.[18] Nevertheless, the moratorium has significant exemptions that have permitted many ministries and agencies to continue regulating – for instance, in urgent cases. So far no real evaluation of the moratorium's effect has been made and its impact on the credibility of the RIA system is unknown.

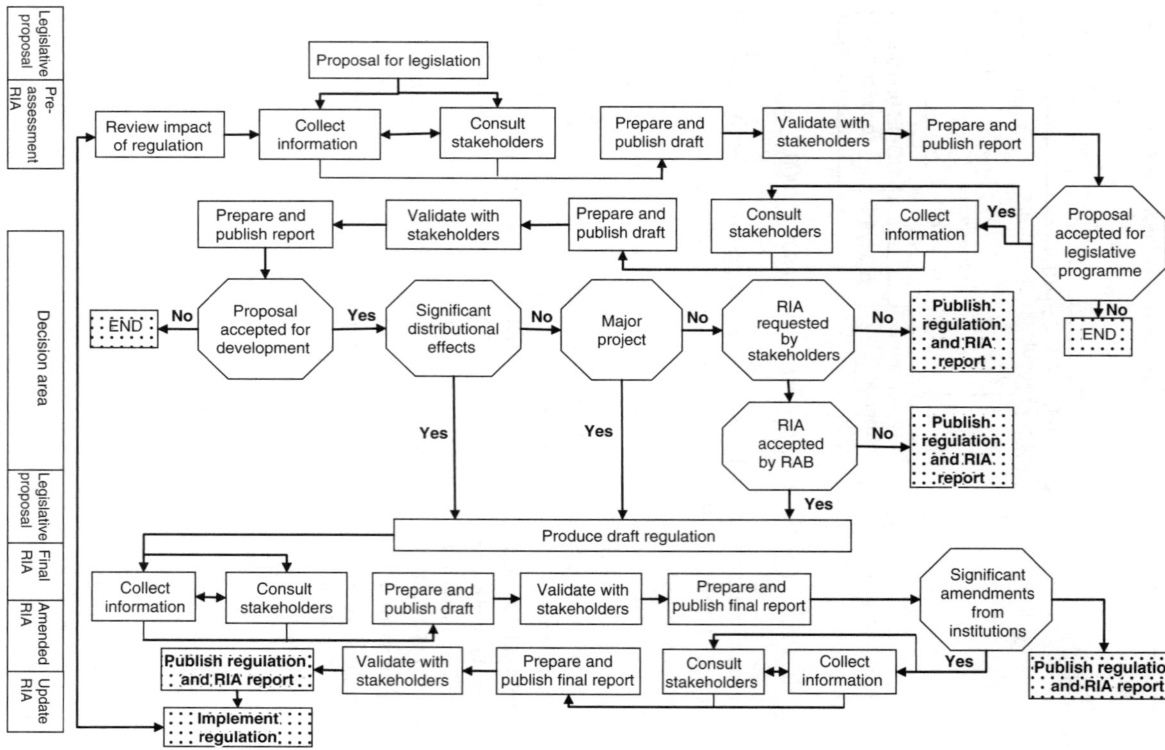

Figure 12.2 Modified process for RIA in Mexico

In tandem with RIA, LFPA ensured that public consultation would be at the heart of the new regulatory policy. Confirming and clarifying the 1996 amendments, the 2000 reform of the law established a 'notice and comment' obligation of 30 working days for all draft federal regulations including technical standards. The 2003 Transparency Law further strengthened this obligation requiring that all draft measures should be available for at least 20 working days on the Internet.[19]

Ministries and agencies can comply with this obligation by using COFEMER's website and requesting COFEMER to certify their fulfilment of the public consultation requirement before proceeding to the next step in the rule-making process. These reforms notwithstanding, the new framework did not set up particular rules on 'active' public consultation mechanisms such as panel tests, hearings or advisory bodies. Neither did it set up criteria to ensure fair participation during the consultation processes.

Nonetheless, the 'publish and comment' mechanism represents an enormous shift in the conduct and perception of the federal public administration in Mexico. Ministries and agencies can no longer prepare in secret and suddenly publish in the *Official Gazette* their pet regulatory proposal. As a result the new rule-making procedure has increased the legal certainty for businesses and individuals and given them a strong incentive to participate in the review process. Many business associations, newspapers and academics now regularly review COFEMER's web page to see which regulatory projects the government is working on. The online system actually sends out personalized alerts, including of proposed measures in specific policy areas or sectors.

These transparency rules have also established stronger incentives for ministries to prepare better-quality RIAs. To a degree it has shielded COFEMER from political pressures since some of the most affected parties (e.g., SMEs or consumers) can vocally address the future impact of the regulations. A main finding of the guillotine review of the formalities of the late 1990s was the extent to which public administrators used their discretionary powers to invent procedures and establish new requirements and obligations without proper legal mandate. Through the special RIA section COFEMER exercises an important legal quality control, which is supplemented by higher-level measures (draft laws, regulations and Presidential decrees by the Legal Counsel).[20]

Imposing programme and administrative rules upon the public administration has historically been a difficult endeavour in Mexico. Strong ministerial independence, a stovepipe approach to public policies (where ministries jockey against each other to launch as many programmes and laws as possible) and an endemic shortage of funds to monitor, evaluate and enforce the rules have plagued the implementation of modern management systems within the bureaucracy. Consequently from the beginning the reformers needed to set up an incentive system to ensure compliance. Two main methods were set up: the LFPA established that the office of the *Official Gazette* would not publish any regulation without ensuring that the proposal had an RIA and a COFEMER opinion attached; and the law also set clear sanctions in case of non-compliance with the new rule-making procedures. The General Controller – later transformed into the Ministry of the Public Administration – was entrusted with the enforcement of these sanctions.

On a more informal level, the unofficial agreement between COFEMER and the Presidential Legal Counsel continues to operate. After more than a decade both bodies have continued to work in parallel: their smooth communication and efficient working relationship ensure the improvement of Mexico's new regulations. This alliance was further expanded with the tactical support of the Competition Authority and Consumer Protection Office.

Mexico is a federal state. Because of the extremely centralized character of pre-reform Mexico, the amount of regulation by states and municipalities was relatively low until the early 1990s. As local government gained increased autonomy during the 1990s, it discovered its regulatory power. While the federal regulatory framework improved, sub-federal regulations attracted increasing criticism from the private sector due to the additional formalities imposed on businesses, creating delays and uncertainties in new investments.

Starting with the 1995 ADAE and reinforced by the 2000 LFPA reforms, Congress mandated COFEMER to promote regulatory reform nationwide through active collaboration with interested local governments. COFEMER's main promotion mechanism has been the organization of annual conferences with all state officials in charge of regulatory reform. Starting in early 2000, selected municipalities were also included in these conferences. The main objectives of these events are to create a sense of peer pressure, raise awareness of similar problems and provide a forum for the exchange of best practices. To facilitate the dissemination of new initiatives like state RIAs COFEMER has launched studies and monitoring exercises across the country. More recently it has been investing heavily, helping states and municipalities to improve their regulatory environments and in particular their business start-up systems.

RESULTS

Mexico's RIA system has made immense progress since its early adoption ten years ago. From a simple checklist used during the guillotine review of formalities, it has evolved into an elaborate process where proposals are scrutinized, published and commented upon according to precise administrative guidelines. Few civil law countries and even fewer developing and transitional countries have achieved such a level of institutionalization and sophistication in their application of RIA.

Among the most significant results in terms of regulatory governance, in 2004 the OECD noted the following:

- The new procedure is achieving initial acceptance by ministries and agencies.
- A world-class online RIA submission system has been in operation since 2002.
- Citizens and business through a single website can consult and provide comments on the full texts of draft proposals along with the RIA and COFEMER's comments.
- Thousands of federal public servants have been sensitized and trained in RIA together with seminars and awareness-raising events in states and municipalities (OECD, 2004).
- In terms of output, over 500 regulatory proposals were reviewed by the UDE from 1995 to 2000. Thereafter, COFEMER has used RIA to appraise hundreds of drafts (see Figure 12.3).

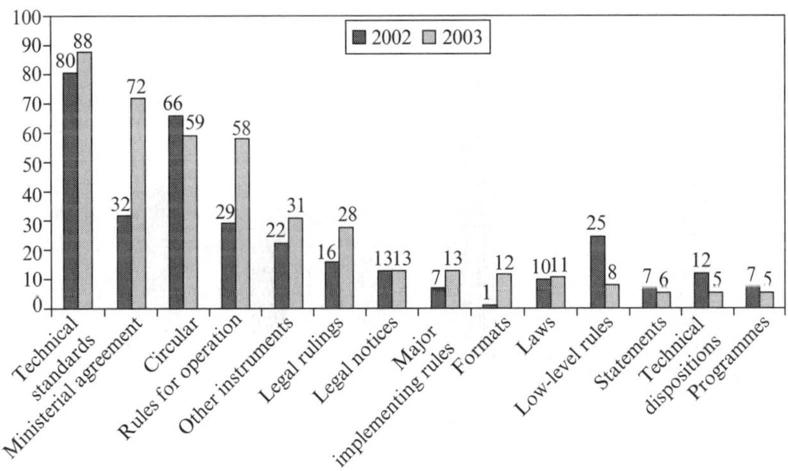

Source: COFEMER in OECD (2004).

Figure 12.3 Regulatory proposals received by COFEMER with an RIA, by type of legal instrument

In terms of outcomes, most commentators agree that RIA has become an effective filter for detecting inadequate regulatory proposals and preventing their publication in the *Official Gazette*. For instance, COFEMER's annual reports indicate that approximately 20 per cent to 30 per cent of proposals received are subject to detailed scrutiny, which involves requesting corrections to an RIA and/or detailed suggestions or comments regarding regulatory content (Cordova and Haddou-Ruiz, 2006). According to Fernando Salas, the first COFEMER director, well-crafted and critical public reviews have postponed the process of issuing a regulation and impeded its entering into force because they have exposed contradictions and legally questionable elements that could have embarrassed higher officials. This challenge function has been particularly effective for poorer-quality secondary regulations and technical standards. Significantly, the RIA filter also reduced the flood of new and hastily drafted proposals that the new administration that came into power in 2001 sought to enact – a typical consequence in many countries of a shift in political power.

The true impact of RIA on the regulatory environment in Mexico is mixed and harder to assess. Various indicators such as those produced by the World Bank indicate that regulatory quality in Mexico has not improved since 2000, though transparency has made great strides (see Figure 12.4). Also, since 1997 important structural and deregulatory reforms have been blocked due to the ever-expanding gridlock between the

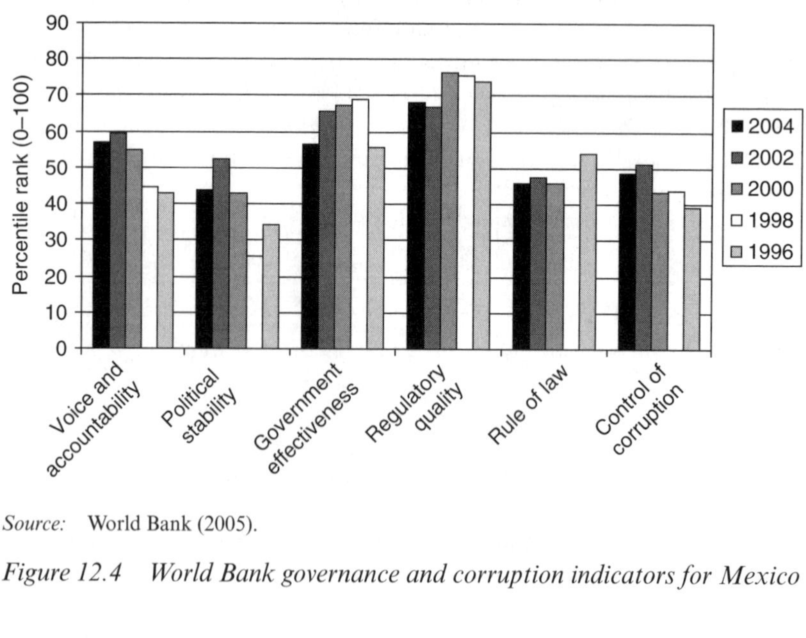

Source: World Bank (2005).

Figure 12.4 World Bank governance and corruption indicators for Mexico

Executive and Legislative powers. The slow progress, and in some cases backtracking, at local level also explain disappointing results.

However, RIA has started to change the culture and practices of the public administration and its regulators. Increasingly, for instance, the courts are using RIA statements during their hearings in solving regulatory controversies. The bad habit of producing regulations without any check and balance has been eradicated. As Salas (2004) indicates, an unexpected result of the RIA effectiveness has been the numerous ministerial attempts to bypass the internal Executive review by going straight to Congress.[21]

Nevertheless, the RIA system has yet to achieve a self-sustained momentum beyond any risks of backtracking and beyond that, an evolving trend based on expanding regulatory governance principles such as efficiency, transparency and accountability. As the system has evolved and matured it has encountered new challenges. First, although the new system tries to use a consensual approach, it has encountered significant friction within a bureaucracy unused to controls and third-party reviews. The process has been prone to leaks and pressures, political motivations and emergencies have allowed some regulations to circumvent the controls. However, the RIA consultation mechanism has raised the cost of pushing through low-quality regulation.

Second, the quality of individual RIA submissions varies enormously. Despite the guidelines and training, RIA drafters still have problems with the practical application of RIA concepts. A case in point is the struggle to define accurately the risk-based objective of a draft measure. Furthermore, the evidence-based section – focusing on the positive and negative impacts of a regulation – is seldom based on primary data collection. The overall level of RIA quantification and data analysis remains quite low, according to a diagnostic study conducted by COFEMER. A third problem is that even though vice ministers must sign off all regulations, RIAs are prepared in practice by medium-level officials. Finally, during the past decade, Congress has increasingly used legislative means (by issuing or amending a large number of acts) to exempt certain regulations from the RIA disciplines.

CONCLUSIONS

RIA has changed the regulatory landscape in Mexico. Law and rule drafters have increasingly started to pay attention to issues like the costs and benefits of regulations and regulatory alternatives, as well as becoming more sensitive to the opinions of the affected groups. Undoubtedly the lawyers' monopoly on the rule-making process has also been breached. Slowly but surely, ministries and agencies have been expanding their capacities and expertise. The fact that the executive and legislature have agreed to continue investing year after year more than $5 million in COFEMER also indicates the degree of multi-party commitment to the regulatory improvement policy.

Certainly many challenges lie ahead but the achievements of Mexico in adopting a policy mechanism such as RIA that is based on efficiency, transparency and accountability are undeniable. Many factors have brought about Mexico's achievement. Among the most important was the institutionalization of COFEMER as an autonomous agency. Its creation, along with the support it received from the President, gave an enormous credibility to the new mechanism – a move unprecedented in many countries with circumstances similar to Mexico's (Cordova and Haddou-Ruiz, 2006). Also, an important lesson is that establishing an RIA system in a transition country requires huge political effort sustained for a long time (often a decade). Only this type of investment may permit the shifting of a regulatory culture and administrative practice deeply ingrained in tradition.

Another important factor was timing. The Mexican reformers knew how to take advantage of the opportunities through innovations and the building of constituencies for reform. The reformers were fortunate to launch RIA after a major crisis and in obtaining the cooperation of key institutions such as the Presidential Legal Counsel. They also used this window of opportunity to build a constituency for reform among the private sector.

This does not mean, however, that RIA in Mexico is secure. No doubt the recent halt in regulatory and structural reforms may be used to discredit the tool. COFEMER needs to be re-energized and a powerful message sent to the federal and local bureaucracy. Nevertheless, the Mexican experiment with RIA should be considered a success story.

NOTES

* Ali Haddou-Ruiz, former Director General of RIA at COFEMER and currently Executive Secretary of the Mexican Federal Competition Commission provided extensive comments to the chapter.

1. Silence is consent consists of the authority granting an automatic approval if the application receives no response after a set time. It is a way to shift the burden of proof on to the bureaucracy: if there is a doubt before authorizing an action, it needs to react before the deadline.
2. Acuerdo Para la Desregulación de la Actividad Empresarial, DOF, Mexico, 24 November, 1995.
3. A formality was defined as a requirement on paper or electronic copy that had to be completed and given to a government agency in order to start operations and for day to day ordinary business operations.
4. An electoral year and the change of administration as well as the enacting of the reforms of the LFPA, explain in part the very long time needed to establish the final Registry.

5. The Presidential Legal Counsel (Consejeria Juridica del Executivo Federal) was set up in 1995 to review the quality of the laws and regulations before being signed by the President and sent to Congress. The signed regulations must afterwards be published in the *Official Gazette* (*Diario Official*).
6. The UDE had the following responsibilities: to propose improvements in regulatory policy to the minister; to act as Technical Secretariat of the Economic Deregulation Board; to review and evaluate current regulations and propose substantive changes; to review regulations and provide advice to issuing ministries; to advise state governments in formulating their respective regulatory policies.
7. Secretariat de Contraloría y Modernization Administrativa or SECODAM.
8. NAFTA, Article 1802.
9. This did not enter into until October 1997, when the guide for producing an RIA was made public.
10. LFPA, Title III-A.
11. Such as the rules and regulations prepared by the Regulatory Energy Commission (Comisión Reguladora de Energía – CRE) or the Federal Telecommunications Commission (Comisión Federal de Telecomunicaciones – COFETEL) and decentralized bodies, such as the Mexican oil company (Petróleos Mexicanos – PEMEX), the Federal Electricity Commission (Comisión Federal de Electricidad – CFE) and the Mexican Institute of Social Security (Instituto Mexicano del Seguro Social – IMSS).
12. This was due to exceptionally strong opposition from the Ministry of Finance, which argued that it was in the process of a major simplification reform. This has so far not happened.
13. Reglamento Interior de la Comisión Federal de Mejora Regulatoria, DOF 28 January 2004.
14. At the end of 2003, the Presidential Legal Counsel and Ministry of Finance reinforced the control by issuing a 'Guide for Executive Proposals within the Executive', which adds the need to do a budgetary impact assessment (DOF 9-IX-2003).
15. This part itemizes the costs and benefits and impacts on market competition, domestic and international trade, consumers' access to goods and services, and small and medium enterprises.
16. Cesar Cordova and Ali Haddou-Ruiz (2006), op. cit.
17. A special procedure permits ministries to use an emergency fast track. However, the regulation adopted is sunsetted after six months. The ministry should use this exceptional period to prepare an 'ordinary submission'.
18. The following cases are considered exceptions to the moratorium: emergencies, legal and regulatory commitments, international obligations, periodic updates where undoubtedly benefits are superior to costs, police and security regulations, and fiscal measures. Acuerdo de Moratoria Regulatoria (DOF 13 May 2004 to 29 April 2005).
19. Ley Federal de Acceso a la Información.
20. In September 2003, the President's Legal Counsel also published new guidelines on the preparation of laws.
21. 'The most salient case was a 2003 reform of the Waters Law that was lobbied by deputies and that was eventually approved by both Houses and then was vetoed by the Executive' (Salas, 2004, op. cit).

REFERENCES

Acuerdo Para la Desregulación de la Actividad Empresarial (1995), DOF, Mexico, 24 November.

Cordova, C. (2005), 'Inspection Reforms in Mexico', Report prepared for FIAS/ World Bank, Washington.

Cordova, C. and A. Haddou-Ruiz (2006), *Case Studies of Reform Implementation Experience: Regulatory Transformation In Mexico*, Washington DC: FIAS/World Bank.

López Ayllón, S. (1997), *Las transformaciones del sistema jurídico y los significados sociales del derecho. La encrucijada entre tradición y modernidad*, Mexico: UNAM.

OECD (1995), 'Recommendations of the Council of the OECD on Improving the Quality of Government Regulation', OCDE/GD(95)95, Paris.

OECD (1997), *The OECD Report on Regulatory Reform*, Paris: OECD.

OECD (1999), *Regulatory Reform in Mexico*, Paris: OECD.

OECD (2002), *Regulatory Policies in OECD Countries: From Interventionism to Regulatory Governance*, Paris: OECD.

OECD (2004), *Progress in Implementing Regulatory Reform in Mexico*, Paris: OECD.

Salas, F. (2004), *Improving Regulation: The Mexican Experience*, Santiago, Chile: Instituto de Economía – Facultad de Ciencias Económicas y Administrativas – Pontificia Universidad Católica de Chile.

World Bank (2005), *Governance Matters IV: Governance Indicators for 1996–2004*, D. Kaufmann, A. Kraay and M. Mastruzzi, Washington DC: World Bank.

13. South East Europe: opportunities and challenges for improving regulatory quality*

Margo Thomas†

INTRODUCTION

South East European (SEE) countries,[1] as with other transition and developing countries, are seeking to increase levels of private investment in order to help stimulate and sustain economic growth. The quality of regulation affecting markets and business activity in general is increasingly viewed as a factor of competitiveness that influences the investment decisions of both foreign and domestic investors.

There is a significant body of work that supports the view that excessive regulations have a negative effect on private investment, international trade and growth. Bolaky and Freund (2004), Dollar and Kraay (2002), Rodrik, Subramanian and Trebbi (2004) have shown that economies with stronger institutions[2] and inexcessive labor and business regulations are more likely to realize higher rates of growth through international trade. As noted by Djankov et al. (2002), the poor quality of institutions and excessive regulation can have a significant negative impact on investment. While it is generally recognized that the impact of foreign direct investment (FDI) is influenced by a range of host country characteristics, Busse and Groizard (2006) have shown that governments must 'tackle the institutional setting and regulatory framework' in order to achieve the positive welfare effects of foreign direct investment (FDI) inflows. In the specific context of SEE, Demekas et al. (2005) concluded that these countries can attract significantly higher levels of non-privatization or greenfield FDI by adopting and strengthening FDI-friendly policies. Moreover, while the principal determinants of the initial wave of

* Special thanks are due to Cesar Cordova-Novian for his comments on the paper and collaboration on Table 13.1.

† This chapter should not be reported as representing the views of the International Finance Corporation (IFC) and/or the World Bank Group (WBG). The findings and views expressed are those of the author and should not be interpreted as those of the IFC and WBG.

greenfield FDI are market size, ease of access and low labor costs, once a certain threshold is achieved institutional development and the quality of the business environment emerge as critical determinants of FDI.

The momentum for regulatory reform appears to be increasing in SEE as governments seek to increase the levels of private investment and growth. The OECD Investment Compact report (2004) noted that there is an increasing recognition of the importance of high-quality regulation at the national, regional and local levels in SEE countries. The findings of this study support that view.

The focus of these countries on possible EU membership as well as the influence of international financial institutions (IFIs) and donors have helped to raise these issues in the economic development agenda. Throughout the region, governments have committed to and/or embarked on some element of systemic regulatory reform aimed at improving the quality of regulations affecting business procedures. This is evident in the action plans submitted under the Investment Compact (the South East Europe Compact for Reform, Investment, Integrity and Growth) of the Stability Pact.[3] Bosnia and Herzegovina's (BiH) Republika Srpska has completed a review of the stock of administrative requirements for businesses and inspections regulations in the Republika Srpska; Croatia recently initiated a comprehensive review of the stock of business procedures and administrative requirements with the objective of reducing and simplifying these requirements and has conducted regulatory impact assessment (RIA) reviews of specific pieces of legislation; Bulgaria has attempted to institute RIA on a pilot basis; Macedonia has passed a decree to establish a regulatory review function at the center of government; Moldova has implemented a Regulatory Guillotine™[4] to review existing normative acts governing entrepreneurial activity and has recently passed a law[5] to institute RIA for new laws and normative acts and a guillotine review of laws; Serbia has established a Regulatory Reform Council and is in the process of institutionalizing RIA; and Romania has established a regulatory governance unit at the center of government to lead the business environment regulatory reform process. The importance of strong championship for effective regulatory reform is clear, given the experience of the OECD countries. Within SEE, championship at the highest level of government is critical for effective implementation and institutionalization of a regulatory quality agenda. There is some anecdotal evidence to support the view that political support or appreciation for systemic regulatory reform as a factor of competitiveness is emerging. For example, in the recent political campaign in Macedonia, at least one party included regulatory reform and tools such as the guillotine as part of its proposed economic program. A similar 'link' is apparent in the pre-election dialog in BiH's Republika Srpska as well.

This chapter focuses on administrative regulations[6] affecting the start-up and operation of business, recognizing that economic and social regulations are also part of the broad regulatory framework. It provides an overview of regulatory governance in the region and looks at the recent experience of three countries – Bosnia and Herzegovina, Moldova and Serbia – that have embarked on regulatory reforms from different strategic approaches. The goal of this chapter is to examine some of the challenges faced by these countries in strengthening the quality of regulation and governance and to draw lessons of experience for other developing countries.

The chapter sets out to make three points. First, while the countries in SEE may not have explicit regulatory governance systems comparable to those of the OECD countries, they have in place elements of regulatory governance systems that are part of the pre-transition legacy or that have been acquired through the reforms associated with the ongoing political and economic transition. Second, these pre-existing legislative, administrative and judicial arrangements, characterized as 'institutional endowments' by Levy and Spiller (1995), influence the design, implementation and effectiveness of regulatory frameworks in a given country. Third, since regulatory governance encapsulates a systemic approach to improving the quality of regulation and the effectiveness of government, it is essentially a process that must be adapted to and aligned with the legal and institutional frameworks, capacities and political realities in a given country. This is important in countries with resource limitations and where there may be limited political capital to support an aggressive regulatory reform agenda. In the case of SEE, it appears that countries are adopting an organic or opportunistic approach to regulatory governance, influenced by resource constraints and political realities.

The chapter is organized in three sections. The first provides an overview of regulatory governance in SEE. This discussion draws on the findings of the OECD Regulatory Governance survey (OECD, 2004) and the 2006 Regulatory Governance survey conducted by the University of Manchester's Centre on Regulation and Competition. The second section focuses on the experience of three SEE countries – Bosnia and Herzegovina, Moldova and Serbia. The third section attempts to draw lessons of experience for other developing and transition economies.

OVERVIEW – REGULATORY GOVERNANCE IN SEE

At the center of the New Public Management (NPM) approach to effective and efficient government in the regulatory state, the concept of regulatory governance moves beyond the narrow objectives of deregulation and slimming the state to emphasize democratic governance factors such as openness, participation, accountability, effectiveness and coherence in the development and implementation of policy. It encompasses the role of government and the interplay of regulatory actors at the legislative, judicial and sub-national levels of the state. This concept is based on two pillars (OECD, 2002):

1. an effective regulatory management system – including the processes and institutions through which regulations are developed, enforced and adjudicated with a focus on the 'stock' of existing regulations and the 'flow' of new regulations;
2. good governance through efficient, transparent and accountable policies and institutions to protect consumers and to achieve sustainable development as well as social and environmental goals.

Within this context, regulatory quality is a defining measure of government effectiveness on the national and sub-national levels. The 2005 OECD *Guiding Principles for Regulatory Quality and Performance* emphasizes the importance of 'a coherent, whole-of-government approach to create a regulatory environment favorable to the creation and growth of firms, productivity gains, competition, investment and international trade'.

It is recognized that the SEE transition economies have a long way to go given their relatively weak institutions and limited capacities. However, some improvement in regulatory quality is evident (see Figure 13.1) based on the first order reforms[7] (Williamson, 2000), institutional strengthening and administrative simplification associated with the transition to market economies. Moreover, the increased levels of FDI and economic growth for most countries in the region (see Figures 13.2 and 13.3) may be attributed to a range of factors including regulatory quality. According to the World Bank (2002), investment flows are likely to be higher for countries with better domestic investment climates, that is, countries with good governance, sound institutions and property rights. The fundamental challenge faced by the SEE countries is deepening reforms in order to generate sustainable growth.

In 2004, the OECD published a comprehensive review of regulatory governance in SEE (OECD, 2004). Drawing on the experience of OECD countries and the OECD Recommendations on Regulatory Quality, this report identified three mutually reinforcing elements of a regulatory governance framework:

1. An explicit policy for systematically improving the quality of regulation and efficiently employing the regulatory authority of the state. This policy should be adopted at the highest level of government.

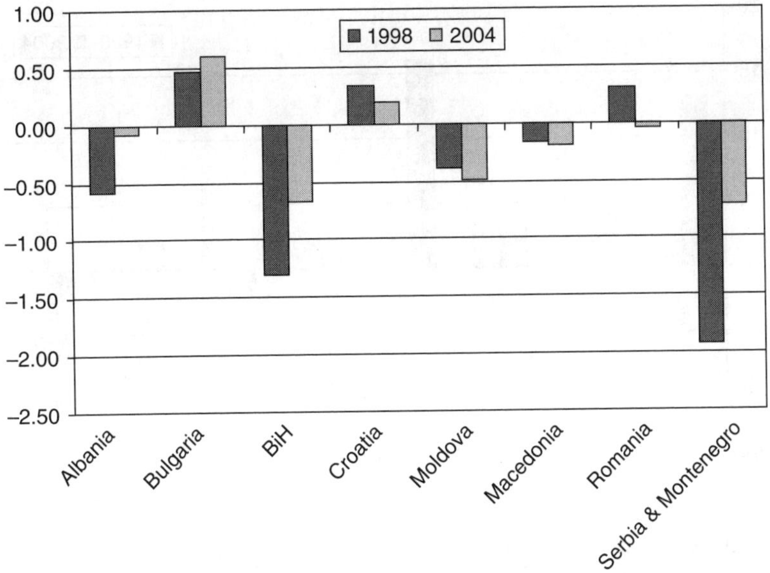

Source: World Bank, *Aggregate Governance Indicators 1996–2004*.

Figure 13.1 SEE regulatory quality

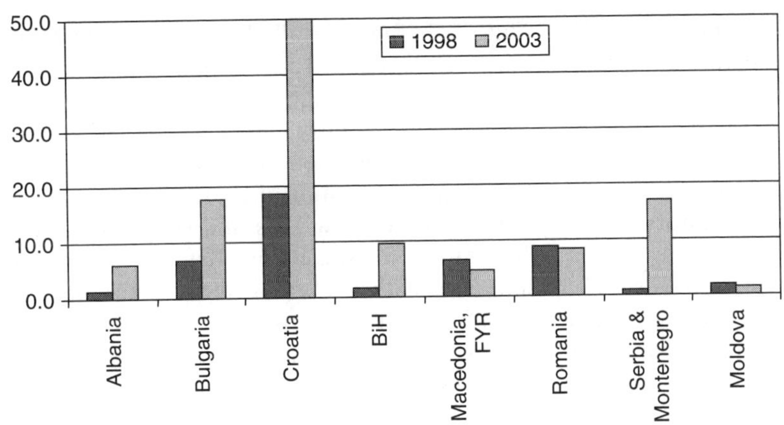

Figure 13.2 SEE per capita FDI inflows (USD '000)

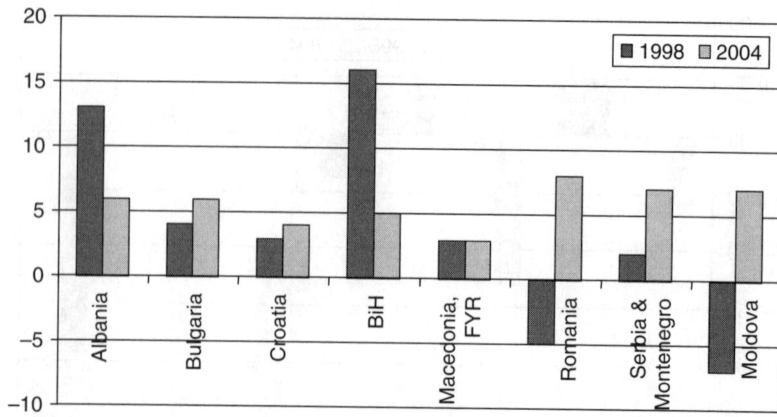

Figure 13.3 SEE annual GDP growth (%)

2. An established capacity or 'oversight body' for leading and implementing the regulatory governance agenda, preferably at the center of government.
3. A strategy for enforcing and implementing the policy. Various tools are available for implementation, including regulatory impact assessment (RIA) and consultation.

While none of the SEE countries has in place all of the three elements of a regulatory governance framework (as defined above), many have instituted different aspects of these elements, as shown in Table 13.1.[8]

With the exception of Moldova, no country has an explicit, overarching policy for ensuring the quality of regulation. In October 2004, Serbia adopted amendments to the Rules of Operation of the Government requiring regulatory impact assessments for new laws and subordinate regulations and established the Council for Regulatory Reform as a starting point for the development of a regulatory reform strategy. Macedonia and Romania have launched initiatives aimed at introducing systematic, ex ante reviews of laws and regulations. In addition, most countries in the region have undertaken ex post reviews of laws and regulations, building on previous administrative simplification reforms of business start-up and operation procedures (e.g., business registration, licensing and permits, inspections, taxation administration, customs and labor regulations).[9]

As noted by the OECD (2004), a central dimension of good regulatory governance is the existence of systematic and mandatory 'checks and balances' to rule-making powers. All SEE countries have established laws and procedures governing the rule-making process and institutions at the center of government that have the responsibility for reviewing proposed laws (see Table 13.1). In Romania and the former Yugoslav Republics, this responsibility rests with legislative councils or secretariats, while in Albania, Bulgaria and Moldova, the Ministry of Justice carries out this function. The authority of these institutions to challenge and comment on the substance of laws or regulations varies and generally the scope of their review is limited to the form, legal quality, constitutionality and conformity with international treaties.

In all SEE countries, at least one institution has this central review function and most have instituted supplemental budgetary and EU compliance reviews, with varying levels of rigor and formality. Each country requires an assessment of the fiscal impact of proposed laws within the context of broader public administration and fiscal reforms. Increasingly, requirements for monitoring the approximation of draft laws with European Union standards are being introduced. Bosnia and Herzegovina, Bulgaria, Croatia and Macedonia have instituted measures to promote EU approximation. In addition, assessments for the potential impact on business activity are being introduced on various levels. Moldova's Ministry of Economy is tasked with assessing draft laws for their potential impact on business and the Regulatory Reform Council plays a similar role in Serbia, while public–private councils in Albania and Montenegro have been charged with providing opinions on the potential business impact of draft laws.

In terms of the tools for implementation, the strategies and application vary quite widely across countries in SEE. As shown in Table 13.1, most countries have basic ex ante regulatory transparency mechanisms for forward planning of laws, notice and comment periods and active consultation. These mechanisms are generally quite weak, with the notable exceptions being Bulgaria's formal system for forward planning and coordination and Romania's robust consultation mechanism that has been formalized under the Sunshine Law[10] and in which private sector bodies (e.g., the Strategic Alliance of Business Associations, the Chamber of Commerce and Industry of Romania) and the Social Dialogue Commissions play an active role in policy dialogs and in providing comments on major legislation. Throughout the SEE, there is a growing network of business advisory councils, business task forces and working groups associated with administrative simplification and business climate reform initiatives (e.g., Albania, Bosnia and Herzegovina, Croatia, Macedonia), foreign investor councils and chambers (e.g., Croatia, Serbia), competitiveness councils (e.g., Croatia, Macedonia, Serbia) and other private sector organizations that can play a critical role in promoting transparent and vigorous consultation in high-quality fora.

Table 13.1 Regulatory governance frameworks in SEE countries

	Policy	Oversight Body			Strategy and Tools Indicators*							
	Explicit policy	Legal controls	Budget controls	Other controls	Forward planning	Notice and comments	Active consultation	Better access	Silence is consent	Licenses elimination	RIA	Inspection reform
Albania	No	Ministry of Justice	Ministry of Finance		NA	NA	1	3	1	1	1	
BiH	No	Legislative Secretariat		Economic Secretariat – EU Directorate	2	1	2	2	1	2	3	3
Bulgaria	No	Ministry of Justice – Legislative Council; Council of Ministers Legal Dept.	Ministry of Finance	Ministry of European Affairs Ministry of Economy and Energy	3	1	2	2	3	2	2	2
Croatia	No	Cabinet Office for Legislation	Ministry of Finance	Ministry of European Integration	2	1	2	3	NA	3	2	3
Rep. of Macedonia	No	Legislative Secretariat	Ministry of Finance	Ministry of European Integration	2	2	1	3	1	3	1	2
Moldova	No	Ministry of Justice	Ministry of Finance	Ministry of Economy	2	1	2	2	2	3	2	1

Romania	No	Legislative Council	Ministry of Public Finance and Court of Auditors		2	2	4	2	3	3	2	2
Montenegro	No	Legislative Secretariat	Ministry of Finance		2	2	2	2	2	2		2
Serbia	Yes	Office of Legal Service; PM's Office; Legislative Secretariat	Ministry of Finance	Council for Economic Regulation Reform	2	1	3	3	NA	3	3	2

Note: * Base scale and rating developed by Cesar Cordova-Novion based on responses to the 2004 OECD review and supplementary information. Updated by author in 2006 based on the University of Manchester's 2006 Regulatory Governance survey and supplementary information. Scale of 1 to 5: 5 indicates performance comparable to OECD good practice.

Source: OECD (2004); 2006 Regulatory Governance survey, University of Manchester Centre on Regulation and Competition.

In 2004, the OECD concluded that SEE experience in the application of RIA as a tool for systematically assessing the impact of policies and regulations is relatively modest. Since then, there has been an increased momentum and focus on the ex ante and ex post application of impact assessment in the region. This momentum may be attributed to a number of factors including increased donor support for systemic regulatory reform following a range of diagnostics of the administrative impediments to business that helped to highlight the fundamental weaknesses in the administrative and regulatory framework.

In terms of ex ante assessments, Serbia is the most advanced in the region, with the introduction of mandatory RIA for legislation proposed by the government. Although the implementation of this requirement has been hampered by limited resources, RIAs are being selectively conducted by the Council for Regulatory Reform (Marušić, Milovanović and Penev, 2006). In the cases of Bulgaria and Moldova,[11] although there are requirements for mandatory RIA for primary and secondary legislation, this tool is not being applied systematically. Croatia has completed pilot RIA exercises and is currently applying the RIA to assess the potential impact of selected draft laws.

There is increasing momentum for the application of ex post application of the RIA methodology for guillotine reviews. In 2005, Moldova carried out an extensive guillotine review of close to 1000 normative acts and, in July 2006, passed a law that established a timetable for the revision and assessment of all laws regulating business activity. In similar fashion, the Republika Srpska in Bosnia and Herzegovina conducted a review of business formalities[12] and inspections procedures and the Government of Croatia has approved plans to launch a similar exercise in September 2006.

REGULATORY REFORM IN THREE SEE COUNTRIES

This section presents three case studies of approaches to systemic regulatory reform in the Balkans. Two of the cases are drawn from countries that were part of the former Yugoslavia – Bosnia and Herzegovina and Serbia. While these countries share the same legal, administrative and regulatory heritage, they have taken two inherently different paths to regulatory reform in terms of the development of a regulatory policy, the sequencing of reforms and the role of the state at the national and sub-national levels. In the case of Moldova, the country's distinct legal and institutional features have shaped the scope and pace of its regulatory reform agenda, compared with Bulgaria and Romania, for example. In all three countries, institutional endowments have influenced the design, implementation and approach to regulatory reform.

Bosnia and Herzegovina

Following the break up of Yugoslavia and the ensuing political and ethnic conflict, Bosnia and Herzegovina (BiH) still faces the costly legacy of the conflict and the combined challenges of post-conflict reconstruction and transition from a centrally planned to a market economy. With the assistance of the international community, BiH has succeeded on a number of fronts. A number of difficult and important institutional reforms have been successfully implemented. BiH has achieved macroeconomic stability and has initiated a range of business environment reforms. However, BiH continues to lag behind its neighbors in the region. Important structural reforms still need to be completed and the administrative procedures associated with market entry, operation and exit need to be further streamlined and simplified. As shown in Figure 13.1, investors still perceive regulatory quality in BiH as relatively poor and the World Bank's 2006 *Doing Business* report ranks BiH as number 87 (of 155 countries) in terms of the ease of doing business.

The complex administrative and decision-making framework, limited technical capacity, and weak policy coordination across the different levels of government further compound the difficulties faced by BiH in the transition process. The government's Medium Term Development Strategy identified a number of reforms that are necessary for sustainable growth including business environment, enterprise and labor market reform.

Legal and administrative framework

The Constitution of BiH provides a framework for a complex governance structure at the state and entity levels. The Constitution spells out the role and responsibilities of the executive, legislative and judicial institutions of the state of BiH *vis à vis* the responsibilities of the entity of the Federation of Bosnia and Herzegovina (FBiH) and the entity of the Republika Srpska (RS). Responsibility for foreign policy, defense, security, refugees and civil affairs, international relations, trade and taxation rests at the state level. The Constitution of BiH and the Constitution of FBiH define the responsibilities of the Federation Government and those of the cantons as well as the responsibilities shared by both levels of government. The responsibilities of the cantons include policy for the regulation and funding of public services, local land use and the regulation and promotion of local business. In parallel, the Constitution of the BiH and the Constitution of the RS spell out the responsibilities of the Government of the RS since there are no cantons in this entity. In addition, Brčko has a status separate from the

FBiH and RS with governmental authority residing within the district and the BiH institutions (Čaušević, 2006). Responsibility for rule-making rests at each level of government within its specific competencies in accordance with the Rules of Procedure. In addition, the Office of the High Representative (OHR), established under the terms of the Dayton Peace Agreement, has the authority to propose and impose laws in cooperation with the BiH Members of Parliament, Council of Ministers, Presidency and Parliament chambers. This complex structure and allocation of authority at the various levels of government necessarily frames the approach to regulatory governance in BiH.

The Rules of Procedure on all three levels of government include provisions for consultation within government. Draft laws must be supported by justifications addressing the constitutionality, legal basis and budgetary impact of proposed laws and opinions from designated bodies. For example, in the case of FBiH, opinions are required from the Legislative Office, Federal Ministry of Justice and Federal Ministry of Finance in FBiH (Penev, 2006). In the RS and FBiH, the Rules of Procedure provide for public consultations to be conducted at the discretion of the relevant legislative committees. Similar provisions are included at the state level in the Rules of Procedure of the House of Representatives and the House of Peoples. Generally, public consultations are conducted only in the case of critical legislation. When consultations are conducted, they are done on a tripartite basis – engaging labor unions and the chambers of commerce.

There is no explicit policy on regulatory quality in BiH and no body (or bodies) charged with systematically assessing the impact of proposed laws and regulations (Penev, 2006). Since much of the authority for regulating the start-up and operation of business resides at the entity and municipal levels in the RS and at the entity and cantonal levels in FBiH, responsibility for improving regulatory quality for business activity effectively rests at the corresponding levels of government.

Administrative simplification

With the assistance of the donor community, a range of activities related to administrative simplification have been undertaken in BiH, covering reforms in areas such as business registration, inspections, business licensing, customs and taxation administration. Improvements are evident in the regulatory quality indicator (Figure 13.1). Despite these improvements, it is clear that further work needs to be done. In terms of the overall ease of doing business,[13] BiH is ranked at number 87 of a total of 155 countries.

Two complementary approaches to promoting administrative simplification have been applied in BiH. They are instructive since they underscore the importance of engaging the appropriate levels of government in designing and implementing regulatory reform, securing ownership and credibility among stakeholders, and marshaling resources to support implementation.

Under the first approach, diagnostic analyses, such as the Review of the Legal Framework and Administrative Barriers to Investment (FIAS, 2000), were carried out at three levels of government, addressing the issues relevant at each level of government and making recommendations for harmonizing entity-level laws and regulations, where appropriate. Comprehensive reforms were designed, implemented and institutionalized with technical support provided by international donors, including, for example, the World Bank's comprehensive Business Environment Adjustment Credit project; USAID's programs on taxation reform, bankruptcy and liquidation, inspections and permits; and UK-DFID's project on business registration streamlining. However, the work of actually implementing change is done at the entity and cantonal levels through various working groups. The outcomes and impact of these reforms varies for a number of reasons including lack of capacity and resistance to change.

Under the second approach, a fast moving 'bulldozer' initiative was launched by the Office of the High Representative (OHR) in 2002. Under the leadership of a committee, which included representatives of the Council of Ministers, OHR, entity governments and the private sector, wide consultations were conducted to target specific aspects of business-related regulations for amendment (World Bank, 2004b). This was a bottom-up approach, driven by a strong institution – the OHR, at the center. Several iterations of the bulldozer have been conducted and efforts have been made to institutionalize this mechanism, a particular challenge related to the need for safeguards to avoid capture or perceptions of capture by special interests. An ex post review of the impact and sustainability of this initiative would provide a better understanding of its challenges and successes.

Regulatory reform in the Republika Srpska

More recently, the Government of the RS initiated several inter-related measures to build on ongoing public sector reform and administrative simplification work and to improve systematically the quality of regulations affecting business activity. In November 2005, the government adopted a policy recommendation for the introduction of regulatory impact assessment (RIA) in reviewing policy proposals and laws. Following a change in political leadership, and the emergence of the new Prime Minister as a strong champion for business environment reform, the government issued a decree to establish a Regulatory Reform Council (chaired by the Prime Minister and including the Ministers of Finance and Economic Relations and

Coordination, the President of Municipalities and representatives of the private sector – the Chamber of Commerce and Association of Employers) and launched an ex post review of business formalities (licensing and permits system) and inspection-related controls and measures. The government has committed publicly to reducing significantly business formalities and inspection measures in order to help reduce the cost of doing business in the entity and garnered extensive support from the business community in this undertaking.

In view of the limited resources and technical capabilities for implementing this guillotine review, a small secretariat was established in the Ministry of Economic Relations and Coordination to support the Regulatory Reform Council and to lead the review process. Although it is not at the center of government, the secretariat effectively reports to the Prime Minister and it works closely with the Legislative Secretariat and other parts of government to facilitate the guillotine review. The staff of the secretariat constitutes a small group of public servants, supplemented by four-person team of consultants – lawyers and economists and international experts.[14] In addition to the coordinating function of the secretariat, the role of the secretariat staff and the consulting team was to review and challenge the submissions of the various ministries of the government, take on board the findings and recommendations of the stakeholder consultations and to make recommendations to the Council for eliminating and streamlining formalities and inspection measures. The electronic registry of 'valid' informalities and inspection measures will be a critical output of the guillotine review. It is expected that this e-registry will be accessible to the general public, thereby increasing transparency and access to information on business regulations.

The guillotine review process includes an energetic public relations campaign and an extensive public consultation component. Starting with the launch of the guillotine, the government undertook a public relations campaign to explain the objectives and expected outcomes of the exercise and to build broad support for the initiative. As part of a structured public consultation mechanism, sectoral inspection working groups established by the Chamber of Commerce under a related donor-funded project, played a critical role in reviewing inspection measures and consulting with the private sector to make recommendations for the guillotine. The sessions of these working groups were open to the public and to the press. The sessions were generally well attended by the business community and often generated vigorous, open discussions about the clarity, consistency and impact of inspection measures and the administration of inspections. One of the emerging points of discussion related to the need for a systematic ex ante review of the impact of proposed laws and regulations. The business community has recognized that the outcome of the guillotine could be undermined if an ex ante review mechanism is not implemented and is now advocating the introduction of RIA. In addition, the leaders of several municipalities have initiated a discussion on the applicability of the guillotine review at the municipal level.

This exercise was completed in September, 2006 and declared a success by the government. Preliminary indications are that all major targets have been successfully met. Some 3000 formalities and inspection-related measures were reviewed and approximately 50 percent were eliminated or recommended for revision. However, a review of the process and outcomes of the guillotine would be necessary to provide a more objective assessment of its impact. At a minimum, the exercise generated support and momentum for regulatory reform.

The process effectively applied some of the key principles of the regulatory governance framework – increased openness, participation, accountability – in helping to improve the coherence and quality of regulations affecting business operations in the RS. Despite the strong political leadership, a number of challenges have emerged as ministries within government sought to protect their turf and vested interests and resisted the reforms aimed at reducing the cost of doing business, and promoting a change in the command and control culture of the public service. This initiative provides the nucleus of regulatory policy that can be further developed and applied more broadly. Moreover, there is strong potential for the RS model to be refined, adapted and applied in the rest of BiH.

Moldova

With the break up of the Soviet Union, Moldova faced a number of challenges in the process of the political and economic transition to a democratic, market-oriented economy. Following a period of political instability and slow growth, Moldova has staged an economic turnaround. Since 2000, the economy has experienced an average real growth rate of 7 percent. However, the major source of this growth has been worker remittances. Private domestic investment is relatively low (roughly 17 percent of GDP), and the government faces the considerable challenge of generating sustainable growth. Since the government views private investment, both domestic and foreign, as an important engine of sustainable growth, it has focused attention on improving the business environment and the quality of regulations affecting business operations in order to reduce the cost and risk of doing business. The Ministry of Economy champions and is spearheading the ongoing regulatory reform initiative.

Legal and administrative framework

The legal system in Moldova is based on the Soviet and continental legal systems. The Law on Legislative Acts and the Law on Normative Acts provide the basic framework for the rule-making process. The Ministry of Justice has the responsibility for reviewing draft laws and preparing legal opinions before discussion in the Cabinet of Ministers and to represent the Cabinet in the relevant parliamentary discussions. In principle, draft regulations are subjected to legal, policy coherence and budgetary impact scrutiny. The laws on legislative and normative acts require the attachment of an informative note with legal and economic analysis to support draft laws and regulations. However, this requirement constitutes a mild scrutiny that is not rigorously enforced. The primary review is legal and focuses on the constitutionality of draft laws. In addition, the Ministry of Finance is responsible for the budget impact review.

Until recently, there was no explicit overarching policy on regulatory quality in Moldova. The 2005 EU Action Plan and the 2006 Law on Basic Principles Regulating Entrepreneurial Activity established a basic policy. As is the case in most SEE countries, Moldova's approach to regulatory governance is rooted in the established institutions and administrative laws and procedures of government. For example, under the rules of the government, there are requirements for consultation with all stakeholders during the law drafting process. However, in practice these requirements are rarely or selectively observed and there is no enforcement. As a result, a draft Law on Full Decision-making Transparency has been prepared to strengthen these requirements. As noted in Table 13.1, Moldova has applied some aspects of the standard regulatory governance tools including forward planning, notice and comments, and consultation. However, clearly there is much room for improving and enforcing the use of these tools in order to improve the quality of regulations and strengthen the rule-making process.

Regulatory reform in Moldova

Starting in 2000, Moldova introduced several regulatory reform initiatives including the passage of legislation for the establishment of a competition agency and administrative simplification programs. The results of these initiatives were mixed and there was considerable resistance to change within the public service and from special interest groups.

In 2004, the World Bank completed a comprehensive assessment of the investment climate in Moldova (World Bank, 2004a). This assessment identified a range of administrative and legal impediments to business activity and stressed that excessive regulations and the risks associated with poor-quality regulations and non-transparent administrative procedures had a significant negative impact on private investment and economic growth in Moldova. Business surveys showed that Moldovan managers spent roughly 19 percent of their time complying with regulatory requirements and the bureaucracy and businesses spent more than 2 percent of their revenues on bribes and facilitation payments, on average. In addition, it was found that the powers and institutions of the judiciary lacked credibility due to corruption, discretionary authority, political influence over the judiciary and the absence of accountability mechanisms (World Bank, 2004a). This report recommended, among other things, that Moldova develop a strategy and institutional framework for deregulation and introduce RIA of government regulations affecting the investment climate.

With the support of the World Bank and bilateral donors, including USAID, Moldova has taken a number of steps to build on the business environment reforms initiated in 2000 and to develop and implement a strategy for regulatory governance. This strategy has been championed by a reformist Ministry of Economy and Trade. The regulatory reform agenda has apparently gained deeper traction with the re-election of the government in 2005 and the political window for pursuing aggressive reforms.

In 2004, the government adopted the policy Decision on the Reform of State Regulation and Entrepreneurship Activity.[15] This decision provided the legal basis for establishing an inter-ministerial commission, a national working group (NWG), and a secretariat to develop a coherent regulatory policy and framework for implementation. The commission was subsequently transformed into the State Commission for Regulatory Reform. The NWG consists of 32 permanent members and 18 ad hoc members drawn from the public and private sectors.

In 2005, the government launched a guillotine review of subordinate regulations with the Decision on the Registry of Normative Acts and the Registry of Authorizations, Permits and Certificates governing entrepreneurial activity.[16] Under the guillotine review, approximately 1000 normative acts were reviewed: 426 were retained and included in the registry; 285 were targeted for amendment; and 99 were eliminated. In addition, the number of authorizations, certificates and permits governing entrepreneurial activity was significantly reduced and a registry has been established.

In 2005, the government adopted the EU–Moldova Action Plan, which articulated Moldova's commitment to economic reform, approximating of Moldovan legislation with that of the EU and its goal of integrating into the EU. This action plan perhaps comes closest to outlining a national regulatory policy and can be interpreted as a first step in this direction. Box 13.1 outlines the major regulatory and administrative reform elements of the action plan.

BOX 13.1 THE EU–MOLDOVA ACTION PLAN

The EU–Moldova Action Plan, signed in February 2005, covers a wide range of issues, including democratization, health standards, legal reform and economics. In the economic area, it includes the following key elements:

Administrative reform and reform of the judiciary:

- adopting an ethics code for civil servants, judges and law enforcement bodies;
- implementing a working program for regulatory reform;
- amending laws concerning the independence and impartiality of the judiciary;
- introducing administrative reform of local government.

Improving the investment climate:

- screening of national legislation to identify barriers to business establishment and progressively abolishing them;
- taking steps to reduce over-regulation, improve transparency and predictability and reduce further the burden of licensing and inspection regimes;
- setting up a dialogue on regulation, enterprise and industrial policy with foreign investors;
- enhancing the prudential regulatory framework for financial markets and supervision to bring it in line with that in the EU;
- creating a national agency for competition protection, providing it with sufficient budgetary means to carry out its mandate.

Trade promotion:

- harmonizing legislation and procedures with EU norms on certification and control of origin of goods in Moldova;
- preparing a plan of steps toward fulfillment of EU requirements on animal health and for the processing of animal products, and for hygiene in food processing.

Source: Moldova Ministry of Foreign Affairs. www.mfa.md/EN/Action_Plan_EU_Moldova.pdf.

In July 2006, the Parliament passed the Law on Basic Principles Regulating Entrepreneurial Activity. This law establishes the legal and institutional framework for the systematic review of existing and proposed laws and regulations affecting business activities. It is based on the principles of predictability, transparency and proportionality and it establishes RIA as one of the primary tools for implementation. This Law provides for a repeat of the guillotine exercise, this time targeting laws affecting business activity.

SERBIA

Following the armed conflicts of the 1990s, international isolation and deterioration of the rule of law, Serbia emerged from the velvet revolution in 2000 and embarked on the second wave of its transformation to a democracy and transition to a market economy. Starting in 2000 and despite a number of subsequent political setbacks, Serbia implemented several major policy steps as part of its transition. These steps, largely consistent with the first generation Washington Consensus reforms, were aimed at stabilizing the economy, integrating Serbia into the global economy and improving economic growth. Since 2000, Serbia has achieved average annual economic growth rates of roughly 5 percent and 2006 growth rates are now projected at around 7 percent, inflation rates have been reduced to single digits from a high of approximately 100 percent in 2000, and annual inward FDI flows have risen steadily, peaking at USD1.4 billion in 2003 driven by privatization. In 2005, Serbia was recognized as one of the top reformers by the World Bank's *Doing Business* report. However, as noted by the World Bank's *Investment Climate Assessment* (2004a), the initial reforms focused on stabilizing the economy and putting critical pieces of legislation in place. The government has now embarked on a range of second-generation reforms aimed at triggering sustained growth, including improving the quality of regulations affecting the business environment, and building institutions and capacity for implementation.

Legal and administrative framework

Serbia's legal system is based on the civil law tradition of the former Yugoslavia, with its foundation on the laws of the former Federal Republic of Yugoslavia except for components superseded by the Constitution. As provided under the Rules of Procedure of the Parliament, the principal actors in the legislative process are the government, Members of Parliament, the Assembly of the Autonomous Province of Vojvodina, and voters constituted in groups of at least 15 000. These actors have the right to propose and amend laws, regulations and general acts. In addition, by government decision, the Council on Regulatory Reform, as part of the government, can make recommendations to ministries for the adoption or amendment of laws, regulations and general acts (Penev and Marušić, 2006).

All draft laws prepared by the government or its constituent bodies are subject to essentially three levels of review before they are presented to the Parliament for adoption. Figure 13.4 provides a summary of the process of enacting laws proposed by the government (Penev and Marušić, 2006).

On the first level, the Rules of Procedure require that draft laws and acts be reviewed for: constitutionality (by the Legislative Secretariat); budget

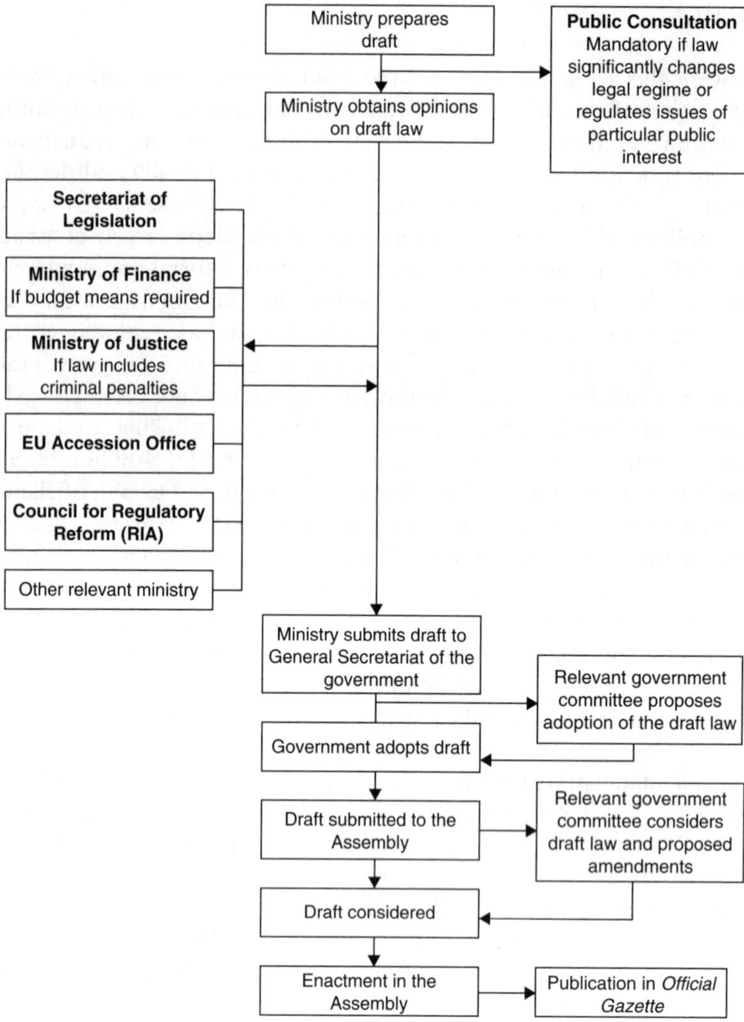

Source: Penev and Marušić (2006).

Figure 13.4 Serbia: rule-making process for laws proposed by the govenment

impact (by the Ministry of Finance); consistency with EU regulations (by the European Integration Office); property rights and national obligations (by the Public Attorney's Office); and criminal implications (by the Ministry of Justice). In 2004, the requirement for an RIA was added by a Decision of the Government. The Council for Regulatory Reform is charged with the responsibility for assisting ministries with the preparation of RIAs and for reviewing the assessments for quality. The opinions produced by these reviews are included in the mandatory justification statements, which are appended to drafts for consideration by the government. The General Secretariat of the government has responsibility for examining the submitted drafts to ensure that the requisite supporting documentation and the draft conform to the requirements.

On the second level, the Committee of the Government with the relevant competence for the law or act presented considers each draft and makes a recommendation to the government for (or against) adoption. The Legislative Secretariat is charged with reviewing laws or acts proposed by the government for enactment by the Parliament. On the third level, the competent committee of the Assembly reviews the draft proposal before it can be sent to the floor for debate.

The levels of review outlined in the process above provide opportunities for strengthening regulatory governance through the enforcement of compliance with the requirements for regulatory quality and public consultation. However, this is contingent upon a fundamental shift in the culture of regulation based on the old command and control approach. Within the existing structure, it appears that there is considerable scope to circumvent these requirements by expediting the passage of legislation or by following an alternative legislative route outside of the government. In addition, it is worth noting that the Regulatory Reform Council is a temporary body and has not been effectively institutionalized or integrated into the rule-making process.

Regulatory reform in Serbia

As noted in the preceding sections, since 2000 Serbia has undertaken a series of economic and legislative reforms to stabilize the economy and to improve the environment for doing business. The first wave of reforms included administrative simplification measures, such as the amendment of the Company Law to eliminate pre-registration inspections, and policy measures such as tax reform, adoption (2001) and amendment (2003) of a Law on Privatization, promulgation of the Law on Public Procurement in 2002, and the promulgation of leasing, collateral and concessions laws in 2003. A second wave of reforms has been launched with a strong focus on effective implementation and deepening administrative simplification. In 2004, the Enterprise Law was promulgated and the Business Registration Law was amended to harmonize the two laws and facilitate effective implementation. Similarly, the Law on Public Procurement was amended to further simplify and streamline the implementing procedures and to harmonize the law with related legislation.

Serbia does not have an explicit, comprehensive regulatory policy. The Regulatory Reform Council has been assigned the task of preparing a regulatory reform strategy for review and adoption by the government. This strategy is expected to incorporate and make explicit many of the elements that already exist as part of the rule-making process and in the various procedures and practices within government, thereby increasing the transparency of the legislative process, strengthening the public consultation mechanisms and increasing public access to information. For example, while there is no formal forward planning system for laws and acts, the ministers of the government are requested to submit annual legislative plans for use within government. In the area of public consultation, the Rules of Operation of the Government were amended in 2004 to permit consultation on all laws at the discretion of the proposing entity, except in cases where the proposed laws are intended to change significantly the legal regime in areas of critical public interest. Generally, the need for and extent of public consultation is determined by the proposing entity and the relevant committee of the government (Marušić et al., 2006).

CONCLUSIONS

Over the past five years, SEE countries have launched a range of initiatives to strengthen regulatory governance and improve the investment climate. Moreover, it appears that government, policy-makers and politicians increasingly share the view that regulatory quality is a determinant of private investment and growth. This was confirmed by the Investment Compact's Ministerial Statement 'Building a New Environment for Private Investment in South East Europe',[17] which recognized that 'high quality regulatory governance guided by a comprehensive and strategic policy is essential for strengthening the confidence of private investors in the region'.

In the absence of explicit strategies for regulatory governance, the SEE countries have adopted an opportunistic approach to regulatory quality – building on administrative simplification initiatives and taking advantage of opportunities to conform to international practice with the assistance of international donors, respond to the 'pull' of EU accession, and comply with international membership requirements (e.g., WTO). In general, they have made considerable progress despite the constraints of politics, capacity and resources for implementation.

When considered in the context of the OECD's Recommendations on Regulatory Quality, it is clear that no country in SEE fulfills the three criteria of a regulatory governance framework – explicit policy, oversight body at the center of government and a strategy for implementation. However, as shown in Table 13.1, all of the countries in the region have in place elements of such a framework. Most have implemented some combination of the regulatory quality tools with varying degrees of sophistication and 'rigor'. As civil law countries with a central administrative law framework, all of these countries, including Moldova and Bulgaria, have institutions at the center of government with some quality control function regarding the review and promulgation of laws, legislative acts and regulations.

SEE countries have in place some of the basic building blocks necessary for regulatory governance frameworks. Institutional endowments include, for example, oversight bodies that carry out a review function in the rule-making process. These bodies include the legislative secretariats, secretariats of the government and government committees such as the Collegium of deputy ministers/state secretaries in Macedonia or Serbia. There is significant potential to strengthen substantially their role in assuring regulatory quality. However, the challenge is to strengthen and supplement these building blocks in order to develop and sustain modern regulatory management systems and to improve regulatory quality systematically. These changes would require a significant shift in the culture of these bodies and, in some cases, it may be necessary to establish new bodies. The experiences of Macedonia and Croatia help to highlight some of the factors that will influence these decisions.

In the case of Macedonia, an effort was made to link an ongoing public service reform program with the fiscal review and the regulatory review function under the General Secretariat of the government. This initiative was facilitated by the ongoing change management program within the secretariat to achieve a shift in the organizational focus to a proactive, quality paradigm in organizing the business of the government and ensuring coherence between the proposals submitted for review with the policy goals and strategic priorities of the government. Croatia offers an interesting example of regulatory reform fueled by an innovative e-government program. In this approach, a regulatory reform capacity has been established at the center of government to drive the initial reforms while the possible role of existing institutions over the long term is being debated.

Institutional endowments also influence the fundamental approach for developing and implementing regulatory management systems (Levy and Spiller, 1995). BiH provides a good example of this. This complex legal and administrative structure and weak policy coordination mechanisms at the state and entity levels has influenced the approach for developing the policy for regulatory quality and the institutional framework emerging at the sub-national entity level. The BiH approach contrasts with that of Serbia and Moldova, for example, where the institutional framework for regulatory reform is being set up at the national level consistent with their legal and administrative mechanisms for rule-making.

A similar view can be taken of the strategies for sequencing of regulatory reforms and deploying a range of tools including public consultation and

RIA. Most countries have employed an organic approach to regulatory reform, starting with administrative simplification and moving on towards systemic mechanisms in order to achieve sustained and deeper reforms and better-quality regulation. This approach is most likely a function of the political economy as well as capacity and resource limitations. Taking this a step further, most countries have opted to introduce systemic regulatory reform initiatives by launching fast-moving, targeted guillotine reviews of existing regulations for demonstration effect and building momentum for extending reforms to include systematic reviews of new regulations 'the flow' over the longer term. To date, five of the countries in the region have launched ex post reviews of the stock of regulations using the guillotine as a first step. For example, in the case of RS in BiH, the guillotine is considered a first step towards a systematic ex ante review and pressure for the next step is coming from stakeholders in the private sector. The exceptions, so far, have been Bulgaria and Serbia where the focus has been primarily on the flow of regulations.

It is worth noting that the broad experience of the SEE countries is similar to that of the OECD countries where the regulatory reform was part of a broader transformation to market-led growth and the regulatory reform agenda included the adoption of 'explicit overarching policies, disciplines and tools, tending to be more permanent than episodic in nature' (OECD, 2005). The implementation of this reform agenda typically happens over an extended period of time and goes through various iterations, influenced by institutional limitations and political reality. In the case of Italy, for example, the regulatory quality program was initiated in the late 1970s with a review of the quality of public administration. It has gone through several phases, including the review of the constitutional framework and the passage of the Administrative Procedures Law in the early 1990s, followed by the 'Bassanini forms', which pushed for deeper administrative simplification and it continues today.

So far, the experience in the countries of South Eastern Europe indicates that regulatory reform is being integrated with the broader governance principles and constitutes an important component of their economic growth and competitiveness strategies. The regulatory reform agendas are being implemented organically – drawing on the international experience, adapting existing institutions where appropriate, building constituencies and capacity for reform, and sequencing reforms to build momentum and support.

NOTES

1. Albania, Bosnia and Herzegovina, Bulgaria, Croatia, FYR Macedonia, Montenegro, Romania, Serbia.

2. The term 'institutions' covers a broad spectrum. On one end as defined by North (1990) it includes formal rules embodied in laws, regulations and enforcement mechanisms (e.g., property rights, contract enforcements and judiciary); on the other end, it includes organizational entities, procedural devices and regulatory frameworks.
3. The Stability Pact was adopted in 1999 by 40 partner countries and organizations to strengthen SEE countries and to support cooperation, sustainable development and peace in the region.
4. Jacobs and Associates, 2005. The Regulatory Guillotine™ is a means of rapidly reviewing a large number of regulations, and eliminating those that are no longer needed without requiring lengthy and costly legal action on each regulation (Jacobs and Astrakhan, 2006).
5. Law on Basic Principles Regulating Entrepreneurial Activity, 11 August, 2006.
6. Administrative regulations are paperwork and administrative formalities through which governments collect information and intervene in individual economic decisions (OECD, 1997).
7. Washington Consensus reforms, including fiscal discipline, tax reform, financial liberalization, openness to foreign direct investment, privatization, deregulation and secure property rights.
8. The data presented in this table are drawn from the OECD 2004 survey and the University of Manchester's Centre on Regulation and Competition 2006 Regulatory Governance survey.
9. The World Bank Group's Foreign Investment Advisory Service (FIAS) has conducted administrative barriers reviews in all SEE countries except Moldova. Various other donors have conducted supplementary diagnostic reviews and have provided implementation assistance in a number of areas.
10. Law on Transparency No. 52/2003.
11. Moldova: Law on Basic Principles Regulating Entrepreneurial Activity.
12. Administrative and regulatory requirements for business start-up and operation through which governments collect information and regulate individual economic decisions.
13. World Bank (2006).
14. The Government of the RS received technical assistance from the Foreign Investment Advisory Service (FIAS) of the World Bank Group and the United States Agency for International Development (USAID).
15. Government Decision No. 141 of 17 February, 2004.
16. Government Decision No. 920 of 30 August, 2005: Monitorul Oficial # 126-128/1047 of 23 September, 2005; Government Decision No. 1030 of 3 October, 2005: Monitorul Oficial # 132-134 of 7 October, 2005.
17. Signed in Vienna on 9 July, 2004.

REFERENCES

Bolaky, B. and C. Freund (2004), 'Trade, Regulations and Growth', World Bank Policy Research Working Paper No. 3255, Washington, DC: World Bank.

Busse, M. and J. Groizard (2006), 'Foreign Direct Investment, Regulations and Growth', World Bank Policy Research Working Paper No. 3882, Washington, DC: World Bank.

Čaušević, F. (2006), 'Jurisdiction and Responsibilities of the Administrative Levels in Bosnia and Herzegovina', in *How to Improve the Legislative Process in Serbia and Bosnia and Herzegovina*, S. Penev (ed.), Belgrade: Investment Compact for South East Europe and Economics Institute, Belgrade.

Demekas, D.G., B. Horvath, E. Ribakova and Y. Wu (2005), 'Foreign Direct Investment in Southeastern Europe: How (and How Much) Can Policies Help?', IMF Working Paper: WP/05/110.

Djankov, S., R. La Porta, F. Lopez-de-Silanes and A. Shleifer (2002), 'The Regulation of Entry', *Quarterly Journal of Economics*, **117** (1), 1–37.

Dollar, D. and A. Kraay (2002), 'Institutions, Trade and Growth', *Journal of Monetary Economics*, **50** (1), 133–62.

FIAS (2000), *Review of the Legal Framework and Administrative Barriers to Investment*, Washington, DC: FIAS.

Jacobs, S. and I. Astrakhan (2006), *Effective and Sustainable Regulatory Reform: The Regulatory Guillotine in Three Transition and Developing Countries*, Jacobs and Associates.

Levy, B. and P. Spiller (1995), 'A Framework for Resolving the Regulatory Problem', in *Regulations, Institutions and Commitment: Comparative Studies of Telecommunications*, B. Levy and P. Spiller (eds), Cambridge, NY: Cambridge University Press.

Marušić, A., D. Milovanović and S. Penev (2006), 'Regulatory Reform and Implementation of Regulatory Impact Analysis', in *How to Improve the Legislative Process in Serbia and Bosnia and Herzegovina*, S. Penev (ed.), Belgrade: Investment Compact for South East Europe and Economics Institute, Belgrade.

North, D. (1990), *Institutions, Institutional Change and Economic Performance*, New York: Cambridge University Press.

OECD (1997), *Report on Regulatory Reform*, Paris: OECD.

OECD (2002), *Regulatory Policies in OECD Countries: From Interventionism to Regulatory Governance*, Paris: OECD.

OECD (2004), *Regulatory Governance in South East European Countries*, Paris: OECD.

OECD (2005), *Background Document on Regulatory Reform in OECD Countries*, Paris: OECD.

Penev, S. (ed.) (2006), *How to Improve the Legislative Process in Serbia and Bosnia and Herzegovina*, Belgrade: Investment Compact for South East Europe and Economics Institute, Belgrade.

Penev, S. and A. Marušić (2006), 'Enactment of New Laws and Revision of Existing Regulations', in *How to Improve the Legislative Process in Serbia and Bosnia and Herzegovina*, S. Penev (ed.), Belgrade: Investment Compact for South East Europe and Economics Institute, Belgrade.

Rodrik, D., A. Subramanian and F. Trebbi (2004), 'Institutions Rule: The Primacy of Institutions Over Geography and Integration in Economic Development', *Journal of Economic Growth*, **9** (2), 131–65.

Thomas, M. and Y. Zhang (eds) (forthcoming), *Regulatory Governance in Transitional and Developing Countries: Survey-Based Studies*, Manchester: Centre on Regulation and Competition, University of Manchester.

Williamson, J. (2000), 'What Should the World Bank Think about the Washington Consensus?', *The World Bank Research Observer*, **15** (2), August, 251–64.

World Bank (2002), *Global Economic Prospects 2003*, Washington, DC: World Bank.

World Bank (2004a), *Investment Climate Assessment, Moldova*, Washington, DC: World Bank.

World Bank (2004b), *World Development Report 2005: A Better Investment Climate for Everyone*, New York: Oxford University Press.

World Bank (2006), *Doing Business*, Washington, DC: World Bank.

Index